COMPREHENSION CHECKUPS GRADES 1-5

COMPREHENSION CHECKUPS
GRADES 1-5
Strategies for Success

Patricia R. Conley
Berdell J. Akin

1991
TEACHER IDEAS PRESS
A Division of
Libraries Unlimited, Inc.
Englewood, Colorado

TEACHER IDEAS PRESS
A Division of
Libraries Unlimited, Inc.
P.O. Box 3988
Englewood, CO 80155-3988

Library of Congress Cataloging-in-Publication Data

Conley, Patricia R., 1950-
    Comprehension checkups grades 1-5 : strategies for success /
Patricia R. Conley, Berdell J. Akin.
    xiii, 297 p. 22x28 cm.
    Includes bibliographical references.
    ISBN 0-87287-874-0
    1. Reading (Elementary) 2. Reading comprehension. 3. Reading
comprehension--Evaluation.   I. Akin, Berdell J., 1950-   .
II. Title.
LB1573.C5562   1991   91-10649
                                                         CIP

CONTENTS

LITERAL COMPREHENSION

CRITICAL EVALUATION

PREFACE

Through the years, we have found ourselves asking the following questions:

1. Can my students tell me "Why"?

2. How often do my students read a selection and then can't talk about it?

3. How often do my students ask, "How do I find the answer?"

4. Why do my students need step-by-step explanations?

5. Why don't my students perform well on standardized tests?

6. Do my students learn "how to" today and forget "how to" tomorrow?

7. How can I help my students to transfer comprehension strategies to content areas?

8. How can I help students to internalize comprehension strategies and become confident, independent readers?

We have come to the realization that before students can become competent, independent readers, they must first have a knowledge of comprehension skills and strategies, such as sequence, main idea, and cause-effect. Second, they need the ability to know when to use these strategies to aid in comprehension.

We reviewed current research in reading, and tried numerous approaches, techniques, and assorted materials to provide students with a foundation to transfer comprehension knowledge to whatever they read. Students, however, continued to have difficulty with comprehension when reading selections on their own. They lacked congruence, the ability to relate ideas, and the knowledge of how to construct meaning.

At this point in our teaching, we began to focus on the idea of using procedures to assist in the initial development of comprehension skills. We realized that this approach could be the "missing link."

We began by focusing on comprehension strategies that were difficult for students. We developed procedures for teaching these strategies through discussions, games, and activities, and also student procedures that could be used as independent strategies when needed. These procedures, and the accompanying practice in using them, gave students a foundation, a tool, and a sense of security. We have observed a carryover and transfer of knowledge. Students have also demonstrated improved comprehension in various contexts.

Our purpose in writing this book was not to debate philosophies but to provide a teaching plan to improve comprehension that can support all philosophies. Common to every teaching belief is the expectation that students will ultimately gain meaning from the written word; this is the goal of any comprehension teaching.

This book presents a paradigm in which functional, not arbitrary, skills are taught. These are presented to students in a relevant framework wherein they think about the skill, its purpose, and its use. Once this is accomplished, the knowledge will become a student strategy that facilitates comprehension. *Comprehension Checkups Grades 1-5: Strategies for Success* provides a teaching plan that will enhance comprehension using procedures, quality literature, and relevant student activities.

ACKNOWLEDGMENTS

A special note of thanks...

To our families, whose love and caring taught us to believe, "When you apply yourself, you can do anything you set out to do."

To our former principal, Mr. Vern Martin, for his support, encouragement, and for "planting the seed."

To Sue Johnson for advancing our thinking.

To the staff at Crawford Elementary who used and tested the procedures in their classrooms.

To our special friends who gave us that much-needed pat on the back and their votes of confidence.

To Elaine Orgill for her never-ending patience through the numerous revisions of our manuscript.

INTRODUCTION

STUDENT STRATEGIES—THE NEED

Increasingly, educators are calling attention to the importance of developing students' thinking ability through their educational experiences in school. The goal of having students become competent thinkers has long been an educational idea. For example, Resnick and Klopfer (1989) state that, "One of the most significant ideas emerging from recent research on thinking is that the mental processes we have customarily associated with thinking are not restricted to some advanced or 'higher order' stage of mental development."

The purpose of reading is to gain meaning. Students need to be taught thinking strategies that good readers use to obtain meaning from what they read. Herrmann (1988) writes, "The teacher's primary role is to teach students how to monitor their comprehension and how to fix a comprehension breakdown." In other words, comprehension and thinking are involved in successful learning for students at the elementary level of reading and can be part of good instruction from the beginning of school.

Students can be taught comprehension strategies by using a systematic, sequential approach which, in turn, provides strategies for them to use in their independent reading. Using a procedure to enhance comprehension has been found to be successful. According to Marzano and Arrendondo (1986), a *procedure* is the "breakdown of [a] whole into parts [or] steps." It is used when one wants to learn how to do something or perform an action. The use of procedures provides students with a system for improving comprehension. More importantly, the focus of the procedure should be on how to apply the knowledge in context. A procedure is a stimulus that prompts students to activate their thinking about a text. It also provides a foundation for the organization of their thinking.

An important element in understanding a procedure is having a working knowledge of the skill concept. Students bring with them varied background experiences that relate directly to the concept. Building upon this concrete knowledge, a procedure gives a student a strategy for dealing with abstract learning. Just as students bring varied backgrounds, they also bring varied ability levels. Procedures give one the flexibility to adjust instruction to meet these various abilities and needs. Through formal and/or informal diagnosis, the teacher can decide what part of the procedure and what background information will need to be taught to meet the needs of the students and their rates of learning.

Procedures are not dependent on reading the written word. Through background knowledge and new experiences, students can develop a strategy using oral language. Beginning at this concrete level will facilitate an understanding of the written word, that is, reading comprehension.

Teacher modeling is crucial if students are to internalize and personalize the procedure. Once students have selected the parts of the procedure that aid comprehension, those parts become the students' strategy. Modeling also plays a crucial role in the students' metacognition. *Metacognition* is the awareness and control of one's own thought processes in attending to, focusing on, processing, comprehending, and remembering information (Baker and Brown 1983). When focusing on reading, metacognition has been referred to as "metacomprehension," whereby students determine what strategies will best help them to comprehend when reading. During modeling, it is important for the teacher to have students verbalize how they used the procedure they have just learned and when it might be used.

1

There are several ways to check the level of a student's metacognition (Palinscar and Brown 1986). First, ask questions (for example, What do you think when you want to be sure you understand the selection? What is the thing to do when you don't understand the selection?). Second, ask the student to tutor another child. Note the directions the student gives, the hints suggested and the cautions provided. Third, ask students to verbalize what they are doing when completing an activity.

Metacognition provides a valuable tool for students not only during reading, but also in everyday life. Students will have been taught to think in the classroom and, as they begin to function in the real world, they may implement their thinking in new situations.

In reading, a strategy is a tool that students can use to help analyze what they read. A strategy also aids in correcting misunderstandings. Traditionally, the comprehension skills, when taught in isolation, have not been thought of as strategies. When students apply the skill through a procedure, however, that process becomes a working strategy. These skill strategies can easily be integrated with other reading strategies, such as SQ3R, DRTA, KWL (**S**urvey, **Q**uestion, **R**ead, **R**ecall, **R**eview; **D**irected **R**eading **T**hinking **A**ctivity; and **W**hat I **K**now, **W**hat I **W**ant to **L**earn, and What I **L**earned).

Students become independent readers when they can make judgments about a text and select appropriate strategies for comprehension. Competency is demonstrated when they self-monitor and self-question to confirm, verify, and check their understanding. This competency enables them to use the new learning and apply it in a different context. It is a teacher's responsibility to provide instruction, material, and guidance to ensure that all students become confident, independent readers.

COMPREHENSION SKILLS LISTING

Teachers must critically review the comprehension strategies they teach and select only the essential ones to incorporate into their comprehension programs (Cooper 1986). By using formal and informal diagnosis, we identified a list of competencies that gave students difficulty in various contents and contexts. We compared our list with various instructional texts and standardized tests. We also asked for input and feedback from teachers at all elementary grade levels.

Through our research, we located a comprehension model that places emphasis on the type of comprehension rather than on isolated skills. Judith I. Schwartz, in her book *Encouraging Early Literacy* (1988), divided comprehension skills into three levels according to "their ranks as lower- to higher-order thinking processes." She defines *literal comprehension* in reading as "the understanding of the direct, primary, and literal meaning of written discourse." Her middle level, *interpretation*, is defined as "understanding what is implied by the written material." The third level of comprehension is *critical evaluation*, during which "the reader evaluates written material by measuring it against some evidence or standard and then making a judgment about its veracity, accuracy, and quality."

In refining our initial list, we found that Schwartz's three divisions fit our targeted procedures and strategies quite well. The list is as follows:

LITERAL COMPREHENSION
Context Clues
Details
Following Directions
Sequence

INTERPRETATION
Cause and Effect
Characterization
Classification
Compare and Contrast
Fact versus Fiction
Figurative Language
Generalization
Inference and Conclusion
Main Idea
Paraphrase
Prediction
Realism and Fantasy
Summarization
Visualization

CRITICAL EVALUATION
Author's Purpose
Author's Point of View
Fact versus Opinion
Narrative and Expository Writing
Propaganda

In this book, we have built a unit around each of these areas, and developed teacher and student checklists that were derived from skill procedures. We observed, during students' use, that these checklists also reinforced Schwartz's model of the three levels of thinking processes.

This listing does not prescribe a sequential order for teaching strategies. It frees the teacher to determine when and what strategies to focus on according to the students' strengths and weaknesses. Teachers also need to consider the content and context of material as part of this decision making.

IMPLEMENTATION FOR PLANNING

The materials presented in each numbered unit may be used as teacher resources when planning instruction. We include in each unit a Teacher Checklist for Planning and a Student Checklist. The Teacher Checklist is a plan for instructional steps. The Student Checklist is the procedure intended to be used by the students as a strategy for independent reading in all content areas and contexts. The content of the Student Checklist is then repeated in a visual representation that can be reproduced for students. An annotated bibliography, directions and patterns for making games and game folders, and additional suggested activities complete the teacher resources in each unit.

Teacher Checklists for Planning

Students will always be at different reading levels. It is important for the teacher to determine where to begin the instruction and, equally important, where to end the instruction to meet the objective. It might be appropriate, for your students, to add or delete steps on these checklists. The teacher will need formal and/or informal assessments to determine each student's knowledge of the skill and how well he or she demonstrates the strategy.

Terms such as *define, teach*, and *review* are used in the checklists to provide flexibility with the beginning or ending of instruction. If students are familiar with the definition, for example, the teacher can begin at the teaching step. These terms are used in the broadest sense. The decisions about how to define, teach, and review are left to you, the teacher.

One strategic technique stressed in the Teacher Checklists is the modeling of the procedure. The important point here is to allow students to observe the procedure and "see" the teacher's thinking. It is important for the teacher to demonstrate verbally how she or he integrated the new information in reading. Modeling minimizes the chance of students misinterpreting the teacher's intentions. This is quite important for students with poor reading ability, because their background knowledge of critical comprehension strategies and how they are used is limited.

The teacher must determine which materials should be used to meet students' needs. Be sure to provide a variety of materials, such as basals, informational books, a wide sampling of fiction, poetry books, and manipulatives.

These checklists are not based on a designated time allotment. Instructional time should be based on the individual needs and abilities of the students. These checklists can be followed when planning instruction for a whole group, small groups, or individuals.

Student Checklists

The Student Checklist is designed to give students strategies to organize their thinking, and to remind them of the steps involved. The teacher must determine whether to model all or part of the procedure according to students' reading abilities and objectives.

Visuals

According to Joyce and Weil (1986), providing a visual representation of a skill along with verbal explanation assists students in following the explanation. Later, at other points in the learning process, the visual representation serves as a cue or prompt. Teachers and researchers have found that presenting students with a visual handout of the procedure, or creating a wall poster of it, enables students to focus their thinking on the steps needed for comprehension, using an identified strategy.

Visuals can be reproduced for student handouts, made into transparencies, or enlarged for wall posters. Modification of the visual may be necessary if the Student Checklist is changed.

Annotated Bibliographies

The annotated bibliographies in each unit are listings of literature that assist teachers in providing students with opportunities to use the comprehension strategies they have learned. Using quality literature to reinforce these comprehension strategies provides advantages for all students. Literature gives an excellent model for reading, gets students actively involved because of their interest in the story, and makes it easier for students to relate knowledge. An integration of strategies can be used when needed for comprehension. Teachers should consider using the following steps:

1. Select literature based on student interest and strategy focus.

2. Read the selection first. Let the students enjoy the illustrations as well as the content.

3. Deal with the selection as a whole. Don't dissect the information.

4. Discuss the story, letting students ask and/or respond to questions.

5. Discuss strategies used for comprehension skills that are reinforced by the selection.

These bibliographies are not complete lists, but ones to which titles can and should continually be added.

Games

Students benefit from active learning. Games and activities are outstanding vehicles for helping students practice, internalize, and apply comprehension strategies. They lend themselves to students helping students in a variety of settings, such as cooperative learning and peer tutoring. The games and activities can serve as models for student-created materials. A major benefit is the replacement of worksheets and workbooks with games and activities that are relevant to the students. In this book, games have been designed to reinforce the strategy focus and to correspond to pieces of children's literature. However, games are not included for every skill unit, because some strategy focuses did not lend themselves to the game format.

Each game has individual directions and a self-checking system. They can be teacher-modeled and/or then completed independently. Here are a few general suggestions for making games:

1. Make copies of game pages (the publisher permits limited photocopying, see copyright statement, p. iv).

2. Collect colored manila folders and library pockets.

3. Cut out selection names and glue onto folder tabs; cut out focus labels and glue onto folder fronts.

4. Cut out answer cards and student directions and store in library pockets that have been glued onto backs of folders.

5. Game pieces can be colored or outlined with color.

6. Some game pieces will be glued onto the insides of folders, and some will be stored in library pockets (see individual games).

7. Extra game pieces are provided for folder decorations or replacement pieces.

8. For longer lasting games, laminate or cover folder and pieces with clear contact paper. This is especially useful for games that ask students to mark answers in grease pencil, as answers can be wiped off after a student completes the game.

Activities

The activities listed in each unit can be used in several ways. They can be developed into bulletin boards, utilized in centers, made the objective for a cooperative learning activity, or used for independent practice, small group/whole group activities, and teacher-directed lessons.

The activities can be presented to the students in various manners. Many can be presented as writing activities. Others lend themselves to classroom displays, exhibits, and presentations. Charts, posters, and overhead transparencies can be utilized. Class or individual books can be created. Although many activities are presented as writing activities for intermediate grades, all the activities can be adjusted to the level of your students. Choose reading materials appropriate to the level. Students do not always have to write, but can draw pictures, use tape recorders, or verbalize their responses to a teacher or group.

Materials come from a variety of sources, so start your collection now—magazines, newspapers, catalogs, student publications, old workbooks, worksheets, old basals, pictures, photographs, and everyday clutter. Teachers do not have to prepare all the activities beforehand. Students can share an active role in the preparation of materials.

IMPLEMENTATION INTO CURRICULUM

In this section, we discuss the implementation of comprehension strategies into various curricula.

Basal Approach

Research on direct instruction indicates that the basal approach is effective in promoting student learning in reading (Joyce and Weil 1986). Since most basal approaches use the direct instruction model, teaching of strategies can be implemented in three basic steps:

1. Teaching
   a. State objective and provide background knowledge.
   b. Model procedure for skill.
   c. Provide guided practice.
   d. Check for understanding.

2. Practicing
   a. Have students use strategy in completion of an activity.
   b. Check and give feedback.

3. Applying
   a. Have students apply strategy to text through guided application.
   b. Have students apply strategy to text through independent application.

Whole Language Approach

In the whole language approach, students can learn the procedures and strategies through the use of mini-lessons, teacher-student conferences, and the like. The teacher can make observations of students' needs and provide them with the necessary guidance and individual support.

The strategies can be reinforced and/or extended through programs around children's literature, writing, and oral language.

Content Areas

The most logical place for instruction in reading and thinking strategies is in social studies and science, rather than in separate lessons about reading. The reason is that the strategies are useful mainly when a student is grappling with important but unfamiliar content (Anderson et al. 1985).

The content areas are ideal places for students to develop a concept and demonstrate a strategy. Cause and effect can be developed through the use of manipulatives in science. Guess and check, a math problem-solving strategy, is very similar to prediction. Social studies topics such as communities, cities, and countries are ideal subject matter for compare and contrast.

Resource Personnel

In a school system that has resource personnel, use of the Teacher Checklist for Planning can provide consistent language for all involved. In planning with teachers, the resource personnel will find out where in the procedure to begin instruction and/or where to end to meet the objectives. This decreases the confusion students could have with terminology and expectations.

At-Risk Students

According to Barton (1988), the classification "at risk" includes students with disadvantaged backgrounds, disciplinary problems, learning disabilities, lack of experience with the English language, and chronic absentee problems. In contrast to students from advantaged homes, at-risk students do not always have the background knowledge or experience with comprehension skills that provides them with the necessary ingredients for comprehension of what they read. More effective comprehension for at-risk students can be facilitated by focusing instruction on critical comprehension skills, such as main idea, sequence, cause and effect, and the like. This instruction gives the student a basic foundation for comprehension, a foundation that can expand for various types of texts.

Gifted and Talented Students

Gifted and talented children are those who, by virtue of outstanding abilities, are capable of high performance. In general, the research and literature on reading instruction support the idea that gifted and creative pupils can attain the highest level of ability—that of evaluation and creative behavior—if they gain the skills that make them independent (Labuda 1985). Implementing the use of procedures and strategies helps create the independence needed for these students to achieve their highest potential. Our teaching plan allows for flexibility in the pace of instruction and extension necessary to meet the needs of these students.

Test Taking

Although standardized tests do not measure a student's true reading ability, they are, at this time, a fact of life. These tests assess skills in isolation, and the material is usually irrelevant. Students who have a solid background in comprehension skill strategies will be able to select the appropriate strategies for designated questions. Consistent use of these strategies in the classroom will foster the independence needed for the testing period.

Evaluation

Evaluation of students' comprehension can be both formal and informal. If there is a "break-down," the teacher can diagnose what part of the procedure or strategy needs extra attention. Remediation can occur through guided practice, peer tutoring, or other reading, writing, and speaking activities. Evaluation needs to be an ongoing process, one that involves the students in reading relevant texts for real purposes.

REFERENCES

Anderson, R. C., E. H. Hiebert, J. A. Scott, and I. Wilkinson, eds. 1985. *Becoming a Nation of Readers: The Report of the Commission on Reading*. [Contract No. 400-83-0057]. Washington, DC: National Institute of Education.

Baker, L., and A. L. Brown. 1983. "Metacognitive Skills and Reading." In *Handbook of Reading Research*, edited by D. Pearson. New York: Longman.

Barton, Jim. 1988. "Reading Instruction in the Accelerated School." Stanford, CA: School of Education, Stanford University.

Cooper, David. 1986. *Improving Reading Comprehension*. Boston: Houghton Mifflin.

Herrmann, B. A. 1988. "Two Approaches for Helping Poor Readers Become More Strategic." *The Reading Teacher* 42: 24.

Joyce, B., and M. Weil. 1986. "Mastery Learning and Direct Instruction." In *Models of Teaching*. 3d ed. Englewood Cliffs, NJ: Prentice-Hall.

Labuda, Michael, ed. 1985. "Gifted and Creative Pupils: Reasons for Concern." In *Creative Reading for Gifted Learners*. 2d ed. Newark, DE: International Reading Association Inc.

Marzano, R., and D. Arrendondo. 1986. *Tactics for Thinking*. Aurora, CO: Mid-Continent Regional Educational Laboratory.

Palinscar, A., and A. L. Brown. 1986. "Metacognitive Strategy Instruction." *Exceptional Children* 53: 188-94.

Resnick, L. B., and L. Klopfer, eds. 1989. "Toward the Thinking Curriculum: An Overview." In *Toward the Thinking Curriculum: Current Cognitive Research*. Alexandria, VA: ASCD Yearbook.

Schwartz, Judith I. 1988. *Encouraging Early Literacy*. Portsmouth, NH: Heinemann Educational Books.

Literal Comprehension

1—CONTEXT CLUES

Objective: The student will identify the <u>meaning</u> of an unfamiliar word in context.

TEACHER CHECKLIST FOR PLANNING

1. Teach students to determine if the unfamiliar word is necessary for the meaning of the sentence.

2. Define context clues—words or phrases around the unfamiliar word that are used to determine the meaning.

3. Define antonyms, synonyms, analogies, multiple meanings, qualifiers, etc.

4. Teach use of antonyms, synonyms, analogies, multiple meanings, qualifiers, etc.

5. Teach use of antonyms, synonyms, analogies, multiple meanings and/or qualifiers as clues for figuring out the unknown word.

6. Teach how knowing the function of the unknown word (action word, naming word, describing word) can be a clue in determining its meaning.

7. Have students read sentence(s).

8. Have students think about the overall meaning of what they read.

9. Have students guess the meaning of the unknown word and substitute their guess(es) in the original sentence(s).

10. Have students reread sentence(s). Ask: Does it make sense?

11. Potential obstacle: Sentences that don't contain enough information to provide clues. Solution: When this situation is unavoidable, teach alternative strategies, such as using a dictionary, thesaurus, or glossary, or asking a peer or teacher.

STUDENT CHECKLIST

1. Read sentence(s).

2. Guess meaning of unknown word using clues.

3. Put guess in place of unknown word.

4. Reread the sentence(s).

5. Ask: Does it make sense?

STUDENT VISUAL—CONTEXT CLUES

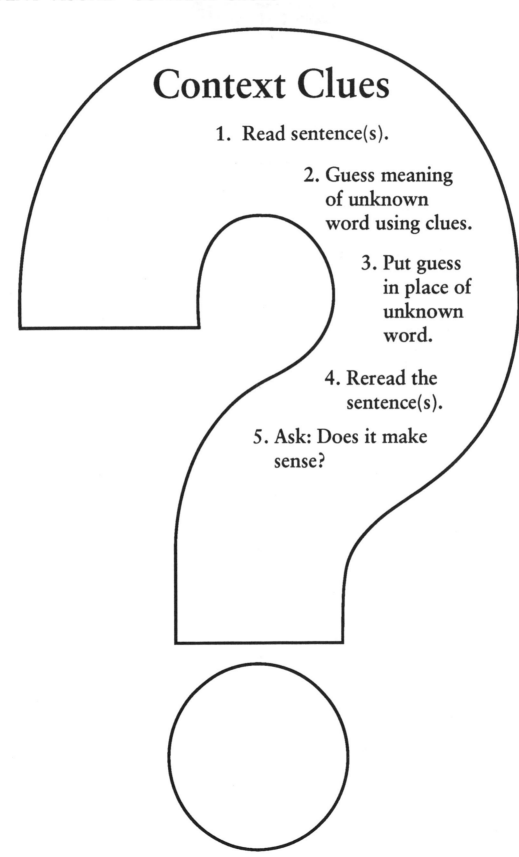

Context Clues

1. Read sentence(s).

2. Guess meaning of unknown word using clues.

3. Put guess in place of unknown word.

4. Reread the sentence(s).

5. Ask: Does it make sense?

ANNOTATED BIBLIOGRAPHY

Basil, Cynthia. *How Ships Play Cards*. Illustrated by Janet McCaffery. New York: William Morris & Co., 1980.
Uses riddles to introduce words that look and sound alike but have different meanings.

Bossom, Naomi. *A Scale Full of Fish and Other Turnabouts*. New York: Greenwillow Books, 1979.
Ten pairs of pictures explore the difference in meaning in pairs of words.

Butterword, Nick. *Nice or Nasty*. Boston: Little, Brown & Co., 1987.
Animal and human characters introduce opposite concepts, such as fast and slow, wet and dry, weak and strong.

Domanska, Janina. *A Scythe, a Rooster and a Cat*. New York: Greenwillow Books, 1981.
Adaptation of a Russian folktale about three brothers who make their fortunes, one with a scythe, one with a rooster, and one with a cat.

Fadiman, Clifton. *Wally the Wordworm*. Illustrated by Lisa Atherton. Owings Mills, MD: Stemmer House Publishers, 1983.
A worm with a voracious appetite for words, who has grown bored with those he finds in the tabloids, discovers the dictionary, where his flagging appetite revives. Includes puns, puzzles, and plays on words.

Goble, Paul. *Iktomi and the Berries*. New York: Orchard Books, 1988.
Relates Iktomi's fruitless efforts to pick some buffalo berries.

_____. *Iktomi and the Boulder*. New York: Orchard Books, 1988.
Iktomi, a Plains Indian trickster, attempts to defeat a boulder with the assistance of some bats, in this story explaining why the Great Plains are covered with small stones.

Grimm, Jacob Ludwig Karl. *The Bearskinner*. Illustrated by Felix Hoffmann. New York: Atheneum Publishers, 1978.
A soldier returning from war promises to do the devil's bidding for seven years in return for as much money and property as he can ever use.

Gwynne, Fred. *The King Who Rained*. New York: Simon & Schuster, 1970.
A little girl pictures the things her parents talk about, such as a king who rained, bear feet, and the foot prince in the snow.

_____. *A Little Pigeon Toad*. New York: Simon & Schuster, 1988.
Humorous text and illustrations introduce a variety of homonyms and figures of speech.

_____. *The Sixteen Hand Horse*. New York: Windmill/Wanderer Books, 1980.
Depicts a little girl's visual images of her parents' talk about such things as bells that peel, banking a fire, and a running nose.

Hanson, Joan. *More Antonyms*. Minneapolis: Lerner Publications, 1973.
Humorous illustrations are used to show the relationship among a number of antonyms.

_____. *More Synonyms*. Minneapolis: Lerner Publications, 1973.
Amusing illustrations are used to show the similarity in meaning among a number of words.

Harris, Joel Chandler. *Jump Again*. Adapted by Van Dyke Parks. Illustrated by Barry Moser. San Diego: Harcourt Brace Jovanovich, 1987.
"Brer Rabbit, He's a Good Fisherman," "The Wonderful Tarbaby," "How Brer Weasel Was Caught," and "Brer Rabbit and the Mosquitoes" are included.

Heller, Ruth. *A Cache of Jewels and Other Collective Nouns*. New York: Grossett & Dunlap, 1987.
Illustrates collective nouns such as "a cache of jewels," "a batch of bread," "a kindle of kittens," and many more.

_____. *Kites Sail High: A Book about Verbs*. New York: Grossett & Dunlap, 1987.
Introduces basic concepts of verbs in a simple verse.

_____. *Many Luscious Lollipops: A Book about Adjectives*. New York: Grossett & Dunlap, 1989.
An introduction to adjectives, their uses, and their forms.

Hoban, Tana. *More Than One*. New York: Greenwillow Books, 1981.
Photographs illustrate words that suggest more than one of an object, animal, or person, such as *stack*, *bundle*, *batch*, and *heap*.

Kundrna, C. Imbior. *Two-Way Words*. Nashville: Abingdon Press, 1980.
Text and drawings introduce homophones and homographs.

Terban, Marvin. *Superdupers!* Illustrated by Giulio Maestro. New York: Clarion Books, 1989.
Explains the meaning and origins of more than a hundred nonsense words that make the English language more colorful, including *flip-flop*, *fuzzy-wuzzy*, *cancan*, and *tutti-frutti*.

Van Allsburg, Chris. *Two Bad Ants*. Boston: Houghton Mifflin, 1988.
When two bad ants desert from their colony, they experience a dangerous adventure that convinces them to return to their former safety.

Vaughn, Marcia K. *Wombat Stew*. Illustrated by Pamela Lotts. Morristown, NJ: Silver Burdett, 1984.
Describes a dingo's attempt at making wombat stew in the outback of Australia while other animals try to trick the dingo.

GAME 1

SELECTION TITLE:

> *Iktomi and the Berries*
> by Paul Goble

FOCUS:

CONTEXT CLUES

HOW TO MAKE: Cut out the boxes containing selection title, focus, student directions, and answer card. Color and cut out all game pieces. Glue title onto folder tab and focus onto folder front. Glue arrow and matching teepee across from each other onto the inside of the folder. Store student directions, answer card, and *grease pencil* in library pocket glued to back of folder.

STUDENT DIRECTIONS:

1. Read sentence on arrow and read words on matching teepee.
2. Circle with grease pencil the word on that teepee that best finishes the sentence.
3. Do all sentences the same way.
4. Check your answers using answer card.

ANSWER CARD:

1. ancestors
2. risen
3. arrow
4. rope
5. reflection
6. temper

PIECES FOR GAME 1—CONTEXT CLUES

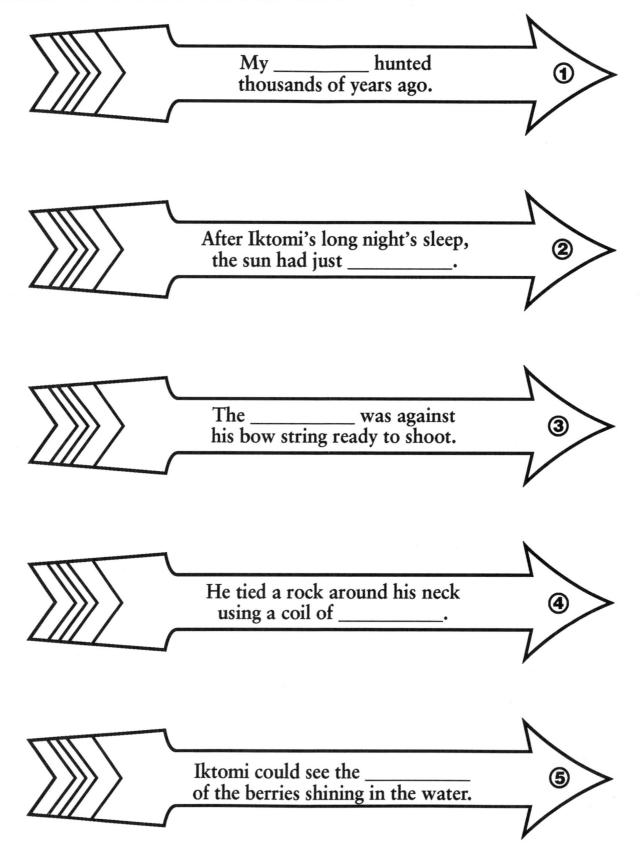

My _____ hunted thousands of years ago. ①

After Iktomi's long night's sleep, the sun had just _____. ②

The _____ was against his bow string ready to shoot. ③

He tied a rock around his neck using a coil of _____. ④

Iktomi could see the _____ of the berries shining in the water. ⑤

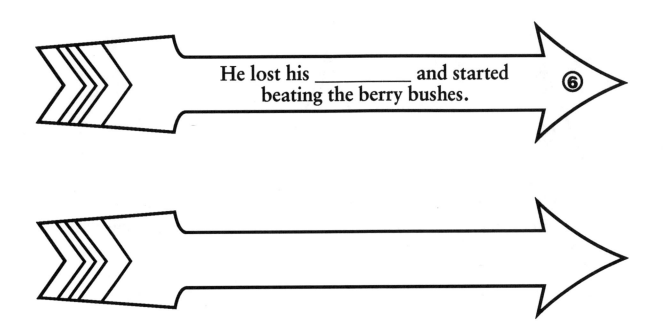

He lost his _____ and started
beating the berry bushes.

6

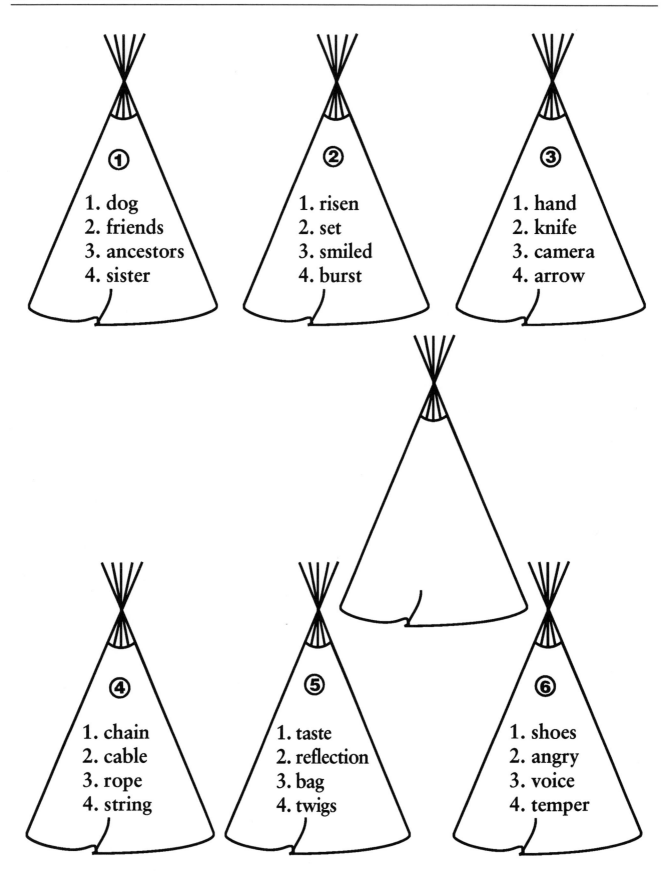

①
1. dog
2. friends
3. ancestors
4. sister

②
1. risen
2. set
3. smiled
4. burst

③
1. hand
2. knife
3. camera
4. arrow

④
1. chain
2. cable
3. rope
4. string

⑤
1. taste
2. reflection
3. bag
4. twigs

⑥
1. shoes
2. angry
3. voice
4. temper

GAME 2

SELECTION TITLE:

> *Wombat Stew*
> by Marcia K. Vaughn

FOCUS:

> # CONTEXT CLUES

HOW TO MAKE: Cut out the boxes containing selection title, focus, student directions, and answer card. Color and cut out all game pieces. Glue title onto folder tab and focus onto folder front. Glue stew pots onto the inside of the folder. Store student directions, answer card, and wombats in library pocket glued to back of folder.

STUDENT DIRECTIONS:

1. Read sentences on stew pots.
2. Think about the meaning of the underlined word.
3. Find the meaning on the wombat for that underlined word.
4. Place that wombat on the stewpot.
5. Check your answers using answer card.

ANSWER CARD:

1. body of water
2. clumps
3. cooking pot
4. kind of tree

5. swallow
6. nuts from a tree
7. dog
8. kind of animal

9. walked

PIECES FOR GAME 2—CONTEXT CLUES

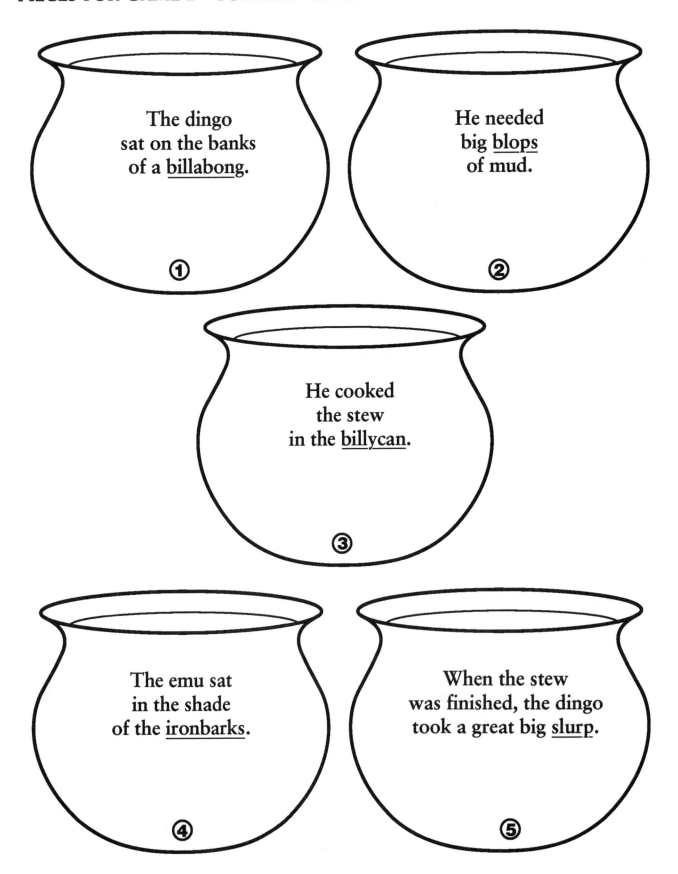

The dingo
sat on the banks
of a <u>billabong</u>.

①

He needed
big <u>blops</u>
of mud.

②

He cooked
the stew
in the <u>billycan</u>.

③

The emu sat
in the shade
of the <u>ironbarks</u>.

④

When the stew
was finished, the dingo
took a great big <u>slurp</u>.

⑤

The <u>gumnuts</u> lay on the ground around the tree.

⑥

The wild <u>dingo</u> howled like a dog.

⑦

The wombat is a <u>marsupial</u>, an animal that carries its young in a pouch.

⑧

Platypus <u>ambled</u> slowly up the bank towards the dingo.

⑨

unused meanings

ACTIVITIES

Reverse the Meaning: Have students select a paragraph from one of their favorite books that has lots of action. Have them rewrite the paragraph substituting opposites for verbs. It will create an entirely new meaning for the paragraph. This activity could also be applied to nouns or adjectives in the paragraph.

Use a Synonym: Have students select a paragraph from a book they have read. Have them rewrite each paragraph using synonyms whenever possible. Put the two paragraphs together. Read the new story and compare it with the original.

Word Bank: When students come across words that have multiple meanings, the words can be added to a class or personal word bank. List each word on a separate 3" x 5" card. Have the students use the words in sentences that demonstrate the different meanings through context, and add these sentences to the card. Students could also draw pictures to help illustrate the words' meanings. Students can then refer to the word bank when they need help.

Children's Own Thesaurus: Instead of making an ordinary dictionary, have the students keep an ongoing thesaurus. Share with them an example of a thesaurus. Develop a list of everyday and overused words that the students have in their vocabulary; some of those words might include *walk, run, like, happy, sad*, and *nice*. When students come across synonyms for these words in their reading, have them add the synonyms to the thesaurus. When they are editing their own writing, the thesaurus will help them choose different words.

Match the Author: Select a paragraph or part of a selection. Write it on chart paper, leaving out several key words as you go. As a group, read the paragraph and brainstorm possible choices for the missing words. Decide upon the best word and write it in the blank. Reread the paragraph. Then hand out a copy of the original paragraph. Read and compare the students' choices to the author's choices. Many times they will be identical.

Mistakes Everywhere: Make a list of sentences that include mistakes that can be found through context. For example, "Tom studied for three hours so that he would flunk his test." Have students find the mistake, cross it out, and substitute a word that makes sense in the context.

Nonsense Makes Sense: Prepare sentences, replacing one word with a nonsense word (for instance, "The drezzil swung from the trees with a banana in his hand"). With younger students, underline the nonsense word. Older students can identify the word that is making understanding difficult. Discuss the meaning of the nonsense word. Write a definition for the nonsense word. Throughout the day or week, make the nonsense word the secret class word and use it in context whenever possible.

A Picture Is Worth a Thousand Words!: Supply an interesting picture and post it on the wall. Create cloze sentences, leaving out a word that can be determined by using the context in the picture. If the task is too difficult, you can also supply the first letter of the missing word.

Scrambled Eggs: Collect plastic eggs similar to those used for pantyhose packages. Write and cut apart several sentences, word by word. Put the words in the eggs, one sentence per egg, leaving out one word in each sentence. Put all the "left-out" words in one egg. Have students open an egg, unscramble the sentence, and then from the last egg locate the missing word. To make the game easier to put away, color code the sentences and the missing words.

Context Captions: Provide students with cartoons that have one or more words cut from the captions. After studying the cartoons, students supply the missing words. Select the cartoons carefully—sometimes the humor is hard for students to interpret.

Simon Says, "What": Play "Simon Says" with students, but increase the difficulty by not naming the item. Instead, give them clues for the item. For example, Simon says, "Clap the things that have five fingers"; Simon says, "Stand on the things found on the end of your feet."

2—DETAILS

Objective: The student will identify details of a picture or written selection.

TEACHER CHECKLIST FOR PLANNING

1. Define details—information that helps readers understand or believe a picture or selection.

2. Teach how to locate words and phrases that tell *who*.
   Examples: Names of people, objects

3. Teach how to locate words and phrases that tell *what*.
   Examples: *That, which, how, how much*

4. Teach how to locate words and phrases that tell *when*.
   Example: Time

5. Teach how to locate words and phrases that tell *where*.
   Examples: Location, position

6. Teach how to locate words and phrases that tell *why*.
   Examples: Reason, cause

7. Teach how to locate words and phrases that tell *how*.
   Examples: Way, method

8. Have students use pictures or written selections to find details.

STUDENT CHECKLIST

1. Look at picture and/or read selection.

2. Identify words and phrases that tell **Who, What, When, Where, Why, and How.**

STUDENT VISUAL—DETAILS

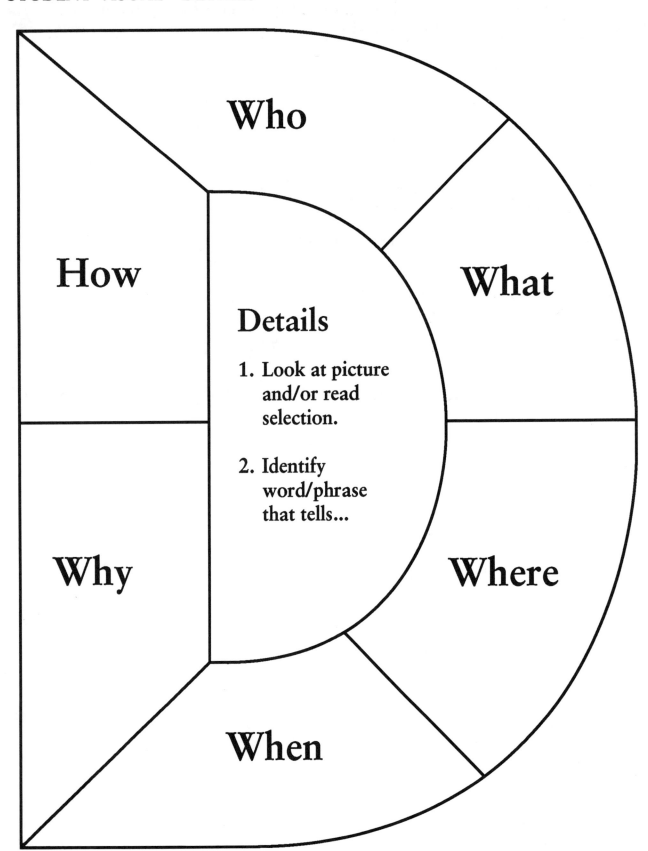

Who

How

What

Details

1. Look at picture and/or read selection.

2. Identify word/phrase that tells...

Why

Where

When

ANNOTATED BIBLIOGRAPHY

Brown, Margaret Wise. *Goodnight Moon*. Illustrated by Clement Hurd. New York: Scholastic, 1947.
A small rabbit acknowledges items in his room and tells each of them goodnight.

Crowe, Robert. *Clyde Monster*. Illustrated by Kay Chorao. New York: E. P. Dutton, 1976.
A young monster is afraid of the dark because he believes that a person may be lurking under the bed or in a corner.

De Paola, Tomie. *The Cloud Book*. New York: Holiday House, 1975.
Introduces the ten most common types of clouds, the myths that have been inspired by cloud shapes, and what clouds can tell about coming weather changes.

Goble, Paul. *The Girl Who Loved Wild Horses*. New York: Bradbury Press, 1978.
Though she is fond of her people, a girl prefers to live among the wild horses where she is truly happy and free.

Hall, Donald. *Ox-Cart Man*. Illustrated by Barbara Cooney. New York: Viking Press, 1979.
Describes the day-to-day life throughout the changing seasons of an early nineteenth-century New England family.

Hogrogian, Nonny. *One Fine Day*. New York: Macmillan, 1971.
An old woman cuts off a fox's tail when he steals her milk, and the fox must go through a long series of transactions before she will sew it back again.

Hutchins, Pat. *The Wind Blew*. New York: Macmillan, 1974.
A rhymed tale describing the antics of a capricious wind.

_____. *You'll Soon Grow into Them, Titch*. New York: Greenwillow Books, 1983.
The tables turn at last for Titch, who has been inheriting his older siblings' outgrown clothes.

Lobel, Arnold. *A Treeful of Pigs*. Illustrated by Anita Lobel. New York: Greenwillow Books, 1979.
A farmer's wife uses drastic measures to get her husband to abandon his lazy ways.

Rylant, Cynthia. *The Relatives Came*. Illustrated by Stephen Gammell. New York: Bradbury Press, 1985.
The relatives come to visit from Virginia and everyone has a wonderful time.

Viorst, Judith. *Alexander and the Terrible, Horrible, No Good, Very Bad Day*. Illustrated by Ray Cruz. New York: Macmillan, 1972.
Alexander's day is filled with mishaps from the time he gets up until the time he goes to bed.

GAME

SELECTION TITLE:

> *Alexander and the Terrible,*
> *Horrible, No Good, Very Bad Day*
> by Judith Viorst

FOCUS:

DETAILS

HOW TO MAKE: Cut out selection title, focus, student directions, and answer card. Color and cut out all game pieces. Glue title onto folder tab and focus onto folder front. Glue silhouettes onto inside of folder. Store directions, answer card, and phrase cards in library pocket glued to back of folder.

STUDENT DIRECTIONS:

1. Read phrase cards and think about the underlined word.
2. Read words on faces.
3. Decide what kind of detail the underlined word is providing.
4. Place the phrase card on the detail categories (faces).
5. Check your answers using answer card.

ANSWER CARD:

Who?	*What?*	*When?*
Audrey got a seat third best friend	sang too loud found a cavity	out of bed this morning while I was punching Nick
Where?	*Why?*	*How?*

sweater in the sink
move to Australia
went to shoe store
	bad day because Mom
	   forgot dessert
	started crying because
	   of mud
	scolded me for being
	   muddy
		sang too loud
		liked Paul's picture
		   better

PIECES FOR GAME—DETAILS

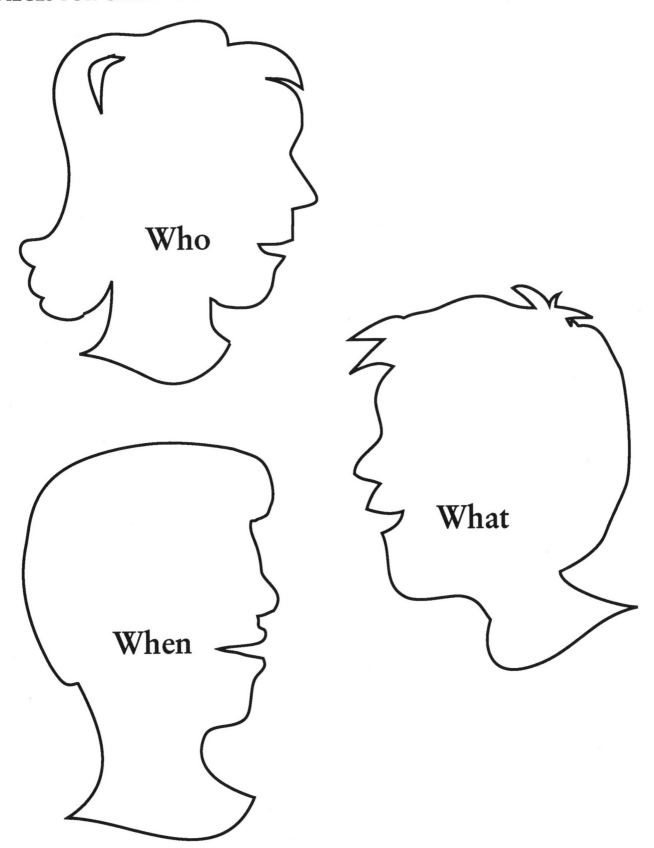

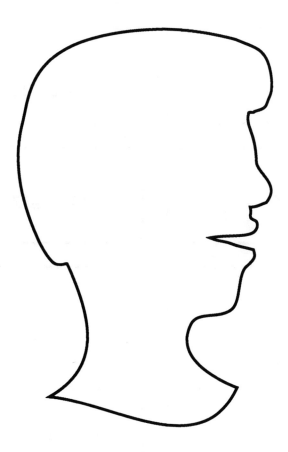

sang too loud	bad day because mom forgot dessert
sweater in the sink	found a cavity
out of bed this morning	started crying because of mud
move to Australia	scolded me for being muddy
Audrey got a seat	went to shoe store
sang too loud	while I was punching Nick
third best friend	liked Paul's picture better

ACTIVITIES

Detail Jeopardy: Have students read a selection. Then give them the answers to detail questions. They will write the appropriate questions. This activity could be used as individual work or expanded into a game modeled after the television game.

Mismatched Details: Find several interesting pictures. Write short paragraphs about the pictures, but make several mistakes (for instance, your paragraph says it was raining hard, but the picture shows a clear, sunny day). Have students look at the pictures carefully and read the paragraphs. After they locate the mistakes in a paragraph, they should circle them and rewrite the paragraph, correcting the mistakes.

Picture Dialogue: Select pictures from magazines, newspapers, etc., that have at least two characters. Have students work alone or in small groups. If they are working in a small group, they should discuss the details they see in the picture. Then they can write a dialogue for the people in the picture, using the details. When they are completed, post the pictures, share the dialogues, and have students match pictures and dialogues.

Sentence Division: Using chart paper or student paper, divide the paper into six columns labeled *who, what, where, when, why, how*. Take sentences from students' reading or their writing, or make up sentences from students' vocabulary. Have students read sentences and divide the sentences into words or phrases that note details. Students write the phrases in the correct columns. An example to get you started is "Six big dogs quickly ate the meat on our table before dinner because they were starved."

Scrambled Phrases: Make a master list of words and phrases that tell who, what, where, when, why, and how. Students can use the phrases to create sentences that include lots of details. In the beginning, you may want to use just two or three phrases to complete a sentence. Have students use the details in the sentences to draw illustrations. Display individual students' pictures and sentences separately around the room. Students will identify the who, what, where, when, why, and how in the sentences. Students will then match these sentences with the appropriate pictures.

Be a Detective: Start a collection of "crime scene" pictures, both funny and serious. For example, the pictures might show a window broken by a baseball, an empty plate and a dog on the floor eating the pizza, or a bank robbery. Students begin by pretending they are police officers. They generate a list of questions to ask about the "crime." After the questions are completed, they answer the questions using the details in the pictures. Some answers may be quite obvious; some may be inferred. Start a book of crime reports for students to share. Your local police or sheriff's department may be a good resource for samples of crime reports or guest speakers.

Hear a Detail: Read a description of an event, such as a birthday party, or a person. The description should include as many details as possible. Have students illustrate the event or person, using as many details as possible. Share the illustrations and talk about similarities and differences.

General-Specific: Set up a blank grid with columns for *who, what, where, when, why*, and *how*. Along the side, have two rows labeled *general* and *specific*. After reading a section, have students chart the details. Under general, they might have "animal," while under specific they might have "a big, black dog."

Irrelevant Details: Tape record or read a selection in which you have added several details that are irrelevant to the selection. Have students listen to the selection and identify the irrelevant details. Another option is to prepare in advance a written selection in which you have added several irrelevant details. After students read the selection, they may cross out the irrelevant details or edit the details so they are relevant to the selection.

3—FOLLOWING DIRECTIONS

Objective: The student will interpret and follow written directions.

TEACHER CHECKLIST FOR PLANNING

1. Discuss the importance of following written directions.

2. Share examples of how directions are used in different contexts.
   Examples: Recipes, games, hobbies, forms, workforce

3. Explain how to locate and identify directions.
   a. Parts—part A, part B.
   b. Numbers—steps 1, 2, 3.
   c. Bold print.
   d. Sections—space left between directions.
   e. Sequence words—first, next, then, last.

4. Explain the importance of skimming all directions before beginning.

5. Teach predicting the outcome of followed directions.

6. Have students predict outcomes.

7. Teach returning to the direction or first set of directions.

8. Teach clue words in a direction.
   Examples: Read, underline, draw, circle, glue, cut, mix, tie

9. Have students find clue words in directions.

10. Teach key information in a direction.
    Examples: What to glue, what to mix, how big, where to start:
    Glue the *small circle* to the *top* of the *page*.

11. Have students find key information in a direction.

12. Teach rereading the direction for understanding.

13. Have students reread and explain the direction.

14. If there is more than one direction, explain and model all directions using the previous steps.

STUDENT CHECKLIST

1. Skim page and look for direction(s).

2. Predict outcome of direction(s).

3. Read direction(s) to find clue words and key information.

4. Reread for understanding.

5. Follow the direction(s).

No game provided in this unit.

STUDENT VISUAL—FOLLOWING DIRECTIONS

Following Directions

1. Skim page and look for direction(s).

2. Predict outcome of direction(s).

3. Read direction(s) to find clue words and key information.

4. Reread for understanding.

5. Follow the direction(s).

ANNOTATED BIBLIOGRAPHY

Arnold, Caroline. *Charts and Graphs: Fun, Facts, and Activities*. Illustrated by Penny Carter. New York: Franklin Watts, 1984.
Explains how charts and graphs are used, and gives directions for a giant pie graph, a block bar graph, a time line, a family tree, a calendar, and other projects.

_____. *Maps and Globes: Fun, Facts, and Activities*. Illustrated by Lynn Sweat. New York: Franklin Watts, 1984.
Explains the uses of maps and globes; includes instructions for making a balloon globe, a model room, a giant compass rose, a contour map, a treasure map, and other projects.

Challand, Helen J. *Experiments with Electricity*. Chicago: Childrens Press, 1986.
A discussion of the properties of electricity, with several related experiments, and an introduction to different kinds of batteries.

Corwin, Judith Hoffman. *Papercrafts*. New York: Franklin Watts, 1988.
Provides illustrated instructions for making a variety of things out of paper, including projects in origami, papier-mâché, and collage.

De Paola, Tomie. *The Popcorn Book*. New York: Holiday House, 1978.
Presents a variety of facts about popcorn and includes two recipes.

_____. *The Quicksand Book*. New York: Holiday House, 1977.
Discusses the composition of quicksand and rescue procedures.

Fletcher, Helen Jill. *Secret Codes*. Illustrated by Michael Cooper. New York: Franklin Watts, 1980.
Presents several easy codes, with messages to decode and directions for making and writing with invisible ink and devising one's own code.

Gibbons, Gail. *Catch the Wind! All about Kites*. Boston: Little, Brown & Co., 1989.
When two children visit Ike's Kite Shop, they learn about kites and how to fly them; includes instructions for building a kite.

Gilman, Rita Golden, and Susan Kovacs Buxbaum. *Boats That Float*. Illustrated by Marilyn MacGregor. New York: Franklin Watts, 1981.
Instructions for making eleven different boats from common items; when finished, all will float.

Gretz, Susanna, and Alison Sage. *Teddybears Cookbook*. Illustrated by Susanna Gretz. Garden City, New York: Doubleday & Co., 1978.
Twenty-three easy-to-follow recipe treats including snacks, salads, desserts, and drinks.

Parish, Peggy. *Let's Be Indians*. Illustrated by Arnold Lobel. New York: Harper & Row, 1962.
Provides instructions for a variety of activities around the theme of Indians. Included are clothing, instruments, models, and games.

Pluckrose, Henry. *Crayons*. Photographs by Chris Fairclough. New York: Franklin Watts, 1987.
   Instructions and illustrations for a variety of crayon art, including resists, rubbings, batiks, and several others.

MacDonald, Suse. *Puzzlers*. Illustrated by Bill Oakes. New York: Dial Books for Young Readers, 1989.
   An introduction to elementary concepts such as "widest," "tallest," and "back-to-back," where the reader is asked to pick out the number with that quality in an animal that is made up of numbers.

Thomson, Neil, and Ruth Thomson. *Fairground Games to Make and Play*. Illustrated by Chris McEwan. Philadelphia: J. B. Lippincott Co., 1978.
   Illustrated instructions for constructing toys, games, and other amusements that recreate the fun of country fairs.

Webb, Angela. *Talk about Sound*. Photographs by Chris Fairclough. New York: Franklin Watts, 1988.
   Allows children to explore the principles of sound with simple activities and experiments using familiar objects and materials.

Winter, Jeanette. *Follow the Drinking Gourd*. New York: Alfred A. Knopf, 1988.
   By following the directions in a song "The Drinking Gourd," taught them by an old sailor, runaway slaves journey north along the Underground Railroad to freedom in Canada.

Zubrowski, Bernie. *Messing around with Baking Chemistry*. Illustrated by Signe Hanson. Boston: Little, Brown & Co., 1981.
   Presents experiments and projects to explore what happens when batter and dough turn into cake and bread. Emphasizes the properties of baking powder, baking soda, and yeast.

ACTIVITIES

Peanut Butter and Jelly: Students will enjoy watching you make a peanut-butter-and-jelly sandwich by following their directions. The trick is that they must give very specific and careful directions. If they don't say "Spread the peanut butter with a knife," but simply say "Put the peanut butter on the bread," put the jar on the bread. Work through the activity together orally first, to illustrate the need for specifics, then do the activity as an individual or small-group writing assignment. When the directions have been completed, make the sandwich again to see if the directions have improved.

Chocolate Sundaes: Many teachers work on a reward system. One way to incorporate the reward and writing is to establish the reward as a chocolate sundae. When the class or individuals have earned a reward, they write sundae-making directions and then follow their own directions to create the reward.

Forms, Forms, Forms: Collect an assortment of forms to be filled out. The collection might include magazine subscriptions, club memberships, job applications, credit card applications, driver's license applications, catalog order blanks, and contest entries. Students will get good practice in following directions with true-to-life paperwork. Your students could also develop applications for classroom jobs or class club memberships, or an entry form for a class contest. Other students must complete the form correctly to be considered for the job, club, or contest.

Everyday Labels: Bring in an assortment of care labels from clothing. Have students read the labels and then tell or write in their own words how to take care of the different garments. They could also draw pictures of the garments to go with the labels.

Warning: Bring in warning labels from household products, along with the products' directions for use. The items might include cleaning products, small electrical appliances, over-the-counter medicines, and childrens' toys. Read the labels and discuss what the warnings and directions mean. Students may wish to design and write their own labels to replace the company's labels.

Recipes: Recipes are a good resource for following direction activities. There are many easy-to-follow recipe books for children that can be used in the classroom. Don't forget the directions readily available on all microwave products.

Treasure Hunts: Working with your school media specialist, set up a treasure hunt in the library with directions for the students to follow. The treasure could be a new book, book marks for the students, or even you waiting to read aloud your favorite book. Students get practice following directions and learn about the library at the same time.

How Did They Do That?: Create a simple picture using circles, squares, and triangles. A clown face is a good possibility. Working with the completed picture, students write the step-by-step directions to make the picture. After the directions are complete, draw a new picture using the directions. Compare the two pictures to see if they are the same. If they are not, find the mistakes in the directions and correct them.

Sign Talk: Many signs in our world give us directions. Take photographs of these signs and display them in the classroom. Discuss the directions on each sign. Have students create new signs for use in your classroom.

4-SEQUENCE

Objective: The student will determine the correct sequence of objects or events in pictures and/or selections.

TEACHER CHECKLIST FOR PLANNING

1. Define sequence—a logical order of objects or events based on a given criteria.

2. Teach picture clues and clue words that are specific to sequence.
   Examples: First, next, last; big, bigger, biggest; before, later, after, ago; in front of, between, in back of

3. Teach context clues that are specific to sequence.
   Examples: Dates, times, seasons, ages

4. Have students determine types of sequential order.
   Examples: Time, size, position

5. Have students arrange, in correct sequence, some objects or events by using pictures and/or clues from a selection.

STUDENT CHECKLIST

1. Look at pictures and/or read selection.

2. Find picture clues/clue words.

3. Find context clues.

4. Determine type of order.

5. Arrange in order.

6. Does the sequence make sense?

STUDENT VISUAL—SEQUENCE

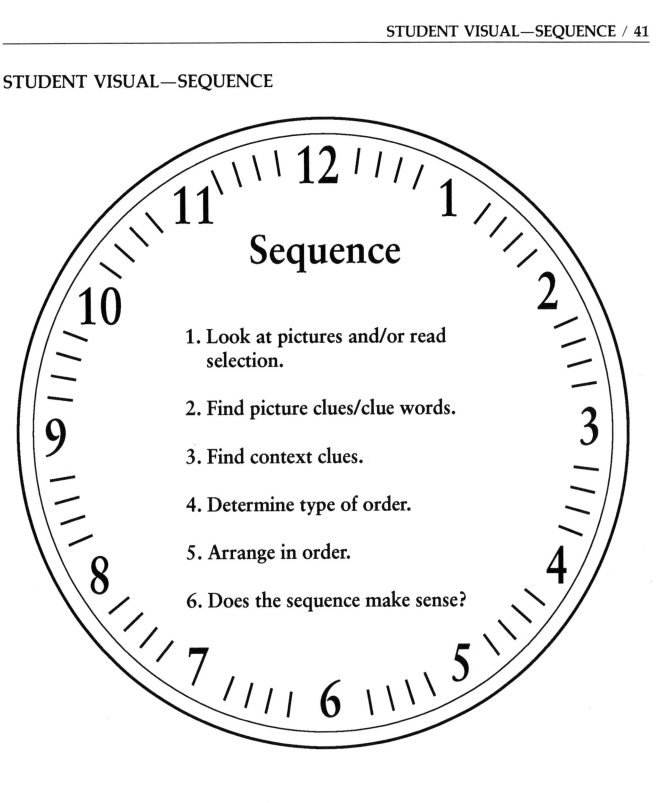

Sequence

1. Look at pictures and/or read selection.

2. Find picture clues/clue words.

3. Find context clues.

4. Determine type of order.

5. Arrange in order.

6. Does the sequence make sense?

ANNOTATED BIBLIOGRAPHY

Bang, Molly. *Ten, Nine, Eight*. New York: Greenwillow Books, 1983.
     Numbers from ten to one are part of this lullaby which observes the room of a little girl going to bed.

Carle, Eric. *The Very Hungry Caterpillar*. New York: Philomel, 1969.
     This picture book tells of the metamorphosis of a hungry little caterpillar who eats his way through ten different things, through a week's time, and becomes transformed into a beautiful butterfly.

De Paola, Tomie. *Charlie Needs a Cloak*. New York: Prentice-Hall, 1974.
     A shepherd shears his sheep, cards and spins the wool, weaves and dyes the cloth, and sews a beautiful new red cloak.

Domanska, Janina. *Busy Monday Morning*. New York: Greenwillow Books, 1985.
     A farm child has a very busy week helping his father with the hay-making. This book is a translation of a Polish folk song that Janina Domanska sang when she was a child.

Gibbons, Gail. *The Pottery Place*. San Diego: Harcourt Brace Jovanovich, 1987.
     Describes the history and process of pottery making by following a potter through a day of work.

Hall, Donald. *Ox-Cart Man*. Illustrated by Barbara Cooney. New York: Viking Press, 1979.
     Describes the day-to-day life throughout the changing seasons of an early nineteenth-century New England family.

Hughes, Shirley. *Noisy*. New York: Lothrop, Lee & Shepard Co., 1985.
     A little girl describes the many noises that can be heard inside and outside her house.

Isadora, Rachael. *I See*. New York: Greenwillow Books, 1985.
     A baby responds to all the things she sees.

Keats, Ezra Jack. *Over in the Meadow*. New York: Four Winds Press, 1971.
     Verses describing the activities of various animals also illustrate the numbers one through ten.

Mack, Stanley. *10 Bears in My Bed*. New York: Pantheon Books, 1974.
     One by one the bears leave the bed, until there are none.

Marshall, James. *Yummers!* Boston: Houghton Mifflin, 1983.
     Emily Pig accepts Eugene Turtle's advice to walk as a way of losing weight, but runs into too many tempting edible diversions.

Murphy, Jill. *What Next, Baby Bear!* New York: Dial Books for Young Readers, 1984.
     While his mother readies his bath, Baby Bear makes a quick trip to the moon.

Sendak, Maurice. *Where the Wild Things Are*. New York: Harper & Row, 1963.
     A mischievous boy takes a boat trip to the land of the wild things and becomes their king.

Selsam, Millicent E. *How Kittens Grow*. New York: Four Winds Press, 1975.
A photographic essay describing four kittens' first eight weeks of life.

_____. *How Puppies Grow*. New York: Four Winds Press, 1972.
Describes the first six weeks of six puppies' lives as they nurse, sleep, learn to walk, eat solid food, and interact with other dogs.

Winter, Jeanette. *The Girl and the Moon Man*. New York: Pantheon Books, 1984.
The retelling of a traditional Siberian tale in which a lonely moon unsuccessfully tries to carry a young girl off into the sky, and then must offer many timeless gifts to win new forgiveness.

GAME 1

SELECTION TITLE:

> *The Pottery Place*
> by Gail Gibbons

FOCUS:

SEQUENCE

HOW TO MAKE: Cut out the boxes containing selection title, focus, student directions, and answer card. Glue title onto folder tab and focus onto folder front. Color and glue, in their entirety, the potter page and buyer page onto the inside of folder. Color and cut out pottery pieces. Store student directions, answer card, and pottery pieces in library pocket glued to back of folder.

STUDENT DIRECTIONS:

1. Read the information on each pottery piece.
2. Starting at the potter, follow the arrows and put the pieces in the correct sequence, ending at the buyer.
3. Check your answers using answer card.

ANSWER CARD:

- Receives dry clay.
- Mixes dry powder and water until clay becomes soft.
- Kneads soft clay to remove air bubbles.
- Puts clay on potter's wheel.
- Designs pottery.
- Puts greenware into kiln for firing.
- Removes cooled pottery and pours on glazes.
- Returns pottery to kiln.
- Removes finished pottery for selling.

PIECES FOR GAME 1—SEQUENCE

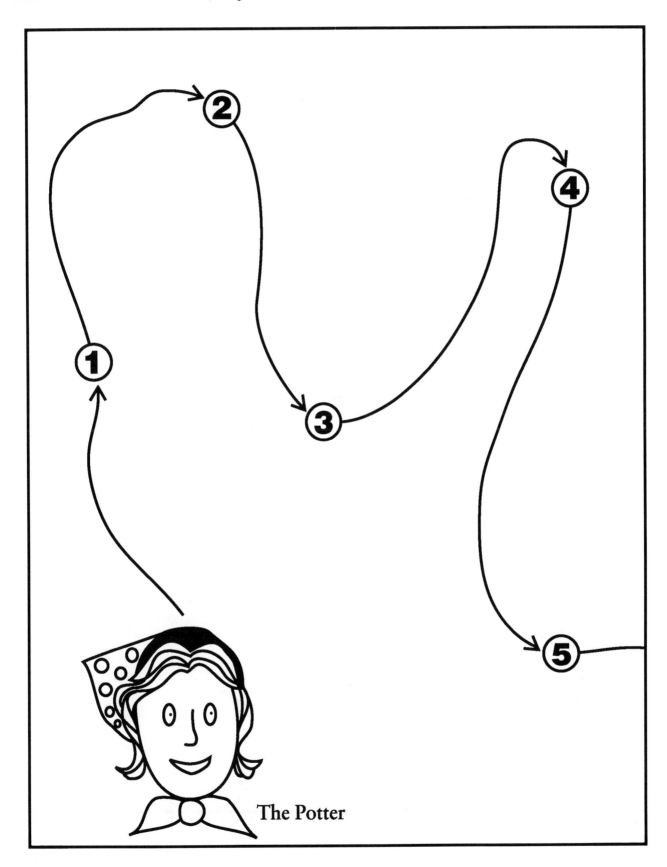

The Potter

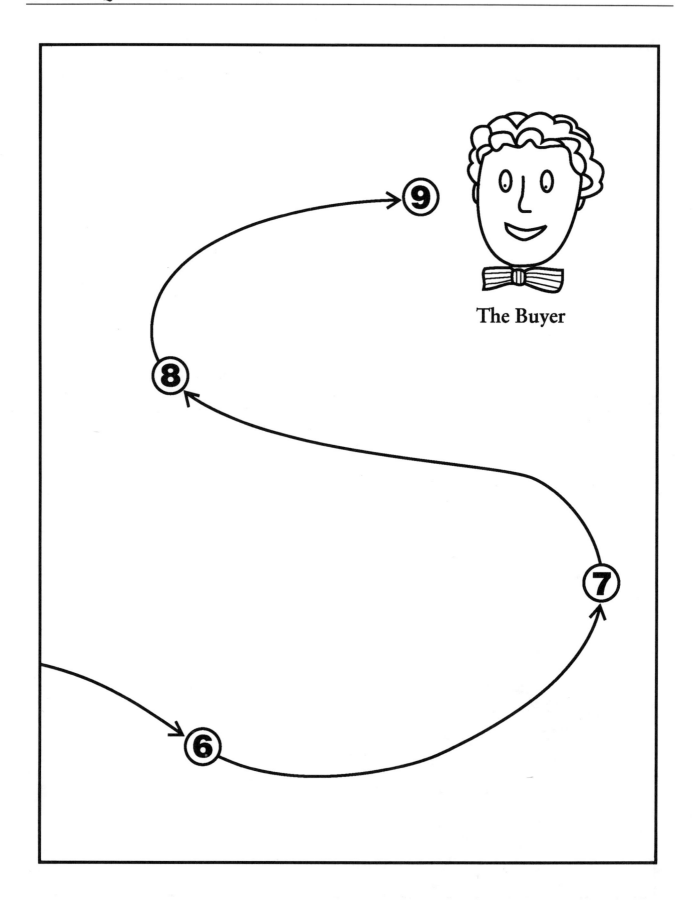

The Buyer

Returns pottery to kiln.

Puts clay on potter's wheel.

Receives dry clay.

Removes finished pottery for selling.

Removes cooled pottery and pours on glazes.

Kneads soft clay to remove air bubbles.

Designs pottery.

Puts greenware into kiln for firing.

Mixes dry powder and water until clay becomes soft.

GAME 2

SELECTION TITLE:

> *The Very Hungry Caterpillar*
> by Eric Carle

FOCUS:

SEQUENCE

HOW TO MAKE: Cut out selection title, focus, student directions, and answer card. Color and cut out caterpillar and glue together onto inside of folder. Cut out sentence boxes. Store student directions, answer card, and sentence boxes in library pocket glued to back of folder.

STUDENT DIRECTIONS:

1. Read all the sentences in the sentence boxes.
2. Decide what happened first and put that sentence on the number 1.
3. Continue putting the sentences in sequence in the same way.
4. Check your answers using answer card.

ANSWER CARD:

1. First there was an egg.
2. Soon a caterpillar popped out.
3. He ate through all kinds of food.
4. He ate through a leaf.
5. The caterpillar became very large.
6. He made a cocoon.
7. Finally he pushed his way through the cocoon and became a butterfly.

PIECES FOR GAME 2—SEQUENCE

First there was an egg.

Soon a caterpillar popped out.

He ate through all kinds of food.

He ate through a leaf.

The caterpillar became very large.

He made a cocoon.

Finally he pushed his way through the cocoon and became a butterfly.

ACTIVITIES

Picture Order: Using old workbooks, cut out a set of sequence pictures. Glue the pictures on pieces of tagboard. The set may be simple (three pictures) or more involved. Have students arrange the pictures in a logical sequence. They should then tell the story or write the story.

If Only ...: Students write a set of sentences that put a simple activity, such as getting dressed, in sequence. Cut the sentences apart and arrange in a wrong order. Draw a picture of what children might look like if their shirts were put on over their coats, or their socks over their shoes. Talk about the problems, correct the mistakes, and draw a picture using the correct sequence.

Sequence Phrase Puzzles: Brainstorm a list of words or phrases that help readers and writers understand sequence. The list might include *first, next, then, last, before, after that, at the same time,* and *later.* Give students two or three sentences that tell about an activity or event. Have students put the sentences and phrases together to complete the puzzle.

Backwards and Forwards: Demonstrate how to make or build something like a tower of blocks. Students write or tell the necessary steps in sequence; then they write or tell the steps to take it apart. Follow the students' directions for taking the project apart to see if the sequence works.

Clock Time: After reading a selection, students complete clocks to show when events in the selection took place. Using selections that have clauses such as "when the sun came up," "after dinner," and "when the stars shone" will really make your students think.

Calendar Time: After reading a selection that spans a longer period of time, have students write the events in the story in the squares of a calendar.

Time Line: Students can create time lines that illustrate events in their own lives. They can also create time lines for events in a reading selection.

Picture Panels: Divide paper into three or four panels. Have students read a selection and illustrate the panels to show "one day in the life of" or "one week in the life of" the main character in the selection. More advanced readers may need more panels. The panels could also be used to illustrate the sequence of a set of directions.

Alphabet Books: Assign one or more letters to each student. Students then design a page for each letter. The pages can be modeled after several well-known alphabet books, and might be similar to "A is for apples eaten by kids." When all the pages are done, students work together to put the pages in alphabetical order before binding.

Small, Smaller, Smallest: Have students illustrate the meaning of a set of adjectives. Students could also use the adjectives in sentences. The illustrated and written pages could be put together for a class book.

Interpretation

5—CAUSE AND EFFECT

Objective: The student will identify cause and effect in a picture/selection.

TEACHER CHECKLIST FOR PLANNING

1. Define effect: *what* happened

2. Define cause: *why* it happened

3. Teach cause and effect clue words.
   Examples: *Because, as a result of, then, so, therefore, due to, when*

4. Have students determine cause and effect.
   Ask: What happened?
        Why did it happen?

5. Have students determine if the relationship makes sense.

STUDENT CHECKLIST

1. Look at picture.

2. Ask: What happened?

3. Ask: Why did it happen?

4. Does it make sense?

5. Read sentence or selection.

6. Look for clue word(s).

7. Ask: What happened?

8. Ask: Why did it happen?

9. Does it make sense?

STUDENT VISUAL—CAUSE AND EFFECT

Cause and Effect

1. Look at picture.

2. Ask: What happened?

3. Ask: Why did it happen?

4. Does it make sense?

5. Read sentence or selection.

6. Look for clue word(s).

7. Ask: What happened?

8. Ask: Why did it happen?

9. Does it make sense?

Find <u>what</u>
Find <u>why</u>
Does it make sense?

ANNOTATED BIBLIOGRAPHY

Aardema, Verna. *Why Mosquitoes Buzz in People's Ears*. Illustrated by Leo Dillon and Diane Dillon. New York: Dial Press, 1975.
A West African tale that reveals the meaning of the mosquito's buzz.

Arkhurst, Joyce Cooper. *The Adventures of Spider*. Illustrated by Jerry Pinkney. Boston: Little, Brown & Co., 1964.
West African folktales: Six humorous stories featuring the crafty spider.

Barrett, Jud. *Cloudy with a Chance of Meatballs*. Illustrated by Ron Barrett. New York: Atheneum, 1978.
Life is delicious in the town of Chew and Swallow where it rains soup and juice, snows mashed potatoes, and blows storms of hamburgers, until the weather takes a turn for the worse.

Carle, Eric. *The Grouchy Ladybug*. New York: Thomas Y. Crowell, 1977.
A grouchy ladybug who is looking for a fight challenges everyone she meets, regardless of size or strength.

_____. *The Mixed-Up Chameleon*. New York: Thomas Y. Crowell, 1975.
A chameleon wishes he could be like each of the animals he sees in the zoo.

Crowe, Robert L. *Tyler Toad and the Thunder*. New York: E. P. Dutton, 1980.
The thunder finally turns the tables on all the animals that tried to persuade Tyler there wasn't anything of which to be afraid.

Dayrell, Elphinstone. *Why the Sun and the Moon Live in the Sky*. Illustrated by Blair Lent. Boston: Houghton Mifflin, 1968.
This African folktale relates how the sun and his wife, the moon, left the earth and water and came to live in the sky.

Gackenbach, Dick. *Harry and the Terrible Whatzit*. New York: Seabury Press, 1977.
Harry, who was going to save his mother, finds out that he is not afraid of the monster after all.

Gross, Ruth Belov (retold from Grimm). *The Bremen-Town Musicians*. New York: Scholastic, 1974.
Four animal friends who are mistreated by their masters set out to become musicians in the town of Bremen and encounter a den of thieves.

Hadithi, Mwenye. *Crafty Chameleon*. Illustrated by Adrienne Kennaway. Boston: Little, Brown & Co., 1987.
A chameleon bedeviled by a leopard and a crocodile uses his wits to get them to leave him alone.

Johnston, Tony. *Pages of Music*. Illustrated by Tomie de Paola. New York: G. P. Putnam's Sons, 1988.
A childhood visit to Sardinia haunts a composer, who returns there one Christmas to repay with his music the kindness of the island's inhabitants.

Lionni, Leo. *Swimmy*. New York: Pantheon Books, 1968.
   A remarkable little fish instructs the rest of his school in the art of protection—swim in the formation of a gigantic fish!

Macaulay, David. *Why the Chicken Crossed the Road*. Boston: Houghton Mifflin, 1987.
   By crossing a road, a chicken sets off a series of wild events, in which the Anderson twins blow up their bathroom and the brave young Hooper lad is rolled up and delivered inside an Oriental rug.

Martin, Rafe. *Foolish Rabbit's Big Mistake*. Illustrated by Ed Young. New York: G. P. Putnam's Sons, 1985.
   As all the animals panic and flee at a little rabbit's announcement that the earth is breaking up, a brave lion steps in and brings sense to the situation.

Noble, Trinka Hakes. *The Day Jimmy's Boa Ate the Wash*. Illustrated by Steven Kellogg. New York: Dial Press, 1980.
   Jimmy's boa constrictor wreaks havoc on the class trip to the farm.

Sendak, Maurice. *Where the Wild Things Are*. New York: Harper & Row, 1963.
   A mischievous boy takes a boat trip to the land of the wild things and becomes their king.

Winter, Jeanette. *The Girl and the Moon Man*. New York: Pantheon Books, 1984.
   A retelling of a traditional Siberian tale in which a lonely moon unsuccessfully tries to carry a young girl off into the sky, and then must offer many timeless gifts to win her forgiveness.

GAME 1

SELECTION TITLE:

> *The Day Jimmy's Boa Ate the Wash*
> by Trinka Hakes Noble

FOCUS:

CAUSE AND EFFECT

HOW TO MAKE: Cut out selection title, focus, student directions, and answer card. Color and cut out all game pieces. Glue title onto folder tab and focus onto folder front. Glue game-piece t-shirts onto inside of folder. Store student directions, answer card, and boas in library pocket glued to back of folder.

STUDENT DIRECTIONS:

1. Read cause phrases on t-shirts.
2. Read effect phrases on boas.
3. Decide which cause and effect phrases go together.
4. Check your answers using answer card.

ANSWER CARD:

1. the cow started crying.
2. the haystack fell over.
3. the pigs ate our lunches.
4. we threw the pig's corn.
5. the chickens started squawking.
6. she threw an egg at Tommy.
7. she started screaming.
8. now Jimmy has a pet.

PIECES FOR GAME 1—CAUSE AND EFFECT

① The haystack fell over, so _____

② The farmer hit the haystack, so _____

the chickens started squawking.

③ We threw the pig's corn, so _____

④ We ran out of eggs, so _____

⑤ The boa was in the henhouse, so _____

⑥ Jenny got mad, so _____

⑦ The farmer's wife saw the boa in the wash, so _____

⑧ A pig didn't get off the bus, so _____

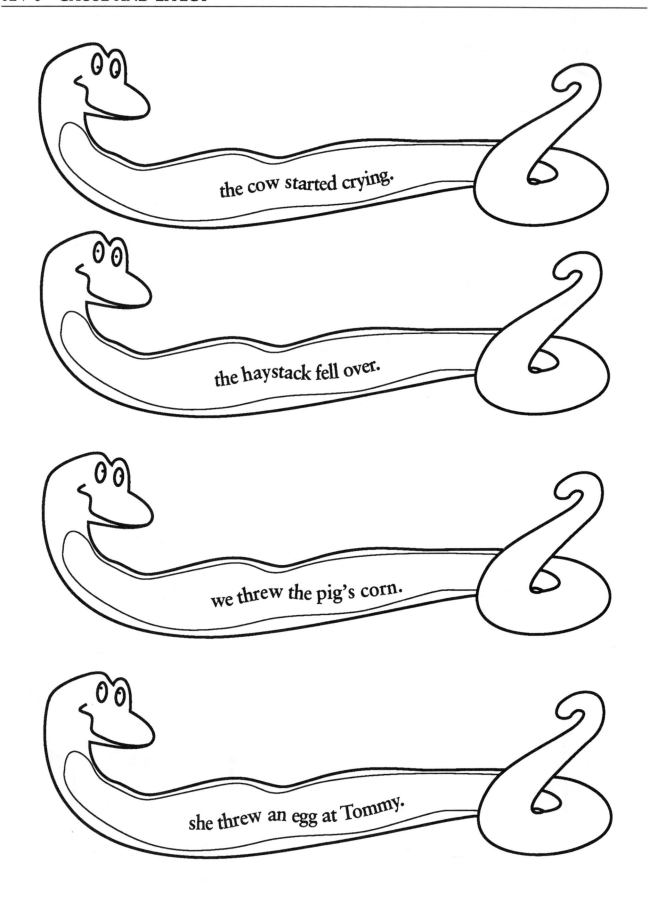

the cow started crying.

the haystack fell over.

we threw the pig's corn.

she threw an egg at Tommy.

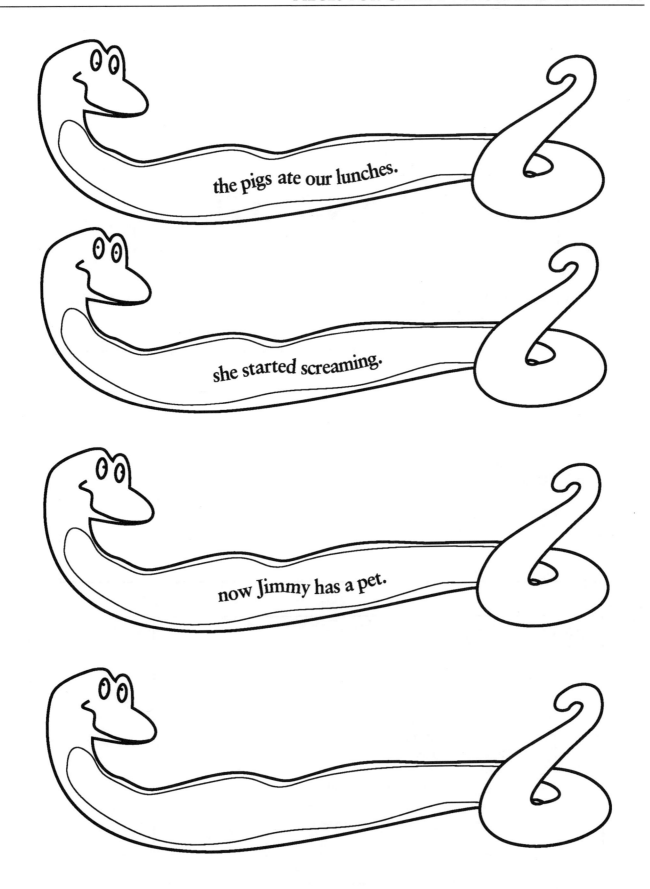

the pigs ate our lunches.

she started screaming.

now Jimmy has a pet.

GAME 2

SELECTION TITLE:

> *Pages of Music*
> by Tony Johnston

FOCUS:

> # CAUSE AND EFFECT

HOW TO MAKE: Cut out selection title, focus, student directions, and answer card. Color and cut out all game pieces. Glue title onto folder tab and focus onto folder front. Glue pages of music onto the inside of the folder. Store student directions, answer card, and musical notes in library pocket glued to back of folder.

STUDENT DIRECTIONS:

1. Read effect phrases on the pages of music.
2. Read cause phrases on musical notes.
3. Decide which cause and effect phrases go together.
4. Place musical notes on top of pages of music to complete the cause and effect statements.
5. Check your answers using answer card.

ANSWER CARD:

1. it was beautiful in spring.
2. the land was not good for growing crops.
3. he loved music.
4. the air was filled with sweet notes.
5. he was a famous composer.
6. he couldn't forget the music of the shepherds' pipes.
7. a procession of wagons was coming.
8. the shepherds arrived from the fields.

PIECES FOR GAME 2—CAUSE AND EFFECT

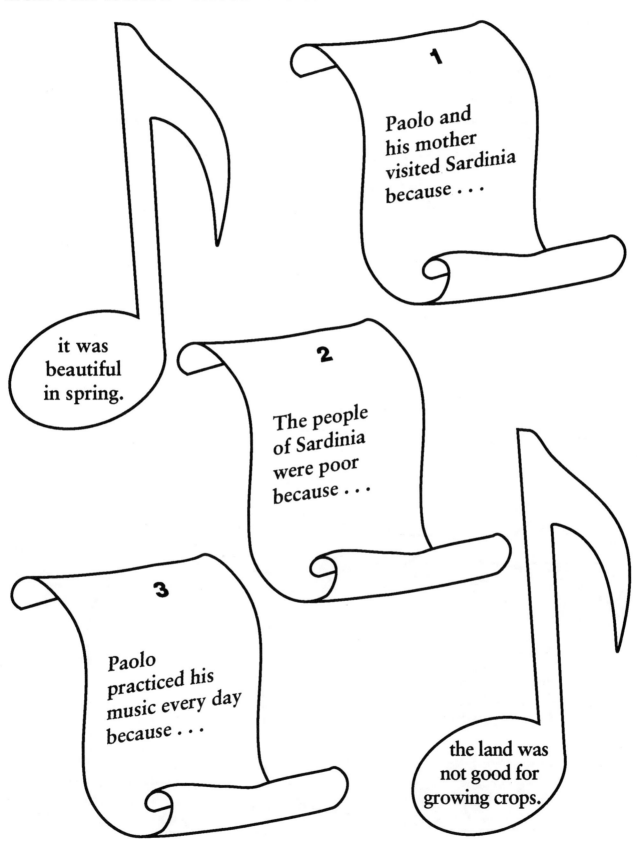

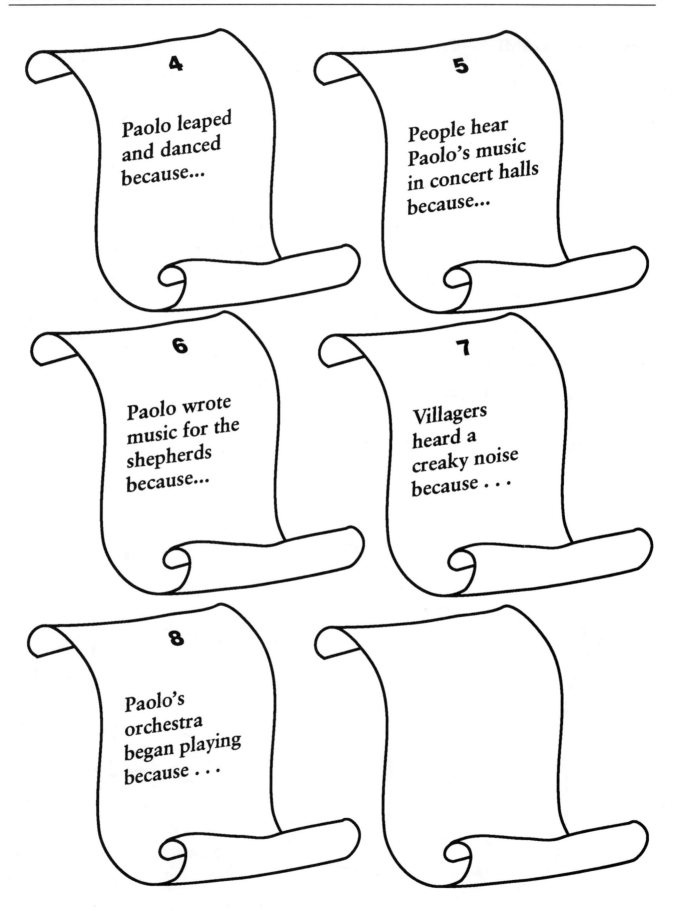

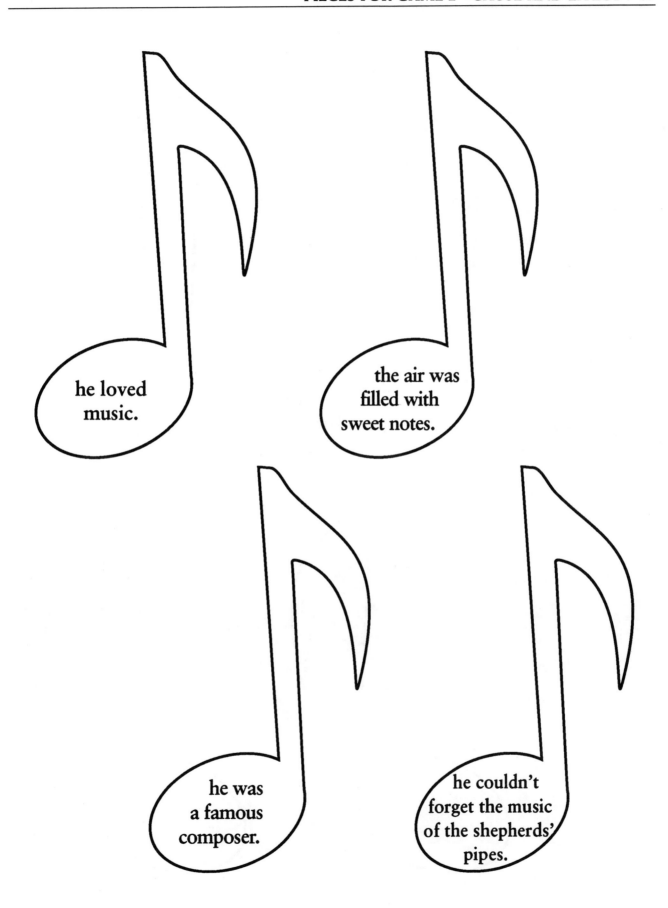

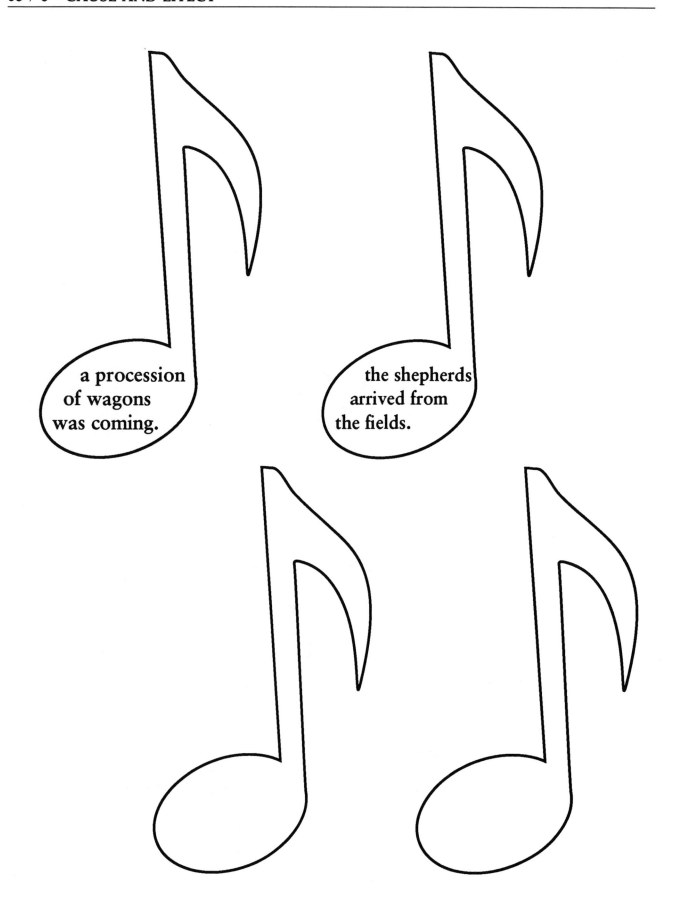

ACTIVITIES

Chain Reaction: Build a chain reaction in the classroom. Start with two or three items. The model might be a ball rolling across the floor, knocking over a paper cup full of water, spilling onto paper towels. Before letting the chain reaction go, discuss what might happen. Release the chain reaction and note what happens. Discuss and chart all the causes and effects in the chain. Students will enjoy creating their own chain reactions and sharing them with the class.

Accident Reports: Use the everyday minor mishaps on the playground as a source for completing accident reports. With students, design a simple accident report form asking what happened (the effect) and why it happened (the cause). When a scraped knee, bruised elbow, or knock on the head occurs, the students involved fill out a report and add to a class records book.

If … Then …: Use the time available while waiting in line, or waiting for students to clean up by presenting students with "If … then …" statements for them to finish. For example, "If it starts raining, then…." Have students brainstorm possible effects. If you want to work on causes, present them with incomplete "because" sentences: "We got wet because…." Students think of and share all the possible causes.

Same and Different: Use two identical items (two flowers or two ice cubes). Put one flower in water, leave the other out. Put one ice cube in the freezer, lay one in the sun. Observe what happens to the items. Discuss in terms of cause and effect. Make a chart listing the results of these mini-experiments. This activity can be done with lots of everyday things.

Does That Make Sense?: Using a list of causes and effects, compiled from worksheets and workbooks, write the statements on strips of paper. Cut the causes and effects apart. Make a sentence pattern: _____ because _____ . Students place an effect on the first blank and a cause on the second blank. They then read the sentence to see if it makes sense. Continue matching until all the pairs have been completed.

Find the Evidence: Locate several pictures illustrating events that have happened. Pictures with many events happening at once are ideal. Students make a list of all the events shown in the picture. They then look for evidence that shows what caused the events. Compile a chart listing events (effects) and causes.

Two-Panel Drawings: Select pictures that illustrate a cause or an effect. Divide a sheet of paper. Glue a cause picture in the second panel. Students complete the activity by drawing an effect in the empty panel so that the drawings make sense. This process could be reversed by gluing an effect picture in the second panel.

Headline Capers: Find newspaper articles with headlines that lend themselves to cause and effect. Cut out articles and cut off the headlines. Put each article and its matching headline into an envelope. Pass out each envelope and have students read the headline to determine if it states a cause or an effect. Have them explain their reasoning. If they think the headline is an effect, have them give possible causes. If they think the headline is a cause, have them give possible effects. Students will then read the accompanying articles to verify their answers.

6—CHARACTERIZATION

Objective: The student will identify the emotions, traits, and attitudes portrayed in a picture or written selection.

TEACHER CHECKLIST FOR PLANNING

Feelings and Emotions

1. Define a feeling: emotion.

2. Develop a list of feeling words.
   Examples: *Happy, sad, worried*

3. Teach action words (body language) that help identify feelings.
   Examples: *Stomped, pouted, marched*

4. Teach clue words (oral expression) that help identify feelings of characters.
   Examples: *Moaned, sighed, laughed, yelled*

5. Review exclamation point and question mark to make connection between punctuation, voice inflection, and emotion.

6. Have students determine feelings and emotions of a character in a selection.

Traits and Attitudes

1. Define a trait: quality or characteristic.

2. Develop a list of trait words.
   Examples: *Greedy, helpful, honest, lazy*

3. Teach how a character's actions help identify traits.

4. Define attitude: manner of acting, feeling, or thinking that shows mood.

5. Teach how a character's actions, feelings, and thoughts can be used to infer the character's attitude.

6. Have students determine traits and attitudes of a character in a selection.

STUDENT CHECKLIST

Feelings and Emotions

1. Look at faces in picture.
   Look at bodies in picture.
   Identify feelings shown.
   Identify reasons for feelings.

2. Listen to selection.
   Identify clues and actions of characters.
   Identify feelings.
   Identify reasons for feelings.

3. Read selection.
   Identify clue words, actions, and/or punctuation.
   Identify feelings.
   Identify reason for feelings.

Traits and Attitudes

1. Identify character's feelings.

2. Identify character's actions.

3. Identify character's traits.

4. Look at character's situation.

5. Look at character's surroundings.

6. Determine character's attitude.

7. Identify reasons for character's traits and attitudes.

STUDENT VISUAL—CHARACTERIZATION

Characterization Feelings and Emotions

1. Look at faces in picture.
   Look at bodies in picture.
   Identify feelings shown.
   Identify reasons for feelings.

2. Listen to selection.
   Identify clues and actions of characters.
   Identify feelings.
   Identify reasons for feelings.

3. Read selection.
   Identify clue words, actions,
      and/or punctuation.
   Identify feelings.
   Identify reasons for feelings.

Traits and Attitudes

1. Identify character's feelings.

2. Identify character's actions.

3. Identify character's traits.

4. Look at character's situation.

5. Look at character's surroundings.

6. Determine character's attitude.

7. Identify reasons for character's traits and attitudes.

ANNOTATED BIBLIOGRAPHY

Balian, Lorna. *Bah! Humbug*. Nashville: Abingdon Press, 1977.
   Two children set a trap for Santa Claus, but only one of them manages to see him.

Blume, Judy. *The Pain and the Great One*. Illustrated by Irene Trivas. New York: Bradbury Press, 1974.
   A six-year-old (The Pain) and his eight-year-old sister (The Great One) see each other as troublemakers and the best-loved in the family.

Byers, Betsy. *The Eighteenth Emergency*. Illustrated by Robert Grosman. New York: Viking Press, 1973.
   When the toughest boy in school swears to kill him, twelve-year-old Mouse finds little help from friends, and must prepare for this emergency alone.

_____. *Good-bye Chicken Little*. New York: Harper & Row, 1979.
   A boy discovers that he doesn't have to feel personally responsible for his uncle's drowning.

Freeman, Don. *Corduroy*. New York: Viking Press, 1968.
   A little bear in a department store had a button missing, but, to his surprise, a girl buys him, sews on a button, and becomes his friend.

Fox, Paula. *One-Eyed Cat*. Illustrated by Irene Trivas. New York: Bradbury Press, 1984.
   An eleven-year-old shoots a stray cat with his new rifle, subsequently suffers from guilt, and eventually assumes responsibility for it.

George, Jean. *Julie of the Wolves*. Illustrated by John Schoenherr. New York: Harper & Row, 1972.
   While running away from home and an unwanted marriage, a thirteen-year-old Eskimo girl becomes lost on the North Slope of Alaska and is befriended by a wolf pack.

Greenfield, Eloise. *She Come Bringing Me That Little Baby Girl*. Illustrated by John Steptoe. New York: J. B. Lippincott, 1974.
   A child's disappointment and jealousy over a new baby sister are dispelled as he becomes aware of the importance of his new role as a big brother.

Greenfield, Eloise, and Tessie James Little. *Childtimes: A Three Generation Memoir*. Illustrated by Jerry Pinkney. New York: Thomas Y. Crowell, 1979.
   Childhood memoirs of three black women—grandmother, mother, and daughter—who grew up between the 1880s and 1950s.

Hill, Elizabeth. *Evan's Corner*. Illustrated by Nancy Grossman. New York: Holt, Rinehart & Winston, 1967.
   Evan, who has a large family, longs for privacy and a place of his own.

Hutchins, Pat. *Tom and Sam*. New York: Macmillan, 1968.
   Two friends try to outdo one another by building beautiful items for their gardens, but jealousy almost destroys their friendship.

Keats, Ezra Jack. *Peter's Chair*. New York: Harper & Row, 1967.
    Many of Peter's things are being taken over by his new baby sister, but before his special little blue chair can be painted pink, he and his dog, Willie, run away.

Kellogg, Steven. *Best Friends*. New York: Dial Books for Young Readers, 1986.
    Kathy feels lonely and betrayed when her best friend goes away for the summer and leaves her alone.

Kuskin, Karla. *Herbert Hated Being Small*. Boston: Houghton Mifflin, 1979.
    Short Herbert and tall Philomel discover that their heights change when they stand next to different people.

MacLachlan, Patricia. *Sarah, Plain and Tall*. New York: Harper & Row, 1985.
    When their father invites a mail-order bride to come live with them in their prairie home, Caleb and Anna are captivated by their new mother and hope that she will stay.

Paterson, Katherine. *The Great Gilly Hopkins*. New York: Thomas Y. Crowell, 1978.
    An eleven-year-old foster child tries to cope with her longings and fears as she schemes against everyone who tries to be friendly.

Rylant, Cynthia. *Miss Maggie*. Illustrated by Thomas DiGrazia. New York: E. P. Dutton, 1983.
    Young Nat is afraid of old Miss Maggie and her rotting log house until her heart conquers his fears.

Sharmat, Marjorie, and Mitchell Sharmat. *I Am Not a Pest*. Illustrated by Diane Dawson. New York: E. P. Dutton, 1979.
    Alicia explains all the ways in which she is not a pest—and besides, her family will think she is sick if she changes her behavior.

Silverstein, Shel. *The Giving Tree*. New York: Harper & Row, 1964.
    A young boy grows to manhood and old age experiencing the love and generosity of a tree which gives to him without thought of return.

GAME 1

SELECTION TITLE:

> *Best Friends*
> by Steven Kellogg

FOCUS:

CHARACTERIZATION

HOW TO MAKE: Cut out selection title, focus, student directions, and answer card. Color and cut out all game pieces. Glue title onto folder tab and focus onto folder front. Glue one hat onto each half of inside of folder. Store student directions, answer card, and stars in library pocket glued to back of folder.

STUDENT DIRECTIONS:

1. Read words on stars.
2. Decide which words describe Kathy or Louise.
3. Place words on the correct hats.
4. Check your answer using answer card.

ANSWER CARD:

Kathy - resentful, jealous, selfish, truthful, thankful

Louise - friendly, caring, unselfish, thoughtful

PIECES FOR GAME 1—CHARACTERIZATION

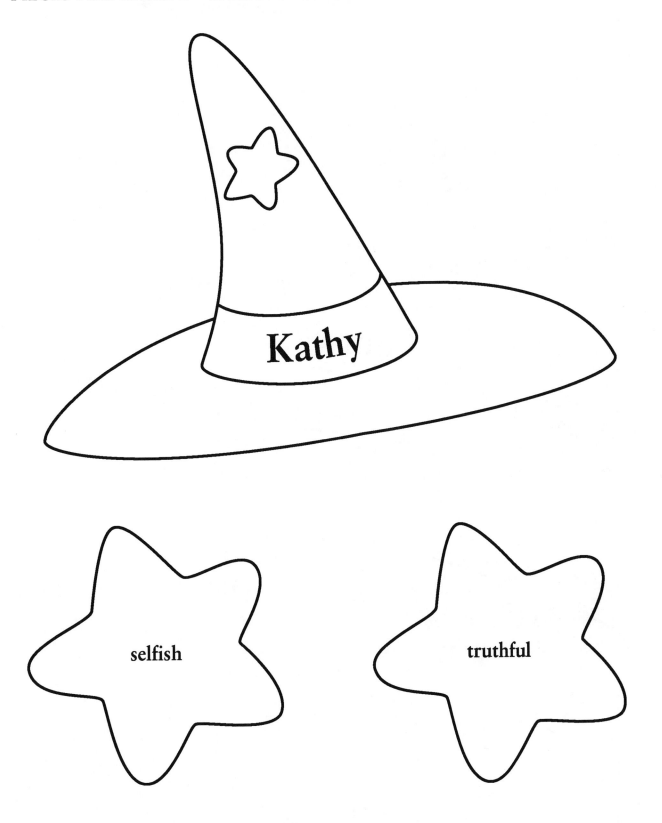

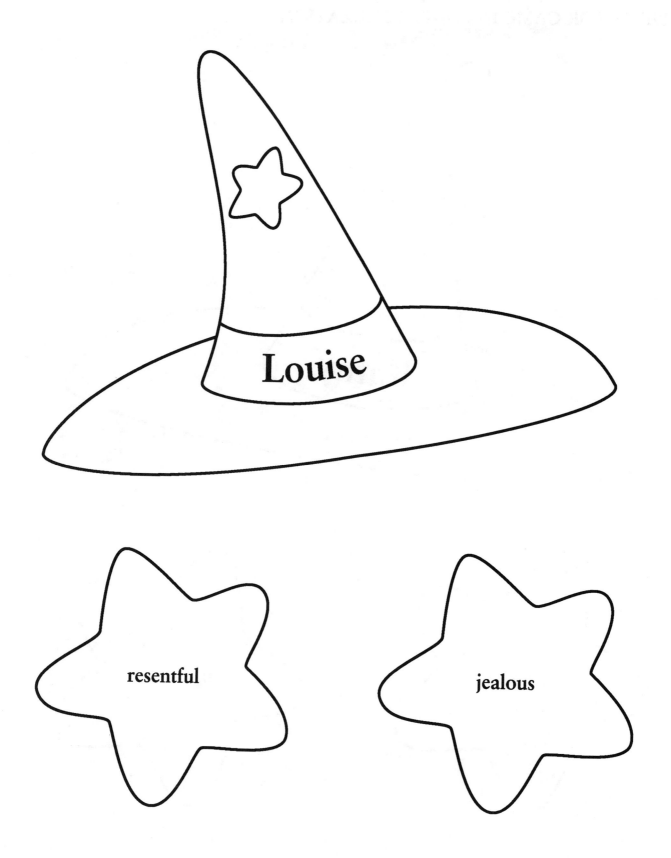

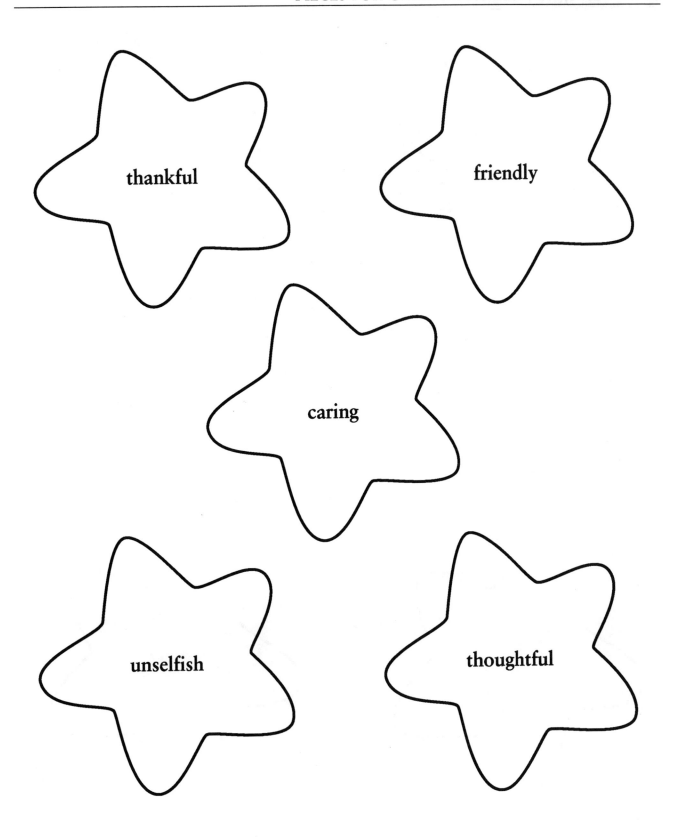

GAME 2

SELECTION TITLE:

> *She Come Bringing Me That Little Baby Girl*
> by Eloise Greenfield

FOCUS:

CHARACTERIZATION

HOW TO MAKE: Cut out selection title, focus, student directions, and answer card. Color and cut out rattle. Glue title onto folder tab and focus onto folder front. Glue both question pages, in their entirety, onto inside of folder. Store student directions, answer card, rattle, and *grease pencil* in library pocket glued to back of folder.

STUDENT DIRECTIONS:

1. Read each question about Kevin.
2. For questions 1 through 7, select a word from the rattle that best describes how Kevin was feeling.
3. Write that word in the box using the grease pencil. For question 8, circle the best answer.
4. Check your answers using answer card.

ANSWER CARD:

1. disappointed
2. unhappy
3. frustrated
4. jealous
5. angry
6. excited
7. proud
8. He was glad he had a little sister.

PIECES FOR GAME 2—CHARACTERIZATION

How did Kevin feel when...

1—...his Mama brought him a baby girl instead of a baby boy?

2—...his Mama hugged him with only one arm because she was holding the baby with the other?

3—...he realized that the baby's fingers were too small to throw a football and that she cried too loud?

4—...his Mama and Daddy looked at her like she was the only baby in the world?

5—...when all the people were bringing presents and crowding around the baby?

6—...Mama put the baby in his lap and said that she needed his help to be a big brother?

7—...he ran to get his friends to show them his little sister?

8—...Which sentence describes how Kevin felt at the end of the story? Circle the sentence.

He didn't care.

He was glad he had a little sister.

He didn't know how he felt about the little girl.

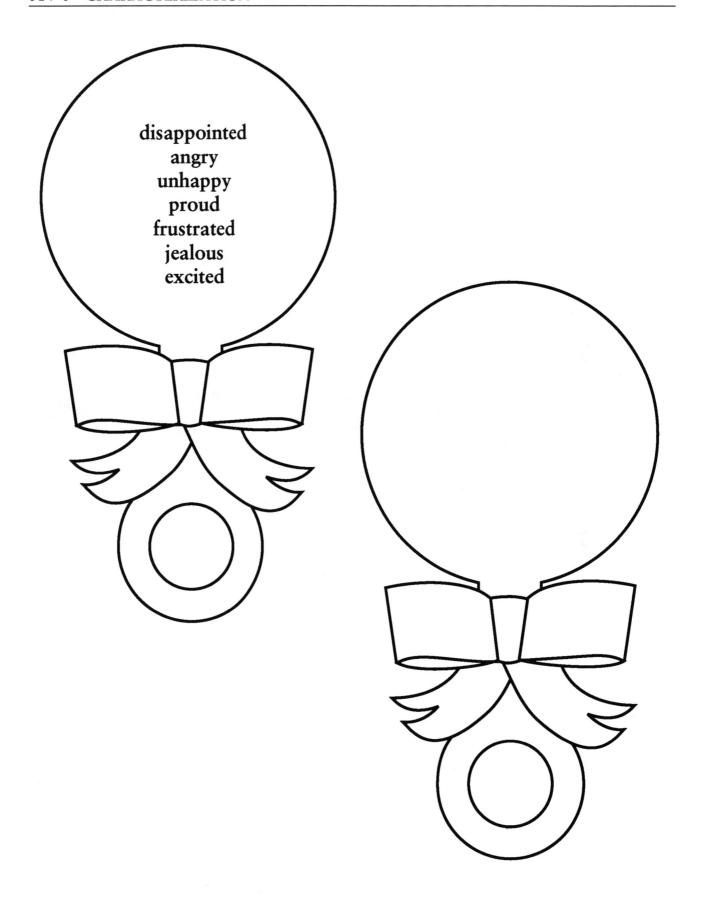

disappointed
angry
unhappy
proud
frustrated
jealous
excited

ACTIVITIES

Character Sketches: After reading a selection, have students write a brief biographical sketch of each character. Share the sketches with the class to see if others can identify the characters from the biographies. Students should include a description of the character, as well as writing about the character's traits and attitudes.

Character Dialogue: Read a selection. Select two or three characters from the selection. Create a new, but similar, situation for the characters. Have students write a dialogue for the characters in the new situation, basing it on their knowledge of the characters learned from the first selection.

Talk Show Interviews: After reading a selection and discussing a character from it, have students work in pairs to prepare interview questions. One student assumes the role of the interviewer, the other assumes the role of the character. Conduct an on-the-spot interview.

Time Lapse: After reading a selection from earlier times, have the students select a character. Bring the character into present time. How would the character dress? What would the character say? How would the character act? This activity could also be reversed by taking a present-day character back in time. The character could even be transported to the future.

Character Diaries: While reading a selection, students pretend they are one of the characters. Students keep a personal diary, using the events in the selection, along with their own backgrounds, to write the character's thoughts as the story moves along.

Letter to a Character: Have students write a letter to a character they have read about. They can give their opinions about the character's traits and attitudes. They might also want to give the character some advice.

Dear Abby: Students write letters, asking for help or advice, to a character in a selection. Other students, assuming the character's identity, answer the letters. Students may write about situations from the selection, or they may want advice about personal problems.

Character Silhouettes: Students trace or draw a silhouette of a favorite character. Without revealing the character's name, they write short descriptions of the character's traits and attitudes. When the class has a collection, display the silhouettes around the room. Have the students read the descriptions to see if they can identify the characters.

Meet the Press: Arrange a press conference in your room. Some students are assigned the role of the characters; other students become the reporters. The reporters develop a set of questions based on events in the story. The characters must respond to the questions, often defending their positions.

Pantomime: While you read a selection aloud (or have a student do so), have selected students pantomime the characters' actions and reactions. After the reading is over, talk about the character portrayals.

7—CLASSIFICATION

Objective: The student will classify objects, pictures, characters, and/or events using a common characteristic.

TEACHER CHECKLIST FOR PLANNING

1. Define classification: arrangement by categories.

2. Teach students to evaluate objects, pictures, characters, events.
   Ask: How are they alike?
   How are they different?

3. Have students sort items into groups using a common characteristic.

4. Have students explain and label groups.

STUDENT CHECKLIST

1. Look at objects, pictures, characters, and/or events.

2. Determine common characteristic(s).

3. Group by common characteristic(s).

4. Label each group.

5. Explain groups.

STUDENT VISUAL—CLASSIFICATION

Classification

1. Look at objects, pictures, characters, and/or events.

2. Determine common characteristic(s).

3. Group by common characteristic(s).

4. Label each group.

5. Explain groups.

ANNOTATED BIBLIOGRAPHY

Adoff, Arnold. *Black Is Brown Is Tan*. Illustrated by Emily Arnold McCully. New York: Harper & Row, 1973.
Describes in verse the life of brown-skinned momma, white-skinned daddy, their children, and assorted relatives.

Balian, Lorna. *Sometimes It's Turkey, Sometimes It's Feathers*. Nashville: Abingdon Press, 1982.
When she finds a turkey egg, Mrs. Gumm decides to hatch it and have a turkey for Thanksgiving dinner.

Blume, Judy. *The Pain and the Great One*. Illustrated by Irene Trivas. New York: Bradbury Press, 1974.
A six-year-old (The Pain) and his eight-year-old sister (The Great One) see each other as troublemakers and the best-loved in the family.

Booth, Eugene. *On the Farm*. Illustrated by Derek Collard. Milwaukee, WI: McDonald-Raintree, 1977.
Questions encourage the readers to look at, think about, and describe scenes from a farm.

Brandenberg, Aliki. *Jack and Jake*. New York: Greenwillow Books, 1986.
A sister complains about the way everyone confuses her twin brothers.

Crews, Donald. *Harbor*. New York: Greenwillow Books, 1982.
Presents the various kinds of boats that come and go in a busy harbor.

Ehlert, Lois. *Eating the Alphabet: Fruits and Vegetables from A to Z*. San Diego: Harcourt Brace Jovanovich, 1989.
An alphabetical tour of fruits and vegetables, from apricot and artichoke to yam and zucchini.

Farber, Norma. *Up the Down Elevator*. Illustrated by Annie Gusman. Reading, PA: Addison Wesley, 1979.
Introduces the numbers one to ten as various tradespeople get on an elevator in ever-increasing numbers.

Green, Mary McBurney. *Is It Hard? Is It Easy?* Illustrated by Len Gittleman. Reading, PA: Young Scott Books, 1960.
Each of the children in this book finds some things hard to do, though their friends can do them easily.

Henkes, Kevin. *Sheila Rae, the Brave*. New York: Greenwillow Books, 1987.
When brave Sheila Rae, who usually looks out for her sister Louise, becomes lost and scared one day, Louise comes to the rescue.

Hoban, Tana. *Dots, Spots, Speckles, and Stripes*. New York: Greenwillow Books, 1987.
Photographs show dots, spots, speckles, and stripes as found on clothing, flowers, faces, animals, and other places.

Noble, Trinka Hakes. *Meanwhile Back at the Ranch*. Illustrated by Tony Ross. New York: Dial Books for Young Readers, 1987.
Looking for some diversion, a bored rancher drives to the town of Sleepy Gulch, little knowing that some amazing things are happening to his wife and ranch during his absence.

Pearson, Susan. *Everybody Knows That!* Illustrated by Diane Paterson. New York: Dial Press, 1978.
A young girl decides to teach her playmate a lesson after he lets her know she can't do certain things because she's a girl.

Robbins, Ken. *City/Country*. New York: Viking Kestrel, 1985.
Photographs and simple text capture the universal images of a car trip, as seen from a child's back-seat perspective.

Rockwell, Anne. *Cars*. New York: E. P. Dutton, 1984.
A simple look at cars and their uses.

Roy, Ron. *Whose Hat Is That?* Photographs by Rosemarie Hausherr. New York: Clarion Books, 1987.
Texts and photographs portray the appearance and function of eighteen types of hats, including a top hat, jockey's cap, and a football helmet.

Scarry, Richard. *Richard Scarry's Best Word Book Ever*. New York: Golden Press, 1963.
A pictorial vocabulary book, with words grouped under common activities, such as mealtime, and basic concepts, such as weather.

GAME 1

SELECTION TITLE:

> *Eating the Alphabet*
> by Lois Ehlert

FOCUS:

CLASSIFICATION

HOW TO MAKE: Cut out selection title, focus, student directions, and answer card. Color and cut out all game pieces. Glue title onto folder tab and focus onto folder front. Glue awnings onto inside of folder. Glue a fruit and vegetable stand under each awning. Store student directions, answer card, and grocery bags in library pocket glued to back of folder.

STUDENT DIRECTIONS:

1. Read name of fruit or vegetable on grocery bags.
2. Classify the item by color, and then by whether the item is a fruit or a vegetable.
3. Place the bag on the correct stand.
4. Check your answers using answer card.

ANSWER CARD:

Red		*Green*	
fruit	*vegetable*	*fruit*	*vegetable*
currant	beet	lime	artichoke
pomegranate	radicchio	ugli fruit	asparagus

Orange		*Yellow*	
fruit	*vegetable*	*fruit*	*vegetable*
kumquat	carrot	grapefruit	corn
nectarine	yam	quince	
persimmon		starfruit	

PIECES FOR GAME 1—CLASSIFICATION

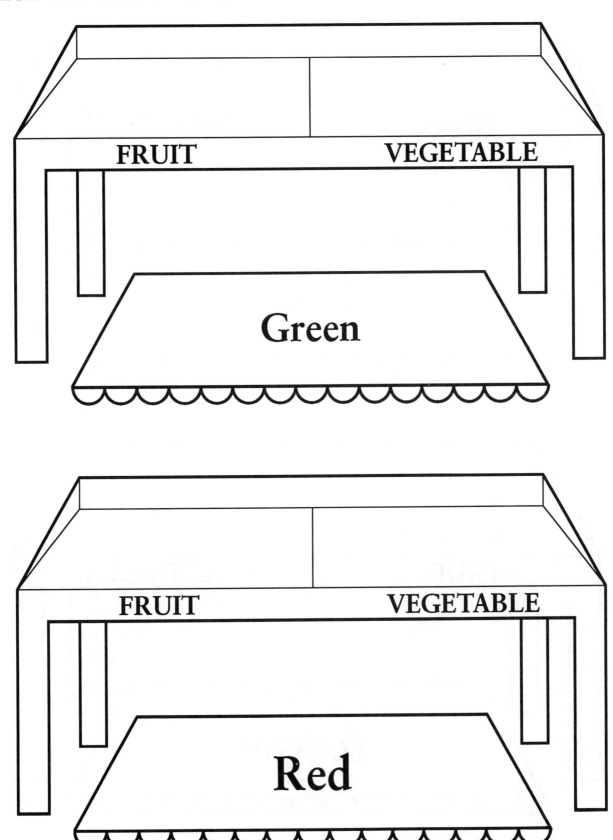

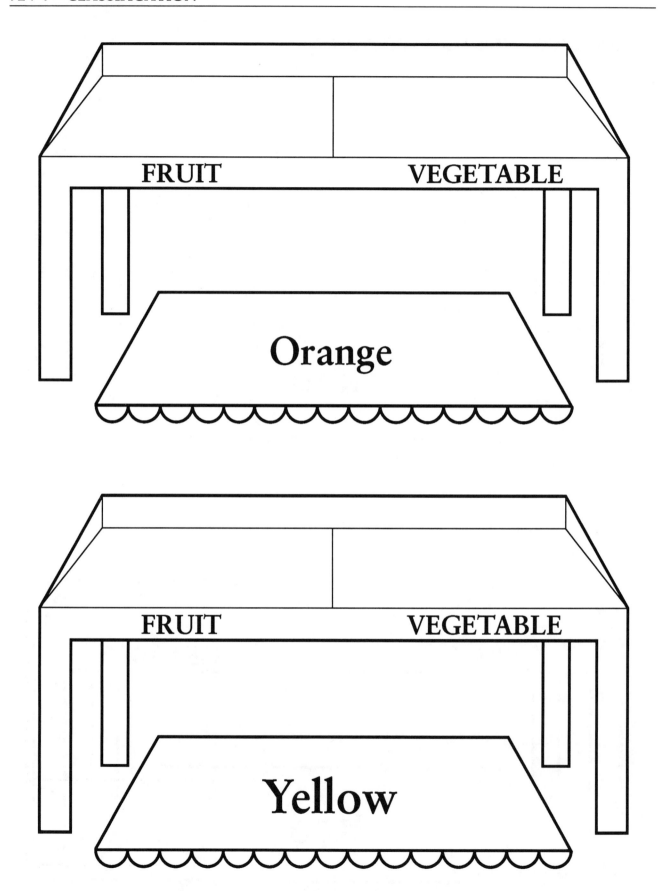

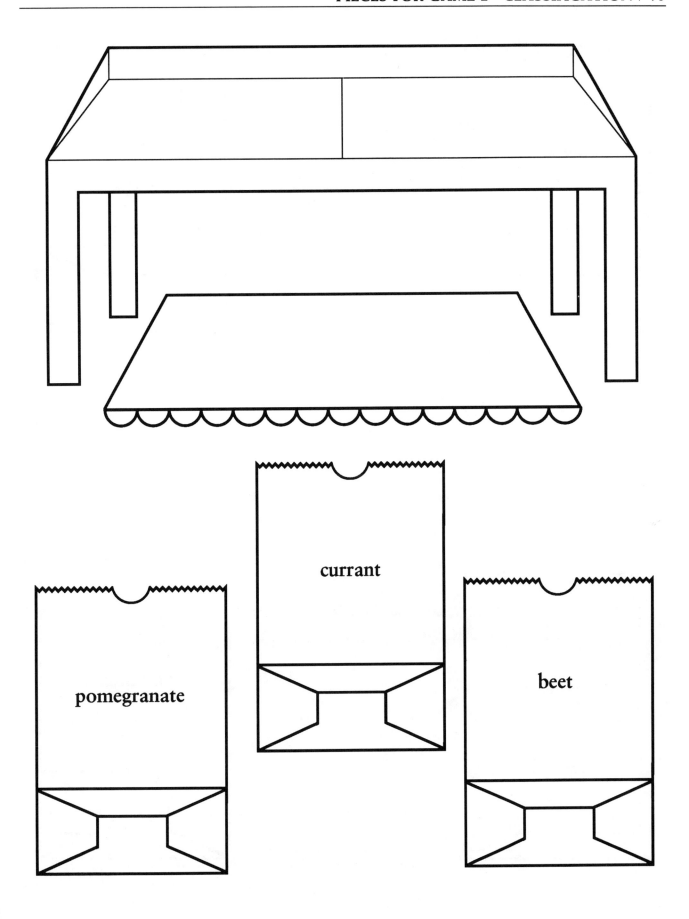

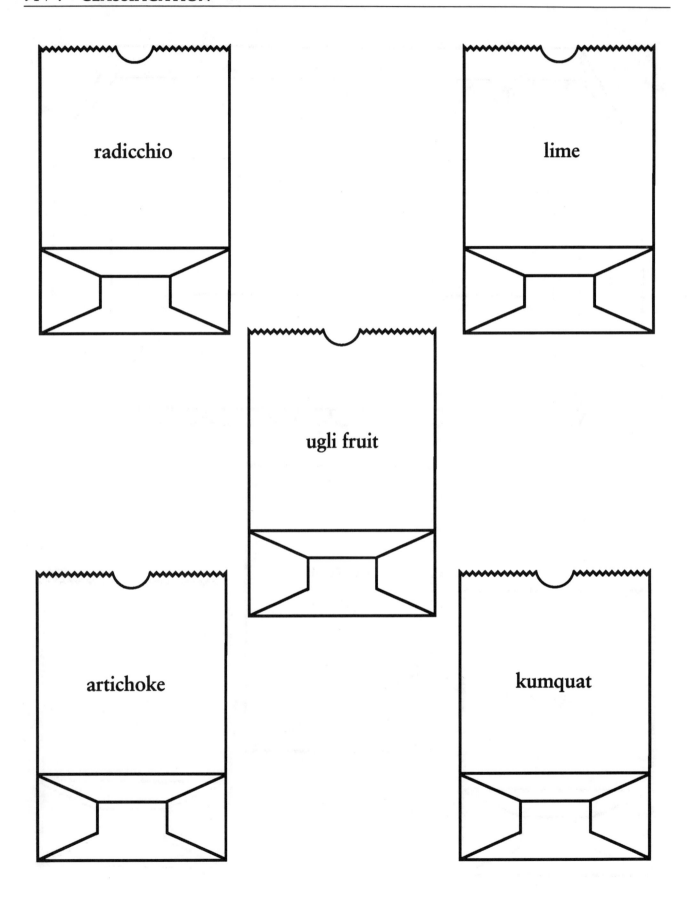

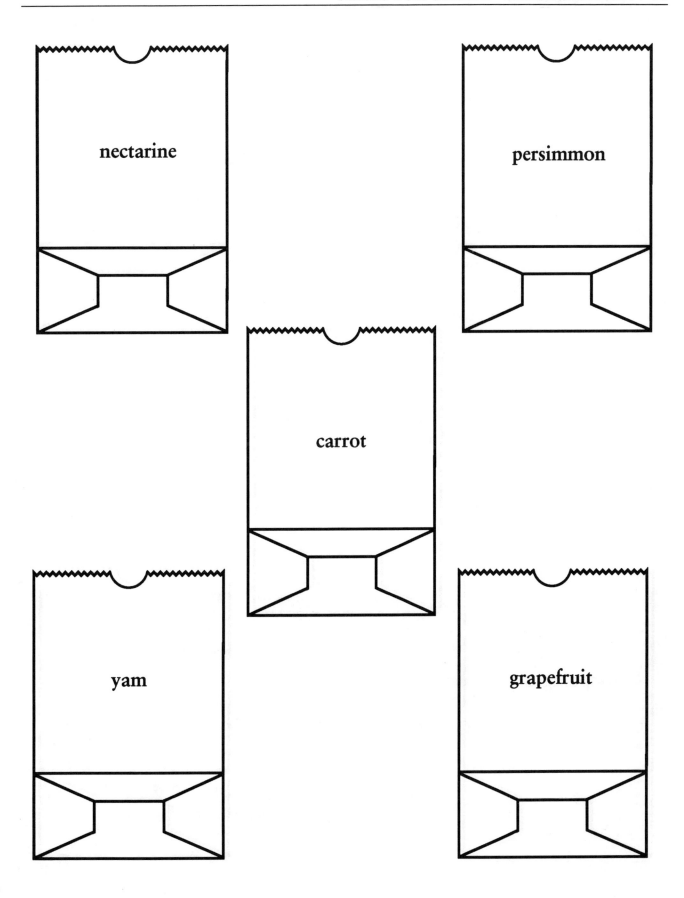

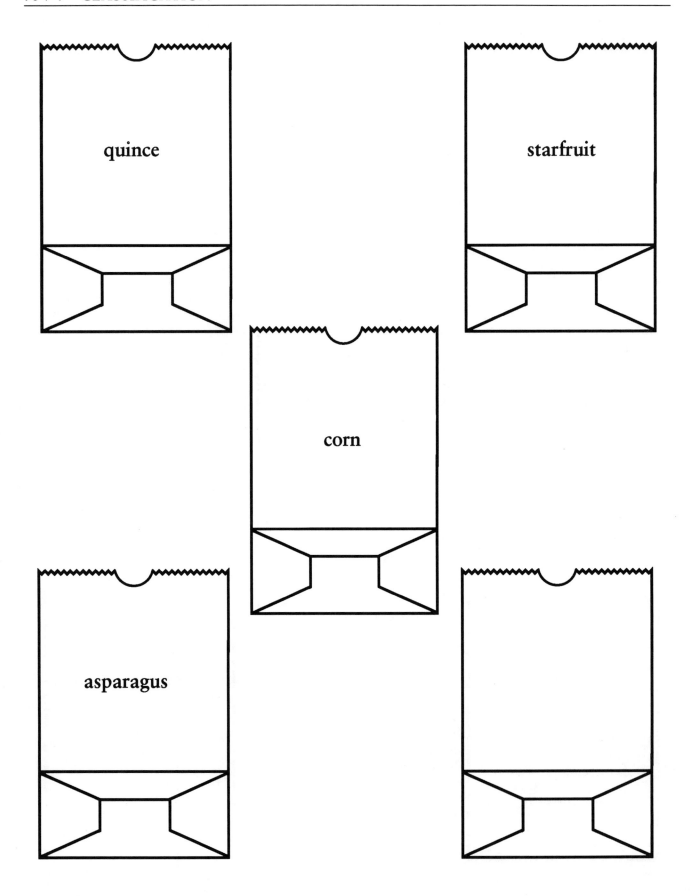

GAME 2

SELECTION TITLE:

> *Whose Hat Is That?*
> by Ron Roy

FOCUS:

CLASSIFICATION

HOW TO MAKE: Cut out selection title, focus, student directions, and answer card. Color and cut out all game pieces. Glue title onto folder tab and focus onto folder front. Glue heads onto the inside of the folder. Store student directions, answer card, and hats in library pocket glued to back of folder.

STUDENT DIRECTIONS:

1. Read categories for hats.
2. Read name of hats.
3. Place names of hats on correct category.
4. Check your answers using answer card.

ANSWER CARD:

Work	*Play*	*Special Occasions*
flight helmet	mouseketeer ears	Easter bonnet
beekeeper's hat	swimming cap	top hat
hard hat	baseball cap	dressy hat
painter's cap	football helmet	graduation cap
chef's hat	hockey helmet	
jockey helmet	bike helmet	*Weather*
surgical cap		ski mask
firefighter helmet		sun bonnet
		rain hat

PIECES FOR GAME 2—CLASSIFICATION

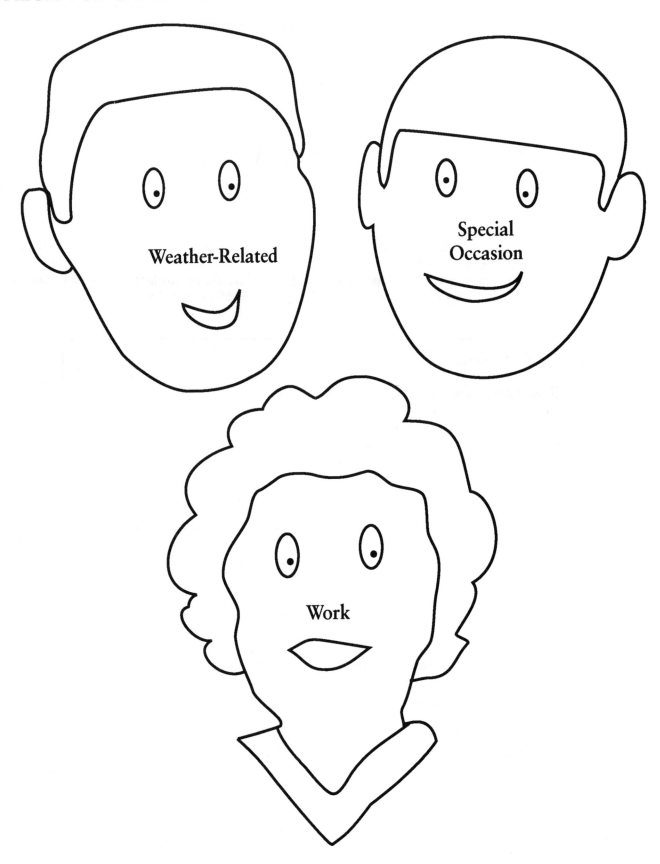

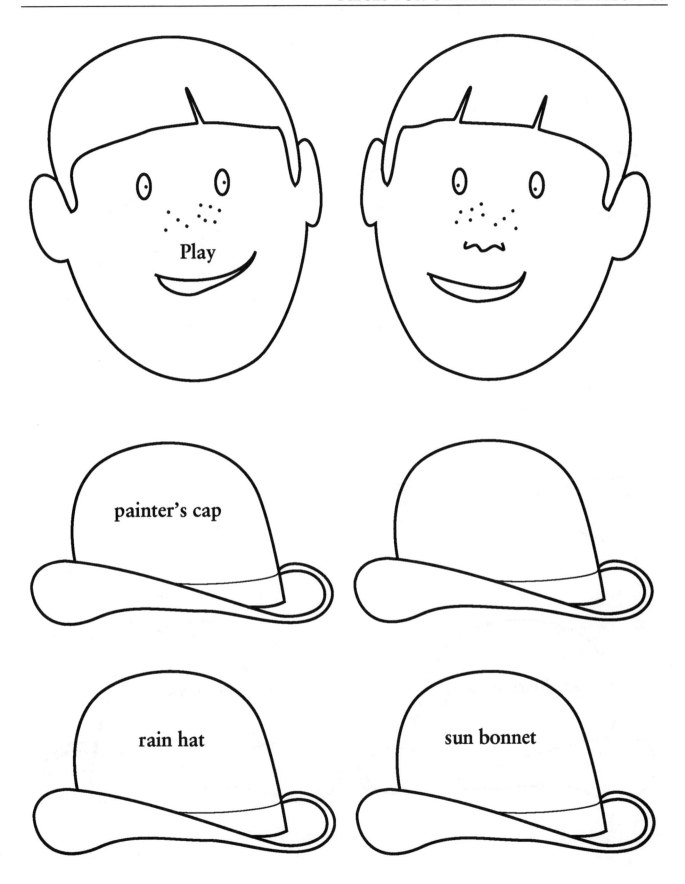

Play

painter's cap

rain hat

sun bonnet

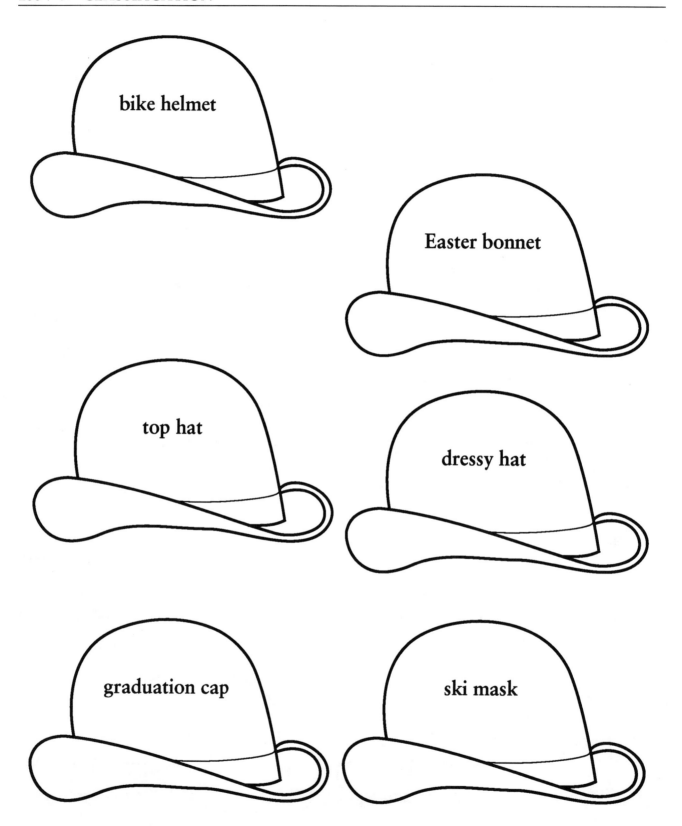

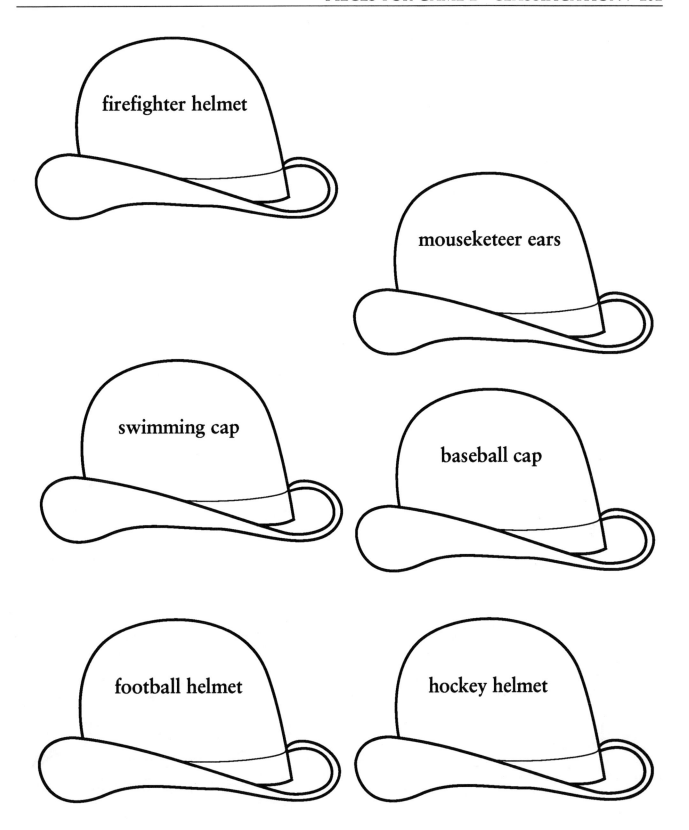

firefighter helmet

mouseketeer ears

swimming cap

baseball cap

football helmet

hockey helmet

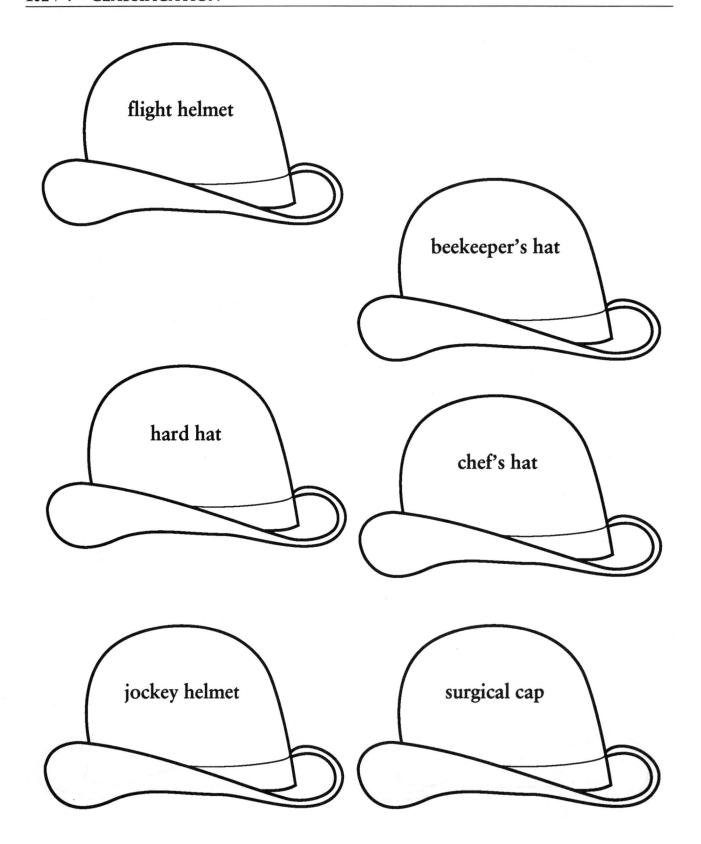

ACTIVITIES

Grocery Store: Using empty food containers, plastic food, or pictures from grocery-store ads, students design their own stores. They decide which items go on the same aisle and the same shelf. They may also develop a store directory for shoppers to use when trying to find a certain item. This activity could also be done with a department store or a sporting goods store.

Design a Zoo: Collect pictures of animals. Students design a zoo, arranging the animals by categories. They might arrange them by species, habitats, continents where found, or even number of legs.

Tasting Party: Bring several common, and some unusual, food items. Have students develop a list of "taste" words. After testing and identifying each item, students assign the items to a specific taste category.

Signs Around Us: Take a short walking trip around the school. Make a list of all the signs you find on the way: street signs, traffic signs, business signs, etc. When you get back to school, classify the signs by their functions.

Classified Ads: Collect an assortment of ads from the local paper. The students then sort the ads, develop headings, and design a layout for their own page of ads. Students may also write their own ads for items they want to sell or buy and develop a page of classified ads for the classroom.

Category Dictionary: Students select a category that interests them, such as dogs, cats, animals, toys, foods. They then develop a list of words that go with their category, alphabetize the words, and write a short definition for each word. They can cut and paste to build their dictionary, adding guide words to the top of the pages. Make a collection of these dictionaries for students to use when they are writing.

Person, Place, or Thing: Keep an ongoing list of persons, places, and things by pulling the information from students' reading. Students can add to the list independently. When the lists gets lengthy, the students can further classify them by breaking down each section. For the "person" section, for instance, they could classify by children, adults, boys, girls, real, or fictional. Similar breakdowns can be developed for other categories.

Twenty Questions: The old, standard game of Twenty Questions can be used to help students develop logical questions to discover what you are thinking of or what might be hidden in a box. Guide the children by helping them develop questions about categories to narrow their choices.

Catalog Publishing: Share with your students examples of catalogs. School supply catalogs are a good source, as are catalogs from department stores or mail-order companies. Students should select a purpose for their own catalog. It might be "Everything Needed for Schools," "The All-American Basketball Catalog," or "A Catalog for an Auto Mechanic." Let students be creative in their choices. Students should decide what is needed in their catalogs and how to arrange the items. They can even develop indexes based on categories.

Good Guys, Bad Guys: Students classify the characters in literature by using the characters' traits. These traits can even be written on white and black hats, like the cowboys in old movies. They could also classify actions using Good Deeds, Bad Deeds.

Build a Library: Students keep an ongoing list of books they have read. They develop a plan for their library using the Dewey Decimal System or a simplified version. Using strips of paper to represent book spines, students write the name of the book, author, and call number on the strip. They then arrange the strips on paper to look like shelving, using their own organizational system.

8—COMPARE AND CONTRAST

Objective: The student will compare and contrast after reading a selection.

TEACHER CHECKLIST FOR PLANNING

1. Explain the relationship between likenesses and differences and comparing and contrasting.

2. Teach using examples.
   Ask: How are things alike?
       How are things different?

3. Teach clue words.
   Examples: *But, unlike, on the other hand, however*

4. Have students group by likenesses and explain their grouping.

5. Have students group by differences and explain their grouping.

6. Have students find relationship between groups.
   Ask: What comparisons and contrasts can be made?

7. Have students explain their thinking.

STUDENT CHECKLIST

1. Ask: How are things alike?

2. Ask: How are things different?

3. Look for clue words.
   Examples: *But, unlike, on the other hand*

4. Group by likenesses.

5. Explain.

6. Group by differences.

7. Explain.

8. Look for relationship(s) between groups.

9. Ask: What comparisons and contrasts can I make?

10. Explain.

STUDENT VISUAL—COMPARE AND CONTRAST

Compare and Contrast

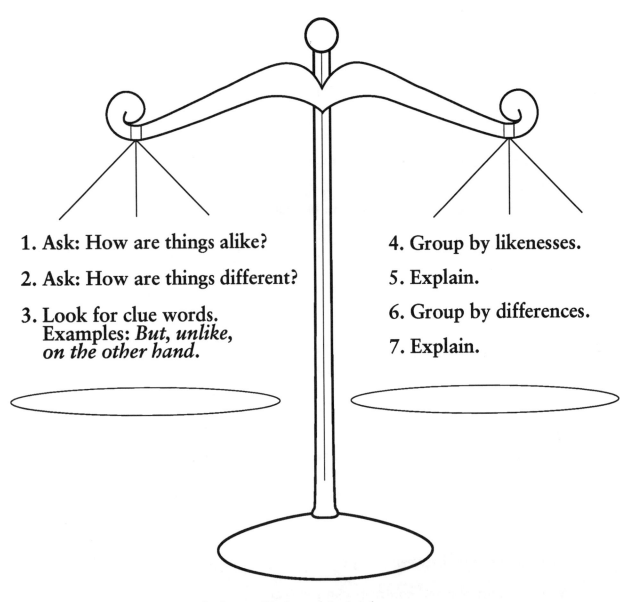

1. Ask: How are things alike?

2. Ask: How are things different?

3. Look for clue words. Examples: *But, unlike, on the other hand.*

4. Group by likenesses.

5. Explain.

6. Group by differences.

7. Explain.

8. Look for relationship(s) between groups.

9. Ask: What comparisons and contrasts can I make?

10. Explain.

ANNOTATED BIBLIOGRAPHY

Burton, Virginia Lee. *The Little House*. Boston: Houghton Mifflin, 1942.
   The little house stood in the country for years and became old and shabby before it got an unexpected new lease on life.

Fair, Sylvia. *The Bedspread*. New York: William Morrow & Co., 1982.
   Two elderly sisters embroider the home of their childhood at either end of a white bedspread, each as she remembers it, with results that surprise them.

Gackenbach, Dick. *Ida Fanfanny*. New York: Harper & Row, 1978.
   Ida lives in a land of no weather until a salesman sells her four magical paintings.

Hughes, Shirley. *Noisy*. New York: Lothrop, Lee & Shepard Co., 1985.
   A little girl describes the many noises that can be heard inside and outside her house.

Lionni, Leo. *Fish Is Fish*. New York: Pantheon Books, 1970.
   When his friend, the tadpole, becomes a frog, and leaves the pond to explore the world, the little fish decides that maybe he doesn't have to remain in the pond either.

McLeod, Emille W. *The Bear's Bicycle*. Illustrated by David McPhail. Boston: Little, Brown & Co., 1971.
   A boy and his bear have an exciting bicycle ride.

Provensen, Alice, and Martin Provensen. *Town and Country*. New York: Crown, 1971.
   Describes life in a big city and on a farm near a village.

Steig, William. *Amos and Boris*. New York: Farrar, Straus & Giroux, 1971.
   Amos, the mouse, and Boris, the whale, have little in common except that they are both mammals and save each other's lives.

Steptoe, John. *Mufaro's Beautiful Daughters*. New York: Lothrop, Lee & Shepard Co., 1987.
   An African tale showing how two daughters were tested for kindness before one was chosen to be the king's wife.

Stevenson, James. *Higher on the Door*. New York: Greenwillow Books, 1987.
   James Stevenson remembers what it was like growing up in a village, sometimes taking the train to New York City.

Wittman, Sally. *A Special Trade*. Illustrated by Karen Gundersheimer. New York: Harper & Row, 1978.
   As the years go by, a little girl is able to help an old man as he helped her when she was very young.

Compare and Contrast between Selections

Grimm, Jacob, and Wilhelm Grimm. *Cinderella*. Illustrated by Otto Svend. New York: Larousse, 1978.
     In this version of the well-known tale, Cinderella is helped to go to the ball by pigeons, turtle-doves, and all the birds of the air.

Louie, Si-Ling. *Yeh-Shen*. Illustrated by Ed Young. New York: Philomel, 1982.
     This version of the Cinderella story, in which a young girl overcomes the wickedness of her stepsisters and stepmother to become the bride of a prince, is based on ancient Chinese manuscripts written a thousand years before the earliest European version.

Perrault, Charles (retold by Amy Ehrlich). *Cinderella*. Illustrated by Susan Jeffers. New York: Dial Press, 1985.
     In her haste to flee the palace before her fairy godmother's magic loses its effect, Cinderella leaves behind a glass slipper.

De Regniers, Beatrice Schenk. *Little Red Riding Hood*. Illustrated by Edward Gorey. New York: Grosset, 1985.
     Retells in verse the adventures of a little girl, on her way to visit her grandmother, who meets a wolf in the forest.

Galdone, Paul. *Red Riding Hood*. New York: McGraw-Hill, 1974.
     A retelling of the folktale about a little girl who finds a wolf in her grandmother's clothing.

Hyman, Trina Schart. *Little Red Riding Hood*. New York: Holiday House, 1983.
     On her way to deliver a basket of food to her sick grandmother, Elizabeth encounters a sly wolf.

De Paola, Tomie. *Tomie de Paola's Mother Goose*. New York: Putnam, 1985.
     An illustrated collection of 204 Mother Goose nursery rhymes, including well-known ones, such as "Little Boy Blue," and less familiar ones, such as "Charlie Warlie and His Cow."

Hague, Michael. *Mother Goose*. New York: Holt, Rinehart & Winston, 1984.
     Hague carefully selected more than forty-five of his favorite rhymes and illustrated all of them with exquisite full-color paintings.

Omerod, Jan. *The Story of Chicken Licken*. New York: Lothrop, Lee & Shepard Co., 1985.
     The fable is retold with illustrations of children performing the story as a school play on stage.

Oxenbury, Helen. *"Henny-Penny"* from *The Helen Oxenbury Nursery Story Book*. New York: Knopf, 1985.
     Includes familiar folktales, such as "Henny-Penny."

De Paola, Tomie. *Fin M'Coul, The Giant of Knockmany Hill*. New York: Holiday House, 1981.
Fin M'Coul's wife, Oonagh, helps him outwit his archrival, Cucullin.

De Paola, Tomie. *Strega Nona*. New York: Prentice-Hall, 1975.
When Strega Nona leaves him alone with her magic pasta pot, Big Anthony is determined to show the townspeople how the pot works.

Galdone, Paul. *Cat Goes Fiddle-I-Fee*. New York: Clarion, 1985.
An old English rhyme names all the animals a farm boy feeds on his daily rounds.

Stanley, Diane Zuromskis. *Fiddle-I-Fee*. Boston: Little, Brown & Co., 1979.
In this cumulative nursery rhyme, a girl gives a special tea party for all her new animal friends.

GAME 1

SELECTION TITLE:

> *Mufaro's Beautiful Daughters*
> by John Steptoe

FOCUS:

> # Compare and Contrast

HOW TO MAKE: Cut out selection title, focus, student directions, and answer card. Cut out daughters' names and glue onto the inside of the folder. Cut out words and phrases. Store student directions, answer card, and words/phrases in library pocket glued to back of folder.

STUDENT DIRECTIONS:

1. Read words and phrases.
2. Compare and contrast words and phrases by placing them under correct daughter's name.
3. Check your answers using the answer card.

ANSWER CARD:

Manyara	Nayasha	Manyara and Nayasha
bad temper	kind	beautiful
teaser	singer	Mufaro's daughters
unhappy	farmer	could be queen
greedy	considerate	lived in Africa
rude	giving	strong
stingy	polite	
servant	queen	

PIECES FOR GAME 1—COMPARE AND CONTRAST

Manyara

Nayasha

Manyara
and Nayasha

bad temper

kind

teaser

singer

unhappy

farmer

greedy

considerate

stingy

giving

rude

polite

servant

queen

beautiful

Mufaro's daughters

could be queen

lived in Africa

strong

GAME 2

SELECTION TITLE:

> *Town and Country*
> by Alice and Martin Provensen

FOCUS:

Compare and Contrast

HOW TO MAKE: Cut out selection title, focus, student directions, and answer card. Color and cut out all game pieces. Glue title onto folder tab and focus onto folder front. Glue town and country silhouettes and the question onto the inside of the folder. Store student directions, answer card, and people in library pocket glued to back of folder.

STUDENT DIRECTIONS:

1. Read sentences on people pieces.
2. Decide which sentences describe the town, which describe the country, and which describe both.
3. Place the sentences on either the town, country, or under the question "How are they alike?"
4. Check your answers using answer card.

ANSWER CARD:

(order of answers not important)

Town - 1, 4, 5, 8, 12, 15
Country - 2, 6, 9, 11, 13, 14
How are they alike? - 3, 7, 10, 16

PIECES FOR GAME 2—COMPARE AND CONTRAST

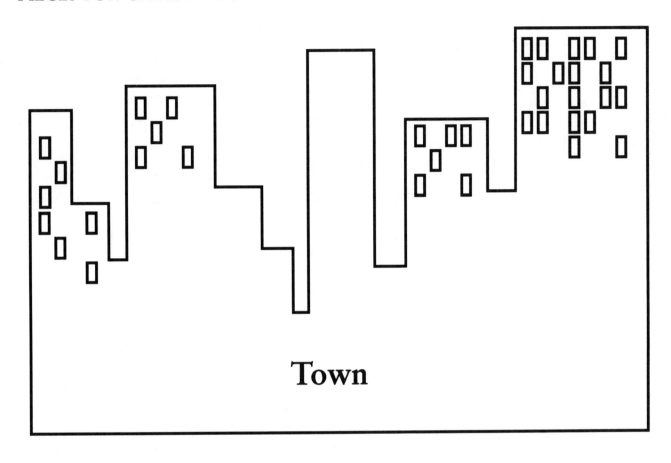

Town

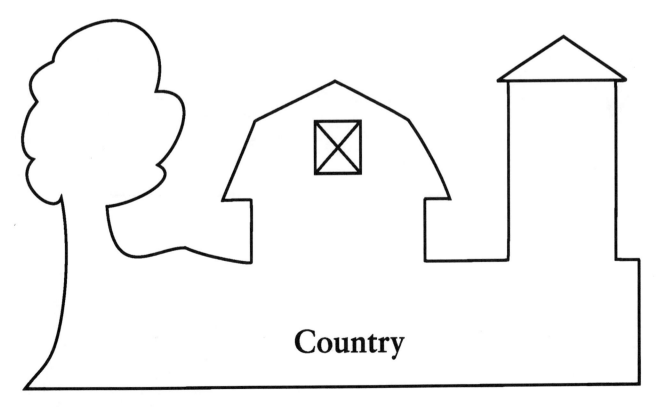

Country

How Are They Alike?

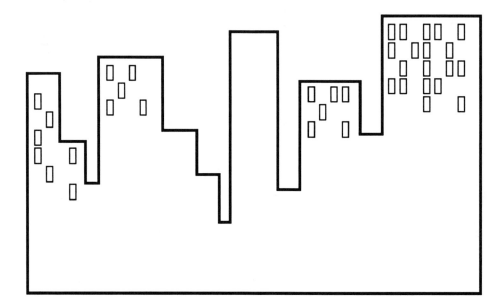

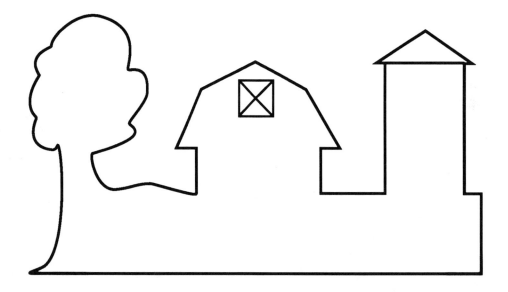

ACTIVITIES

How Are They Alike and Different?: Have students make two lists after reading or listening to several thematically related selections. One list will be of characters that are alike. The other list should be characters that are different. Students should make notes on the lists explaining how the characters are alike or different. The activity can also be done with settings or events from the selections.

Different Versions: Read two or more versions of the same folk tale, tall tale, or fairy tale. Make a chart of their likenesses and differences. Have a discussion about why the versions are different.

Real Life or Not: While reading a selection, have the students compare and contrast how different situations were handled in the reading to how they themselves would have handled the same situation. They could discuss, write about, or draw illustrations showing their thinking.

Two Books: Share with your students two different selections about the same topic. One selection might be the story of the three pigs. The other selection might be *Charlotte's Web*. Have the students make a chart comparing and contrasting the pigs in each selection.

What's in a Picture: Examine the work of several illustrators from books on the same subject. Look for likenesses and differences. Discuss how appropriate the work is to the text. Discuss how the story would change if the illustrations were switched. Students may illustrate a paragraph or selection using different styles and then compare and contrast their own work.

News Coverage: Videotape news coverage of a major news event from several local or national networks. View the videotapes with your students. Compare and contrast the reports. Extend the activity by having students write and present a news report about an event at school or an event from a reading selection. After all have presented their reports, compare and contrast the news.

What a Difference a Day Makes: Students might enjoy keeping track of the weather. Temperatures, sky conditions, precipitation, and appropriate clothing and activities could be recorded. This recordkeeping leads right into finding likenesses and differences and comparing and contrasting.

Sneaker Tracks: Begin by making crayon or chalk rubbings of everyone's (including the teacher's) sneaker soles. Cut out the rubbings and lay them on the floor. Look for likenesses and differences among the tracks. Make a class poster and display the tracks along with a list of likenesses and differences.

Flying High: Bring into the classroom examples of items that go in the sky (model airplanes, birds, kites, gliders). Have students create a chart to show how all the items are alike and how the items are different. This activity can be done with other similarly related items (automobiles, trains, shoes, kitchen utensils).

9—FACT VERSUS FICTION

Objective: The student will identify whether a statement is fact or fiction.

TEACHER CHECKLIST FOR PLANNING

1. Define fact: information that can be observed and/or checked by using reference material.

2. Define fiction: information made up by the author.

3. Compare similar fact and fiction statements.
   a. Probable versus improbable.
   b. Observable versus unobservable.
   c. Verifiable versus unverifiable.

4. Have students determine if statements are fact or fiction and explain why.

5. Compare similar fact and fiction selections.

6. Have students determine if selections are fact or fiction and explain why.

7. Compare fact and fiction statements in the same selection.

8. Have students determine which statements are fact and which are fiction.

STUDENT CHECKLIST

1. Read selection.

2. Think about individual statements.

3. Ask: Is the statement probable or improbable?
   Is the statement observable or unobservable?
   Is the statement verifiable or unverifiable?

4. Determine if the statement is fact or fiction.

5. Explain the reason.

STUDENT VISUAL—FACT VERSUS FICTION

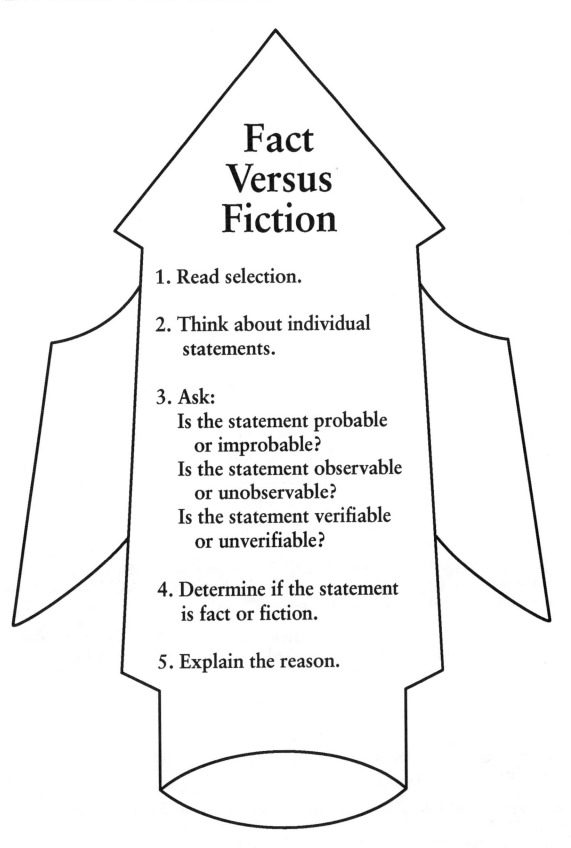

Fact
Versus
Fiction

1. Read selection.

2. Think about individual
   statements.

3. Ask:
   Is the statement probable
   or improbable?
   Is the statement observable
   or unobservable?
   Is the statement verifiable
   or unverifiable?

4. Determine if the statement
   is fact or fiction.

5. Explain the reason.

ANNOTATED BIBLIOGRAPHY

Compare and Contrast between Selections

Briggs, Carole S. *Ballooning*. Minneapolis: Lerner Publications Co., 1986.
   Surveys the history of ballooning, explains how hot-air and gas balloons work, and describes races, rallies, and a typical ride in a balloon.

Calhoun, Mary. *Hot-Air Henry*. Illustrated by Erick Ingraham. New York: William Morrow & Co., 1981.
   A sassy Siamese cat stows away on a hot-air balloon and ends up taking a fur-raising flight across the mountains.

Burton, Jane. *Chester the Chick*. New York: Random House, 1988.
   Text and photographs follow a baby chick through his first year of life, as he learns how to peck for food, plays with other chicks, and develops into a rooster.

Ravilious, Robin. *The Runaway Chick*. New York: Macmillan, 1987.
   A mischievous chick has an exciting and dangerous adventure when he wanders away from his mother, though no one in the barnyard will believe him afterwards.

Freeman, Don. *Corduroy*. New York: Viking Press, 1968.
   A little bear in a department store has a button missing, but, to his surprise, a girl buys him, sews on a button, and becomes his friend.

Rosenthal, Mark. *Bears*. Chicago: Children's Press, 1983.
   Briefly describes different kinds of bears, how they behave, and how they should be treated.

De Paola, Tomie. *Tony's Bread*. New York: G. P. Putnam's Sons, 1989.
   A baker loses his daughter but gains a bakery in the grand city of Milano after meeting a determined nobleman and baking a unique loaf of bread.

Turner, Dorothy. *Bread*. Illustrated by John Yates. Minneapolis, MN: Carolrhoda Books, 1988.
   Describes how bread is produced, prepared, and eaten, and presents some background history as well as two recipes.

Holling, Holling Clancy. *Pagoo*. Boston: Houghton Mifflin, 1957.
   Provides a peek into the life of a hermit crab named Pagoo, told against a factual background of tide-pool life.

Pohl, Kathleen. *Hermit Crabs*. Photographs by Hidekazu Kubo. Milwaukee: WI: Raintree Publishers, 1987.
   Text and photographs describe the life cycle and behavior patterns of the hermit crab.

Goffstein, Brooke. *An Actor*. New York: Harper & Row, 1987.
    A small actor presents herself to the audience and shows the roles she plays on stage.

Greenberg, Keith Elliot. *Michael J. Fox*. Minneapolis, MN: Lerner Publications Co., 1986.
    Follows the life and career of the diminutive Canadian actor who has achieved phenomenal success in both television and film work.

Linn, Margot. *A Trip to the Dentist*. Illustrated by Catherine Siracusa. New York: Harper & Row, 1988.
    Simple questions and answers introduce the procedures, instruments, and routines involved in a visit to the dentist.

Steig, William. *Dr. De Soto*. New York: Farrar, Straus & Giroux, 1982.
    Dr. De Soto, a mouse dentist, copes with toothaches of various animals except those with a taste for mice, until the day a fox comes to him in great pain.

Collins, James L. *Exploring the American West*. New York: Franklin Watts, 1989.
    Recounts the exploits of explorers of the American West, from Daniel Boone in the late 1700s to John Charles Fremont in the 1850s.

Gammell, Stephen. *Git Along, Old Scudder*. New York: Lothrop, Lee & Shepard, 1983.
    Old Scudder doesn't know where he is until he draws a map and names the places on it.

De Paola, Tomie. *The Cloud Book*. New York: Holiday House, 1975.
    Introduces the ten most common types of clouds, the myths that have been inspired by their shapes, and what clouds can tell about coming weather changes.

Ray, Deborah Kogan. *The Cloud*. New York: Harper & Row, 1984.
    A little girl struggles to hike up a mountain with her mother in hopes of seeing a beautiful white cloud.

Gibbons, Gail. *Thanksgiving Day*. New York: Holiday House, 1983.
    Presents information about the first Thanksgiving and the way that holiday is celebrated today.

Stevenson, James. *Fried Feathers for Thanksgiving*. New York: Greenwillow Books, 1986.
    Mean witches Dolores and Lavinia try to spoil Thanksgiving for everyone else, but nice witch Emma and her friends outwit them.

Fischer-Nagel, Heiderose, and Andreas Fischer-Nagel. *A Puppy Is Born*. New York: G. P. Putnam's Sons, 1983.
Photographs and text portray the birth and first few weeks of four wirehaired dachshunds.

Saltzberg, Barney. *Cromwell*. New York: Atheneum, 1986.
Cromwell is not like other puppies, since he wears clothes and digs with a shovel, but his new owner expects him to behave like a regular dog.

Dorros, Arthur. *Ant Cities*. New York: Thomas Y. Crowell, 1987.
Explains how ants live and work together to build and maintain their cities.

Van Allsburg, Chris. *Two Bad Ants*. Boston: Houghton Mifflin, 1988.
When two bad ants desert from their colony, they experience a dangerous adventure that convinces them to return to their former safety.

Burton, Virginia Lee. *Mike Mulligan and His Steam Shovel*. Boston: Houghton Mifflin, 1967.
Mary Ann, the steam shovel, is old fashioned, but she and her owner prove they can still dig and be of use in the town of Popperville.

Potter, Tony. *Earth Movers*. Illustrated by Robin Lawrie. New York: Macmillan, 1989.
Simple text and detailed illustrations with see-through pages introduce the characteristics and functions of various machines that move earth.

GAME 1

SELECTION TITLE:

> *A Trip to the Dentist* by Margot Linn
> *Doctor De Soto* by William Steig

FOCUS:

Fact versus Fiction

HOW TO MAKE: Cut out selection title, focus, student directions, and answer card. Color and cut out all game pieces. Glue title onto folder tab and focus onto folder front. Glue teeth numbered 1-6 in vertical order onto left side of folder. Glue teeth numbered 7-12 in vertical order onto right side of folder. Draw arrow between teeth on the left side and teeth on the right side (1⟷7). Store student directions, answer card, and toothbrushes in library pocket glued to back of folder.

STUDENT DIRECTIONS:

1. Read sentences on teeth, a pair at a time.
   1⟷7, 2⟷8, 3⟶9, 4⟶10, 5⟶11, 6⟷12
2. Decide which sentence in the pair is fact and which is fiction.
3. Place fact toothbrushes on fact sentences and fiction toothbrushes on fiction sentences.
4. Check your answers using answer card.

ANSWER CARD:

1.	fact	7.	fiction
2.	fact	8.	fiction
3.	fiction	9.	fact
4.	fact	10.	fiction
5.	fiction	11.	fact
6.	fact	12.	fiction

PIECES FOR GAME 1—FACT VERSUS FICTION

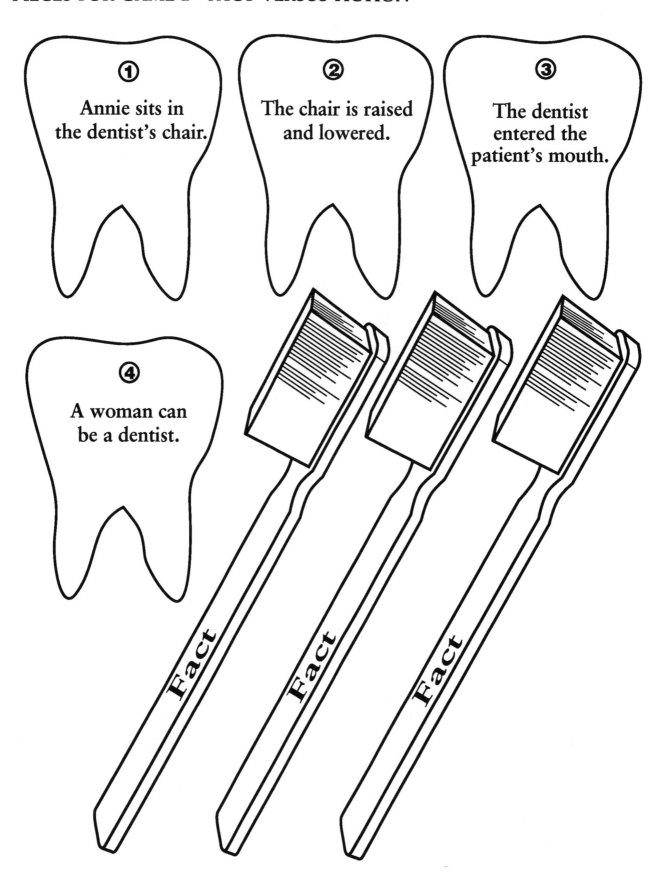

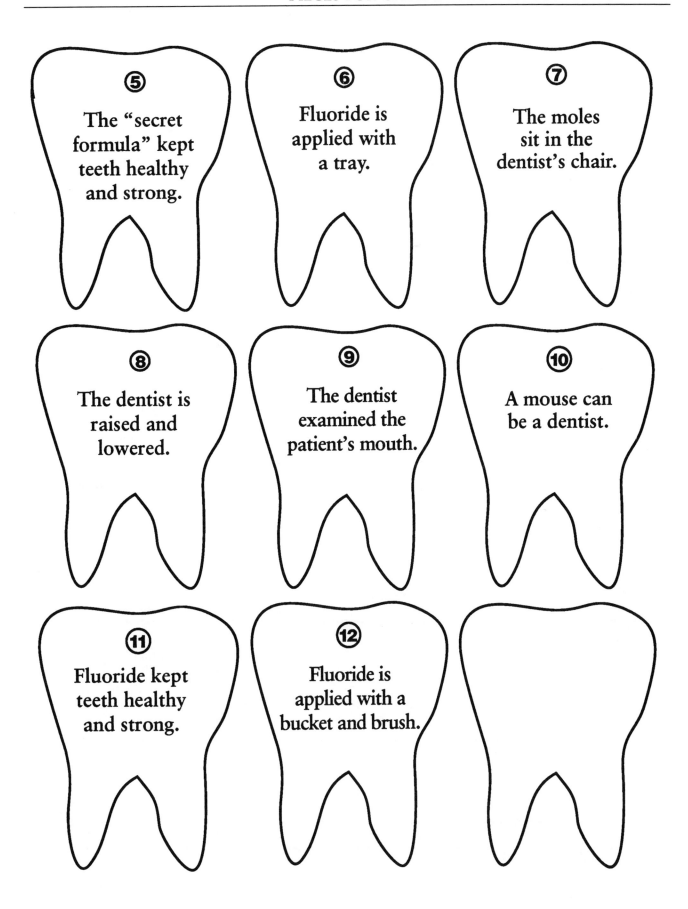

⑤ The "secret formula" kept teeth healthy and strong.

⑥ Fluoride is applied with a tray.

⑦ The moles sit in the dentist's chair.

⑧ The dentist is raised and lowered.

⑨ The dentist examined the patient's mouth.

⑩ A mouse can be a dentist.

⑪ Fluoride kept teeth healthy and strong.

⑫ Fluoride is applied with a bucket and brush.

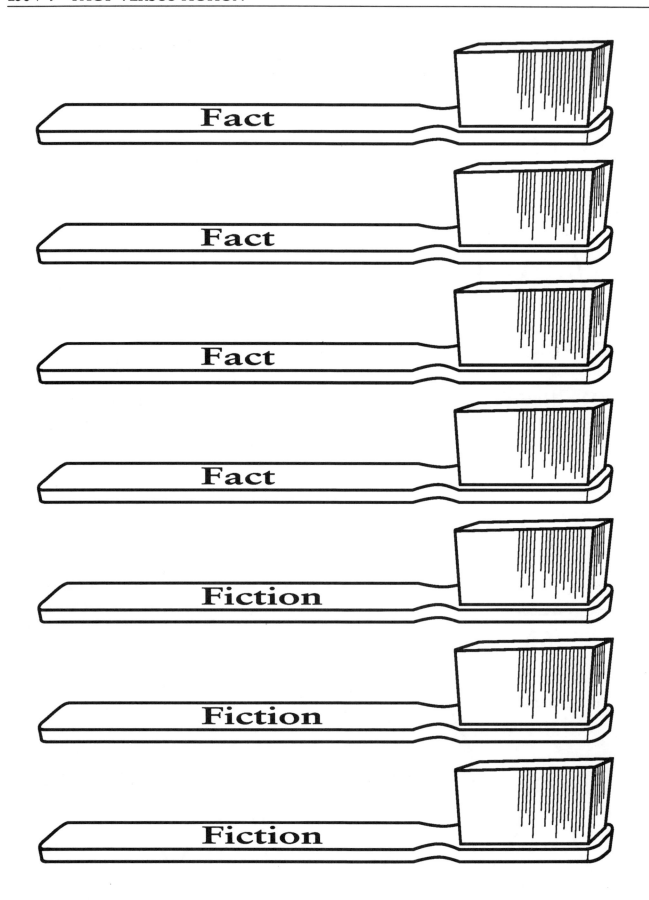

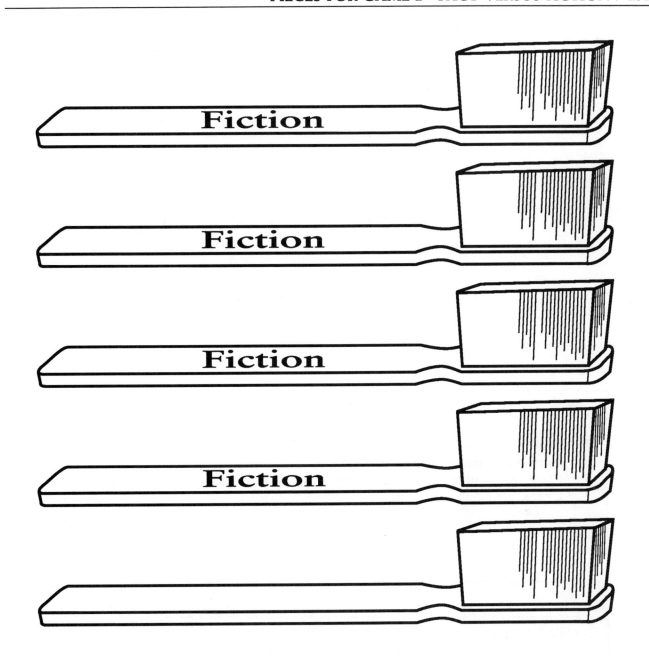

GAME 2

SELECTION TITLE:

> *The Cloud Book*
> by Tomie de Paola

FOCUS:

> # Fact versus Fiction

HOW TO MAKE: Cut out selection title, focus, student directions, and answer card. Color and cut out all game pieces. Glue title onto folder tab and focus onto folder front. Glue telescopes onto the inside of the folder. Store student directions, answer card, and clouds in library pocket glued to back of folder.

STUDENT DIRECTIONS:

1. Read sentences on telescopes.
2. Decide if sentence is fact or fiction.
3. Place fact clouds on fact sentences and fiction clouds on fiction sentences.
4. Check your answers using answer card.

ANSWER CARD:

1.	fact	7.	fact
2.	fact	8.	fiction
3.	fiction	9.	fact
4.	fact	10.	fiction
5.	fiction	11.	fact
6.	fiction	12.	fact

PIECES FOR GAME 2—FACT VERSUS FICTION

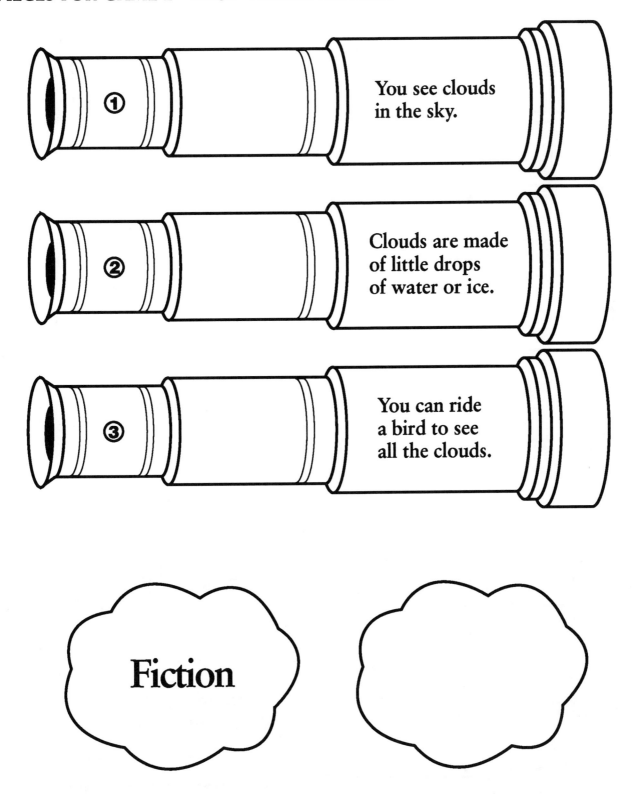

① You see clouds in the sky.

② Clouds are made of little drops of water or ice.

③ You can ride a bird to see all the clouds.

Fiction

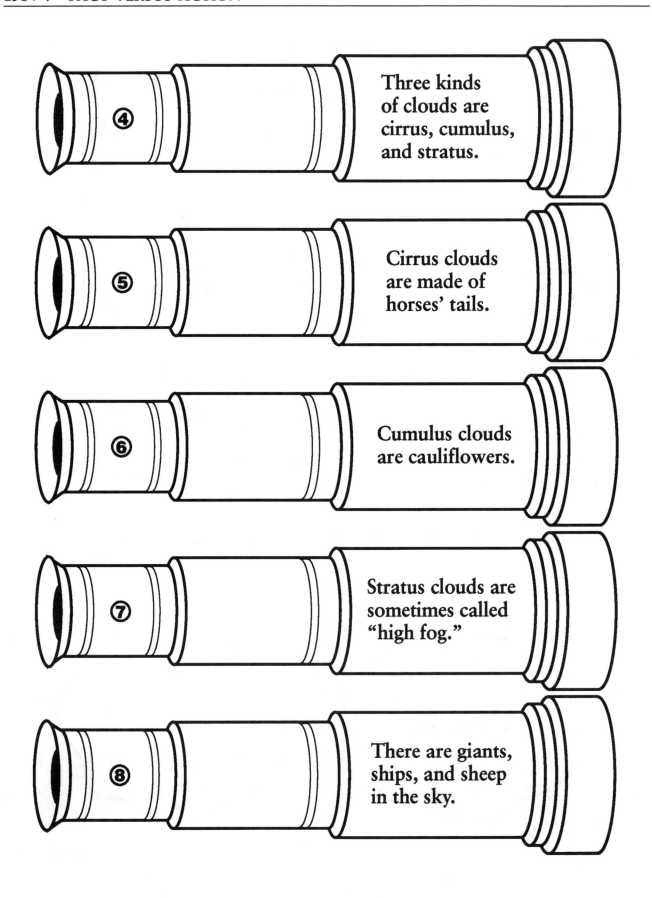

④ Three kinds of clouds are cirrus, cumulus, and stratus.

⑤ Cirrus clouds are made of horses' tails.

⑥ Cumulus clouds are cauliflowers.

⑦ Stratus clouds are sometimes called "high fog."

⑧ There are giants, ships, and sheep in the sky.

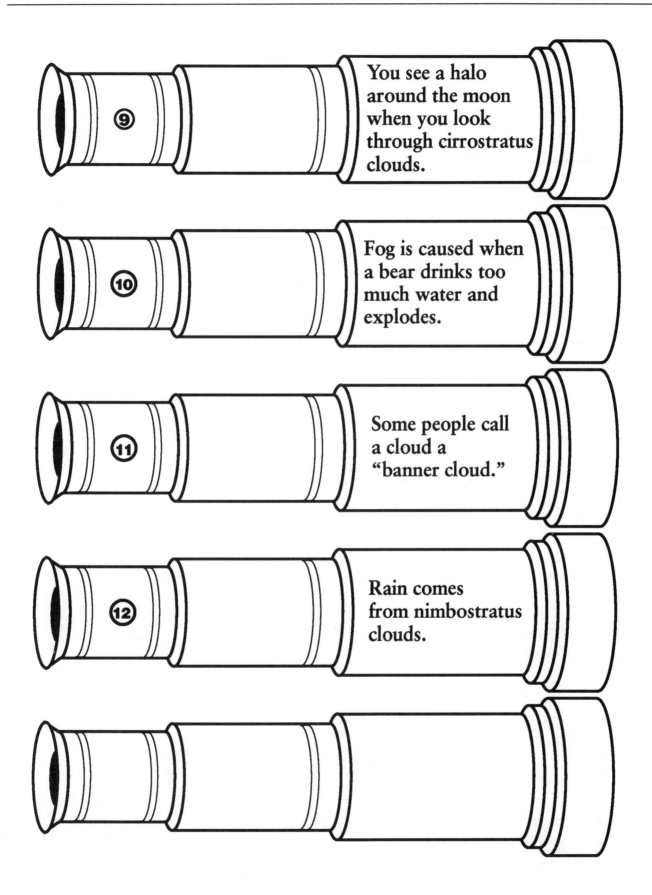

9 You see a halo around the moon when you look through cirrostratus clouds.

10 Fog is caused when a bear drinks too much water and explodes.

11 Some people call a cloud a "banner cloud."

12 Rain comes from nimbostratus clouds.

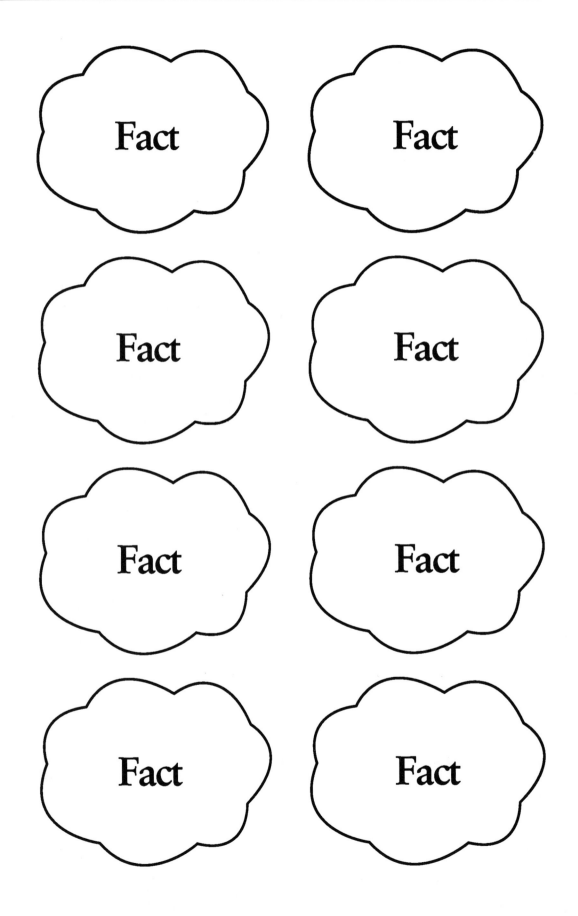

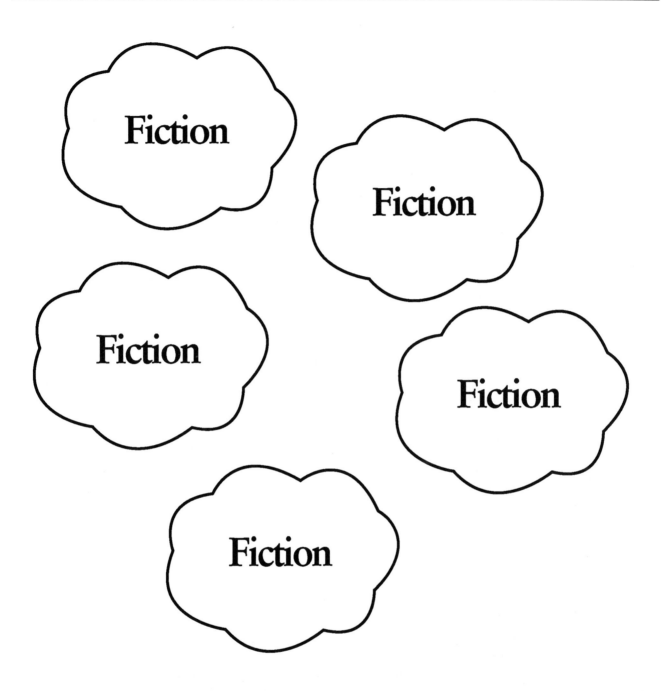

ACTIVITIES

Probable versus Improbable: Write probable statements on paper strips. Have students write, or state orally, an improbable statement about the same subject. (The child turned off the light and went to bed. The child turned off the light and jumped into bed before the room got dark.) This activity could be done with verifiable versus unverifiable statements, or observable versus unobservable statements.

Chef's Special: Turn your classroom into a restaurant. Have the students, your chefs, create luncheon menus with factual or fictional items on it. Have students pair up. Pass out play money to students. When ordering items from their partner's menu, they will only order and pay for factual items.

What's in a Title?: Compile a list of fact and fiction titles (*All about Snakes, Flight to the Center of the Earth, The Utes of Colorado, Marvelous Marvin on Mars*). These titles can be titles of popular literature or invented titles. Put the titles on cards. Students choose a card from the top of the pile, read the title, decide if it is fact or fiction, and verbalize statements that might be found in the selection.

Title Trivia: Prepare cards having several fact or fiction statements on them. The sentences on each card need to be about the same topic and need to be *either* fact or fiction. Students select a card from the pile, tell whether the statements are fact or fiction, and create a title to match the statements.

Dreaded Chores: Most students have some chores they have to do at home, and there are usually ones they hate to do. Students write descriptions of how to complete the dreaded chore. Then, using their imaginations, they create a new, imaginary plan for completing the chore. Compare the two descriptions for factual and fictional elements.

Job Descriptions: With your class, brainstorm a list of occupations. Also brainstorm a list of facts about each job. Students may select an occupation to research. They might interview someone, use reference materials, and/or write letters asking for information to determine facts and fiction about the occupation. They could share the information with the class through reports, charts, or role-playing.

Animal Crack-ups: Have students bring pictures of their favorite animals to class. Students write or share orally lists of facts about the animals. Then cut all the animal pictures into pieces (head, body, tail, legs). Pass out the mixed-up pieces and have students create a fictional animal. Have students name the new animal and share fictional information about the animal.

Pig Pairs: Find a picture of Porky Pig and a picture of a real pig. Glue them onto a piece of chart paper that has been divided in half. Have students write factual and fictional statements to glue under each picture. Other pairings could be used (an astronaut and Captain Kirk, yourself and Miss Nelson).

10—FIGURATIVE LANGUAGE

Objective: The student will recognize and relate the meaning created by the use of figurative language in a written selection.

TEACHER CHECKLIST FOR PLANNING

1. Define figurative language: words having symbolic or hidden meaning rather than literal meaning.

2. Define types of figurative language.

    a. Imagery—descriptions used to make poems and stories more interesting to read and to express ideas more vividly.
        Example: The sun sent fingers of light into the room.
    b. Idiom—expression in which the actual meaning of the individual words is different from the meaning of the whole expression.
        Example: Hit the road!
    c. Simile—comparison using "like" or "as."
        Example: The sun is like a ball of fire.
    d. Metaphor—direct comparison between things *not* using like or as.
        Example: The snowflake is a dainty flower.
    e. Hyperbole—greatly exaggerated ideas.
        Example: I'm scared to death of spiders.
    f. Personification—human traits used to describe non-human things.
        Example: The tree branches waved hello as we walked by.

3. Teach the recognition of figurative language in context by using examples and non-examples.

    a. Evaluate sentence for truthfulness by using context clues and/or picture clues.
        Ask: Does it really mean exactly what it says?
    b. Identify part of sentence that is figurative.

4. Have students determine meaning of figurative language.
    Ask: What literal picture does this sentence create?
    Ask: What is wrong with the picture?
    Ask: What is the hidden meaning of the sentence?

5. Have students check to see if the hidden meaning fits into the context.

STUDENT CHECKLIST

1. Read sentence.

2. Determine if figurative language is used by looking at context clues and pictures.
    Ask: Does it really mean exactly what it says?

3. Determine meaning of figurative language.
    Ask: What literal picture does this create?
           What is wrong with the picture?
           What is the hidden meaning of the sentence?

4. Check to see if hidden meaning fits into context.

STUDENT VISUAL—FIGURATIVE LANGUAGE

Figurative Language

1. Read sentence.

2. Determine if figurative language is used by looking at context clues and pictures.

   Ask: Does it really mean exactly what it says?

3. Determine meaning of figurative language.

   Ask: What literal picture does this create? What is wrong with the picture? What is the hidden meaning of the sentence?

4. Check to see if hidden meaning fits into context.

ANNOTATED BIBLIOGRAPHY

Adoff, Arnold. *Flamboyan*. Illustrated by Karen Barbour. San Diego: Harcourt Brace Jovanovich, 1988.
One sunny afternoon while everyone is resting, Flamboyan, a young girl named after the tree whose red blossoms are the same color as her hair, dreamily flies over her Caribbean island home.

_____. *OUTside INside Poems*. Illustrated by John Steptoe. New York: Lothrop, Lee & Shepard Co., 1981.
Poems reflect a child's thoughts inside and outside, describing what he sees and feels.

Agard, John. *Lend Me Your Wings*. Illustrated by Adrienne Kennaway. Boston: Little, Brown & Co., 1987.
A fish who longs to fly and a bird who longs to swim trade fins and wings for a new look at life.

Bauer, Caroline Feller. *Snowy Day: Stories and Poems*. Illustrated by Margot Tomes. New York: J. B. Lippincott, 1986.
A collection of stories and poems with snow as a common theme.

Fox, Siv Cedering. *The Blue Horse and Other Night Poems*. Illustrated by Donald Carrick. New York: Seabury Press, 1979.
A collection of fourteen poems about sleeping, dreaming, and waking.

Hanson, Joan. *Similes*. Minneapolis, MN: Lerner Press, 1973.
A child uses similes to describe his neighborhood friends.

Hilgartner, Beth. *Great Gorilla Grins*. Illustrated by Leslie Morrill. Boston: Little, Brown & Co., 1979.
A collection of alliterative descriptions of a variety of animals.

Hopkins, Lee Bennett. *Click, Rumble, Roar*. Photographs by Anna Held Audette. New York: Thomas Y. Crowell, 1987.
A collection of eighteen poems about machines by Myra Cohn Livingston, Eve Merriam, David McCord, and others.

Livingston, Myra Cohn. *Sky Songs*. Illustrated by Leonard Everett Fisher. New York: Holiday House, 1984.
Fourteen poems about the various aspects of the sky, such as the moon, clouds, stars, storms, and sunsets.

O'Neill, Mary. *Hailstones and Halibut Bones*. Illustrated by Leonard Weisgard. Garden City, NY: Doubleday & Co., 1961.
Twelve poems reflect the author's feelings about various colors.

Parnall, Peter. *Alfalfa Hill*. Garden City, NY: Doubleday & Co., 1975.
Describes the coming of winter and its effects on the animal inhabitants of a New Jersey hill.

Prelutsky, Jack. *Ride a Purple Pelican*. Illustrated by Garth Williams. New York: Greenwillow Books, 1986.
A collection of short nonsense verses and nursery rhymes.

_____. *The Sheriff of Rottenshot*. Illustrated by Victoria Chess. New York: Greenwillow Books, 1982.
A collection of sixteen humorous poems, including "The Sheriff of Rottenshot," "The Soggy Frog," and "The Ghostly Grocer of Grumble Grove."

Radin, Ruth Yaffe. *High in the Mountains*. Illustrated by Ed Young. New York: Macmillan, 1989.
A young child describes a day spent near grandpa's house in the mountains.

Rylant, Cynthia. *Night in the Country*. Illustrated by Mary Szilagyi. New York: Bradbury Press, 1986.
Text and illustrations describe the sights and sounds of nighttime in the country.

Sandburg, Carl. *Rainbows Are Made*. Illustrated by Fritz Eichenberg. San Diego: Harcourt Brace Jovanovich, 1982.
Seventy humorous and serious poems dealing with people, word plays, everyday things, nature, night, and the sea.

Silverstein, Shel. *The Giving Tree*. New York: Harper & Row, 1964.
A young boy grows to manhood and old age experiencing the love and generosity of a tree which gives to him without thought of return.

Stolz, Mary. *Storm in the Night*. Illustrated by Pat Cummings. New York: Harper & Row, 1988.
While sitting through a fearsome thunderstorm that has put the lights out, Thomas hears a story from Grandfather's boyhood, when Grandfather was afraid of thunderstorms.

Terban, Marvin. *Mad as a Wet Hen!* Illustrated by Giulio Maestro. New York: Clarion Books, 1987.
Illustrates and explains over one hundred common English idioms, in categories including animals, body parts, and colors.

Zolotow, Charlotte. *The White Marble*. Illustrated by Deborah Kogan Ray. New York: Thomas Y. Crowell, 1963.
Two children find beauty and wonder in the park on a hot summer night.

GAME 1

SELECTION TITLE:

> *Flamboyan*
> by Arnold Adoff

FOCUS:

Figurative Language

HOW TO MAKE: Cut out selection title, focus, student directions, and answer card. Color and cut out all game pieces. Glue title onto folder tab and focus onto folder front. Glue suns onto the inside of the folder. Store student directions, answer card, and canoes in library pocket glued to back of folder.

STUDENT DIRECTIONS:

1. Read sentences on the suns.
2. Read sentences on the canoes.
3. There are two sentence canoes that go with each sun, one that is literal and one that states the "hidden" meaning of the sentence.
4. Choose the sentence that tells the hidden meaning for the sentence on the sun.
5. Check your answers using answer card.

ANSWER CARD:

1. Flamboyan's skin is very dark.
2. Flamboyan's eyes are big and round.
3. The rooster is crowing in the morning.
4. The branches are long.
5. Flamboyan can't fly.
6. She sat in the shade of a tree.

PIECES FOR GAME 1—FIGURATIVE LANGUAGE

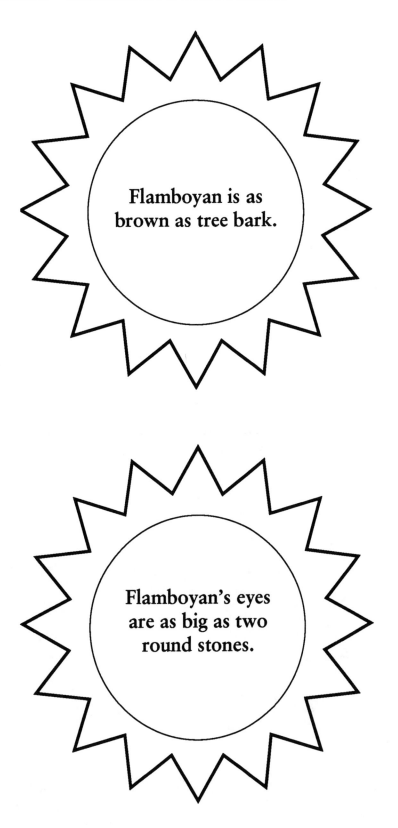

Flamboyan is rooted
to the ground.

She sat under an
umbrella of branches
and leaves.

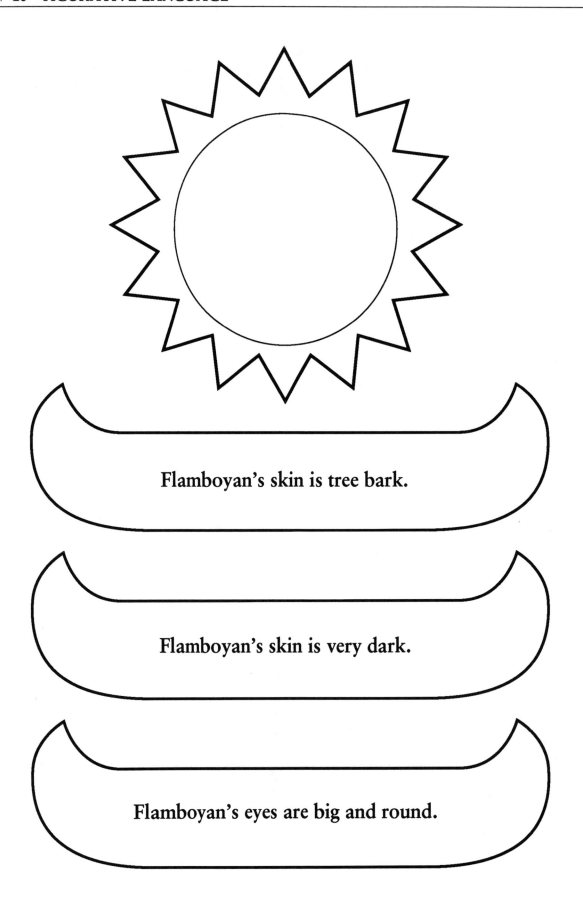

Flamboyan's skin is tree bark.

Flamboyan's skin is very dark.

Flamboyan's eyes are big and round.

Flamboyan's eyes are stones.

The rooster invites the sun to come up.

The rooster is crowing in the morning.

The branches are long.

The branches are as tall as the sky.

Flamboyan is a plant with roots.

Flamboyan can't fly.

She sat under an umbrella.

She sat in the shade of a tree.

GAME 2

SELECTION TITLE:

> *Hailstones and Halibut Bones*
> by Mary O'Neill

FOCUS:

Figurative Language

HOW TO MAKE: Cut out selection title, focus, student directions, and answer card. Color and cut out all game pieces. Glue title onto folder tab and focus onto folder front. Glue one crayon box onto each half of the inside of the folder. Store student directions, answer card, and crayons in library pocket glued to back of folder.

STUDENT DIRECTIONS:

1.   Read sentences on the crayons.
2.   Decide if sentence is an example of figurative language.
3.   Put figurative language sentences on the "Yes" box and others on the "No" box.
4.   Check your answers using answer card.

ANSWER CARD:

(order of answers not important)

Yes - 1, 5, 6, 8, 10, 12
No - 2, 3, 4, 7, 9, 11

PIECES FOR GAME 2—FIGURATIVE LANGUAGE

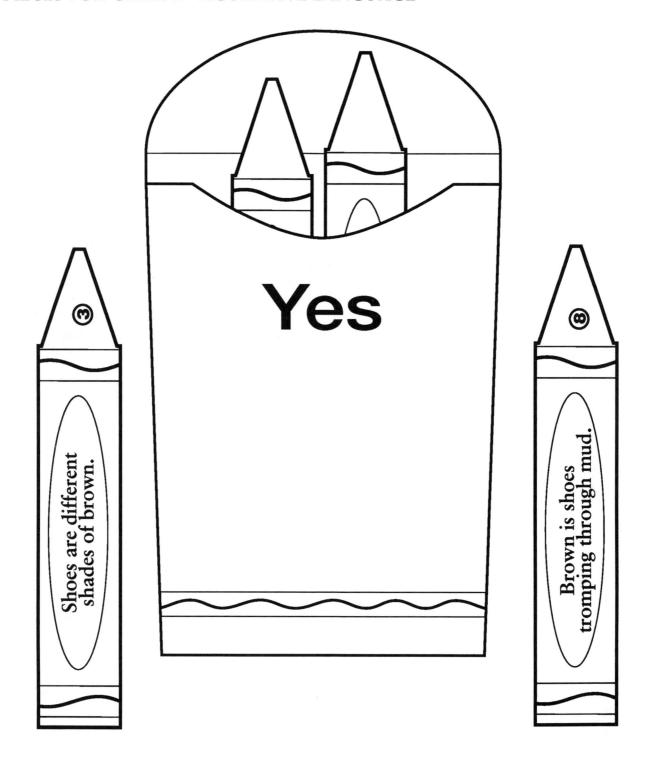

Yes

③ Shoes are different shades of brown.

⑧ Brown is shoes tromping through mud.

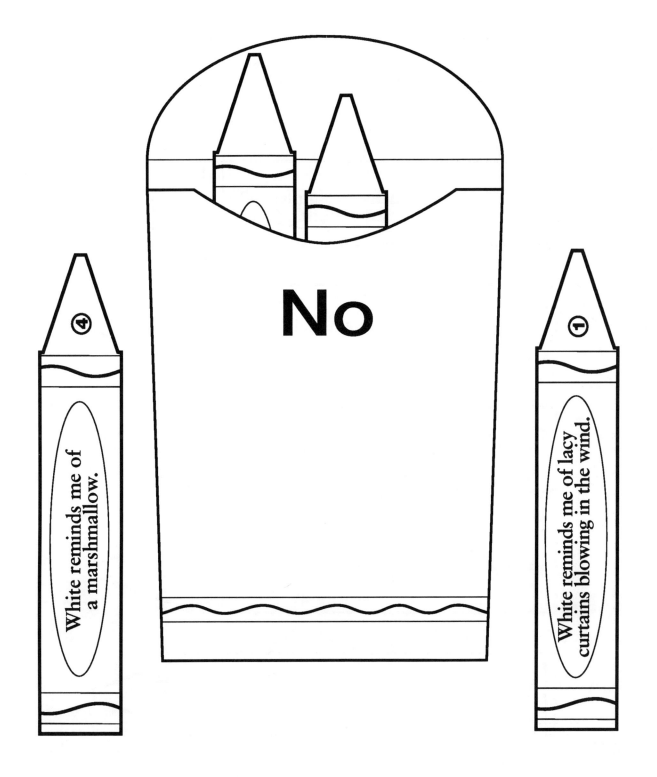

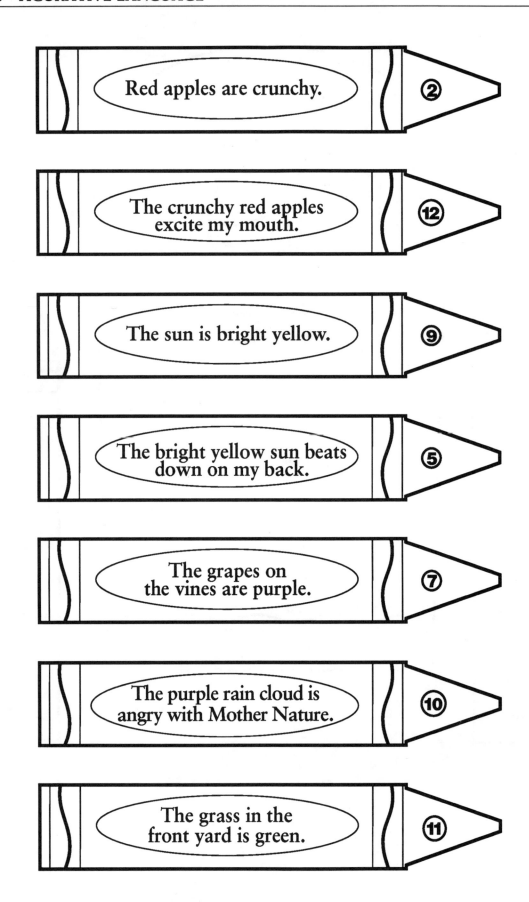

Red apples are crunchy. ②

The crunchy red apples excite my mouth. ⑫

The sun is bright yellow. ⑨

The bright yellow sun beats down on my back. ⑤

The grapes on the vines are purple. ⑦

The purple rain cloud is angry with Mother Nature. ⑩

The grass in the front yard is green. ⑪

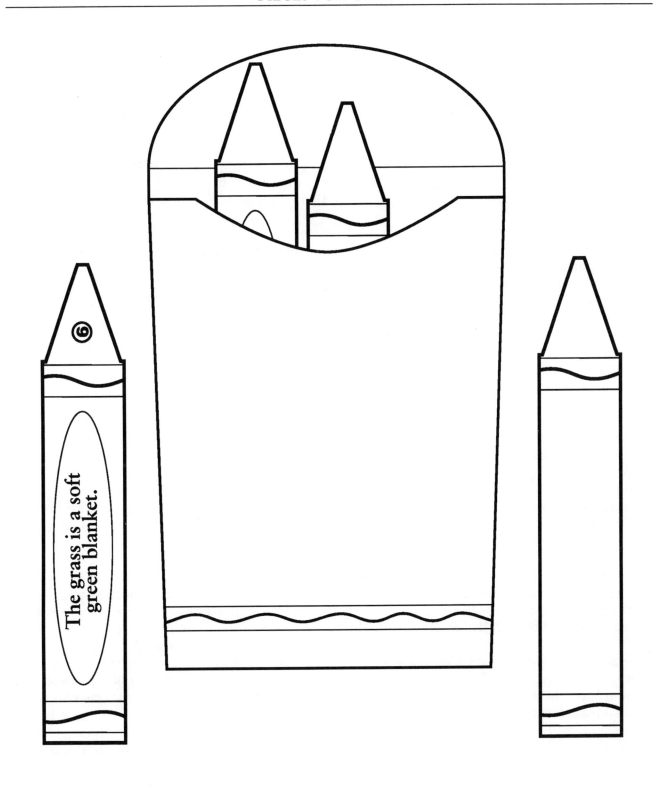

The grass is a soft green blanket.

ACTIVITIES

Colorful Language Dictionary: Start a class dictionary with examples of colorful language found in poetry that students enjoy. Be sure to include a short definition or description of each example. This dictionary can be added to throughout the year whenever students come across other examples in their reading.

Literal Meanings: Select idioms or colorful language phrases from a selection students are going to read. Have them draw an illustration to show the *literal* meaning. When the students come upon the idiom in the selection, have them compare their illustrations to what is actually meant in context.

Sense Chart: While working with literature that uses figurative language, use a class chart divided into five parts. Label each part with one of the senses (seeing, hearing, tasting, smelling, touching). When the students come across figurative language in their reading, have them decide which sense is being used in the description. The example is then listed on the Sense Chart under the appropriate category.

Vacuum Cleaner Similes: Bring a vacuum to the classroom. Note details about its looks, its function, or its sound. Make a book of similes about the vacuum cleaner ("A vacuum cleaner is like a hungry dog devouring its food"). Students might write and illustrate their similes to create a class book. This activity can be done with an assortment of household appliances.

Mood Metaphors: Brainstorm with your class a list of words that describe people's moods (*lonely, sad, excited*). Have students divide into working groups. Have them select one mood word to think about. In the working group, have them brainstorm a list of objects that remind them of the mood (Excited—marbles bouncing in a pinball machine; Lonely—a hot dog with no bun). Students then create mood metaphors using the brainstormed list (She is lonely. She is a hot dog without a bun). These metaphors are a great starter for poetry. The metaphors can be developed for class or individual books.

Come Alive: Have students think of a personification for a familiar object. Play this activity like charades, but have students draw their personifications on the chalkboard or poster paper, while other students try to guess the personification. The student who guesses the correct answer states the comparison between the object and the human.

Hide and Seek: Help students generate a list of figurative language statements (statements using imagery, metaphors, similes). Cut the statements apart. Place them in empty containers and hide them around the room. Divide the students into teams. Have each team look for one container. When a team locates a container, its members first decide what kind of figurative language is used (imagery, simile), and then write three statements using that type of figurative language. Have students share their statements, which can be saved and used for the next game of Hide and Seek.

Mystery Box: Collect an assortment of interesting objects (rocks, shells, pencils, leaves, ribbons). Each student reaches into the box and selects one object. The student then writes a sentence, using figurative language, about the chosen object. These sentences can then be put in the mystery box. Another group selects a sentence from the mystery box and tries to decide what object was written about.

11—GENERALIZATION

Objective: The student will make and test a generalization.

TEACHER CHECKLIST FOR PLANNING

1. Define generalization: a broad statement that puts related facts and details together.

2. Teach how to determine subject matter of information based on finding the relationship of details.

3. Teach how to determine a pattern or trend using the subject matter.

4. Teach how to use the pattern or trend to make a generalization.

5. Have students make generalizations from given information.

6. Teach clue words that make a generalization invalid.
   Examples: *All, always, never, no*

7. Teach clue words that make a generalization valid.
   Examples: *Sometimes, usually, most, many, some, as a rule*

8. Teach how to make invalid generalizations valid.

9. Have students make invalid generalizations valid.

10. Have students make a valid generalization using clue words based on given information.

11. Teach how to test a generalization.
    Ask: Are there clue words?
    Ask: Is there a sufficient amount of evidence in the information?
    Is there other evidence that supports or contradicts the statement?

STUDENT CHECKLIST

1. Determine relationship of details.

2. Find a pattern or trend of subject matter.

3. Make a generalization using clue word(s), if needed.

4. Test generalization.
   Ask: Are clue words used?
   Ask: Is there enough evidence in the information?
   Ask: Is there other evidence that supports or contradicts the statement?
   Ask: Is the generalization valid or invalid?

STUDENT VISUAL—GENERALIZATION

Generalization

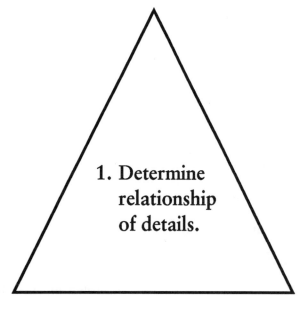

1. Determine relationship of details.

2. Find a pattern or trend of subject matter.

3. Make a generalization using clue word(s), if needed.

4. Test generalization.
   Ask: Are clue words used?
   Ask: Is there enough evidence in the information?
   Ask: Is there other evidence that supports or contradicts the statement?
   Ask: Is the generalization valid or invalid?

ANNOTATED BIBLIOGRAPHY

Barrett, Judi. *A Snake Is Totally a Tail*. Illustrated by L. S. Johnson. New York: Aladdin Books, 1983.
Words and pictures show essential characteristics of a number of animals ("a porcupine is a pile of prickles" and "a crab is conspicuously claws").

Baylor, Byrd. *Everybody Needs a Rock*. Illustrated by Peter Parnall. New York: Aladdin Books, 1974.
Describes the qualities to consider when selecting the perfect rock for play and pleasure.

_____. *When Clay Sings*. Illustrated by Tom Bakti. New York: Aladdin Books, 1972.
The daily life and customs of prehistoric southwest Indian tribes are retraced from the designs on the remains of their pottery.

Blume, Judy. *The Pain and The Great One*. Illustrated by Irene Travis. Scarsdale, NY: Bradbury Press, 1984.
A six-year-old (The Pain) and his eight-year-old sister (The Great One) see each other as troublemakers and best-loved in the family.

Buchanan, Joan. *Nothing Else, But Yams for Supper*. Illustrated by Jerinia Marton. Ontario, Canada: Black Moss Press, 1988.
Alice will not eat anything other than soft, mucky, and gummy yams, until she finds out that other foods can have that same texture and are good.

De Paola, Tomie. *Oliver Button Is a Sissy*. San Diego: Harcourt Brace Jovanovich, 1979.
His classmates' taunts don't stop Oliver Button from doing what he likes best.

Kline, Rufus. *Watch Out for These Weirdos!* Illustrated by Nancy Carlson. New York: Viking Press, 1990.
Wanted posters introduce a gallery of offbeat characters, including Erin "Starin" McCarron, who looks in people's windows, and Bob "The Slob" McCobb, who was once buried under the mess in his room.

Lester, Alison. *Rosie Sips Spiders*. Boston: Houghton Mifflin, 1989.
Each child in this group of seven likes to do everything in an individual way, whether it's working, taking a bath, playing, or going to sleep.

Peet, Bill. *The Luckiest One of All*. Boston: Houghton Mifflin, 1982.
Wishing to be a bird, a little boy learns that there are benefits and drawbacks to every condition, and that being a little boy is the best of all.

Raskin, Ellen. *Nothing Every Happens on My Block*. New York: Aladdin Books, 1966.
As Chester sits and complains about the boring block where he lives, all sorts of exciting and even strange things are going on behind his back.

Shaw, Charles G. *It Looked Like Spilt Milk*. New York: Harper & Row, 1947.
Describes what you might see when you look at clouds.

Smith, William Jay. *Ho for a Hat*. Illustrated by Lynn Munsinger. Toronto, Canada: Little, Brown & Co., 1989.
A young boy and his dog observe and try on a variety of hats.

Spier, Peter. *Bored-Nothing to Do*. New York: Doubleday & Co., 1978.
On a lazy afternoon, two bored brothers keep themselves busy by building and flying an airplane.

_____. *People*. New York: Doubleday & Co., 1980.
Emphasizes the differences among the four billion people on earth.

Stevenson, James. *Could Be Worse*. New York: Mulberry Books, 1977.
Everything is always the same at Grandpa's house, even the things he says—until one unusual morning.

GAME 1

SELECTION TITLE:

> *People*
> by Peter Spier

FOCUS:

GENERALIZATION

HOW TO MAKE: Cut out selection title, focus, student directions, and answer card. Color and cut out all game pieces. Glue title onto folder tab and focus onto folder front. Glue one square onto each half of the inside of the folder. Store student directions, answer card, and people in library pocket glued to back of folder.

STUDENT DIRECTIONS:

1. Read sentences on people.
2. Decide if they are valid or invalid generalizations.
3. Put generalizations on the correct box.
4. Check your answers using answer card.

ANSWER CARD:

(order of answers not important)

Valid - 1, 2, 6, 9, 10
Invalid - 3, 4, 5, 7, 8

PIECES FOR GAME 1—GENERALIZATION

Valid
Generalizations

Invalid
Generalizations

GAME 2

SELECTION TITLE:
> *Rosie Sips Spiders*
> by Alison Lester

FOCUS:
GENERALIZATION

HOW TO MAKE: Cut out selection title, focus, student directions, and answer card. Color and cut out all game pieces. Glue title onto folder tab and focus onto folder front. Glue plates onto inside of folder. Store student directions, answer card, and apples in library pocket glued to back of folder.

STUDENT DIRECTIONS:

1. Read sentences on the plates.
2. Decide how the sentences are related.
3. Read the generalizations on the apples.
4. Select the valid generalization.
5. Check your answer using answer card.

ANSWER CARD:

Food provides us with the vitamins and minerals that keep us healthy.

PIECES FOR GAME 2—GENERALIZATION

For supper, mom always cooks beans.

Some children get sick because they do not eat properly.

My Uncle Joe never eats lunch.

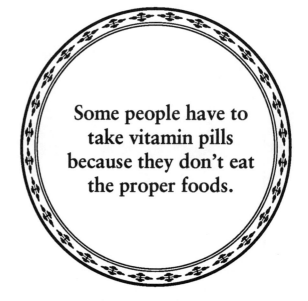

Some people have to take vitamin pills because they don't eat the proper foods.

Philip enjoys fresh vegetables in his salad.

I eat carrots so my hair will be healthy.

My mom won't let me eat three candy bars because too much sugar is not good for me.

Billy drinks orange juice for vitamin C.

Susie drinks milk at every meal for calcium.

Eating liver helps to keep our blood healthy.

Jane eats lunch at noon.

Food provides us with the vitamins and minerals that keep us healthy.

Everyone needs a garden to grow healthy food.

Every person eats three meals a day.

All foods make you healthy.

ACTIVITIES

Everybody Does It: Listen for the generalizations your students use in conversation ("Everybody has a pencil"). Make a list of their generalizations. Share the list with your class. Have students decide if generalizations are valid or invalid. If a generalization is invalid, make it valid.

Soup's On: Prepare two or three different flavors of soup (chicken noodle, tomato, chowder). Pour into bowls. While enjoying the soup, have students find similarities and differences between the soups (liquid, eat with spoon, hot). Chart the findings on the blackboard. From the findings, have students make generalizations. Discuss whether the generalizations are valid or invalid. For a variation, do a similar follow-up with cans of soup, or use soup that is prepared in different ways (from scratch, canned, dry mix).

Critical Issues: Using an issue that is relevant to students (for example, pollution), select material pertaining to the issue. Students should read the materials and make a chart of the main ideas gathered. They then look for similarities and think about why the ideas are similar. Repeat the procedure by looking for differences in the main ideas listed. Have the students write a statement, in broad terms, that explains the main ideas.

Measuring Success: Assemble a set of selections (short stories, old basals) in which the characters are successful in completing a task or solving a problem. Share orally or have students read the selections. Compile a list, with students, of tasks completed and problems solved. Add to the list what the characters did that made them successful. Have students look for similarities or differences in the ideas on the list. Based on the ideas, similarities, and differences, have students generalize about being successful.

Geographic Terms: Post as many pictures as possible of a natural landform (island, peninsula, mountain). Have students, working in small groups, look for details in an individual picture. Have the small groups share the information with the rest of the class. Put this information on a chart. Have students look for similarities and differences in the ideas shared. Have students broadly define a term ("What is an island?") using the similarities and differences. The definition is a simple generalization.

High Fashion: Bring clothes from your family's closets or observe the students' clothing. Have students find similarities about the print on the fabrics, the notions (lace, trim, etc.), necessary items (buttons, zippers, elastic waist), lengths (sleeves, pants), and so forth. Make a list of generalizations about the students' clothing. Try this on two or three different days to see if the generalizations stay the same or change. This activity provides an opportunity for students to test generalizations.

Math Motives: Work through, with your students, several math story problems that use the same operation for solving (addition, subtraction, multiplication, division). After working all the problems, have students find relationships between the problems. Using the relationships, have students make generalizations about the operation (addition is putting things together).

A Common Thread: If you are planning a thematic unit (astronauts, Indians, bears), you can have the students complete diagrams illustrating the similarities and differences they find during the study. Then have the students use the diagrams to make generalizations about the topic.

12—INFERENCE & CONCLUSION

Objective: The student will make an inference and/or draw a conclusion about a selection.

TEACHER CHECKLIST FOR PLANNING

1. Define inference: details and personal experiences used to figure out something the author did not state.

2. Define conclusion: relationship between details, personal experiences, and inference.

3. Use examples to show how to make an inference.
   Ask: What do I "know" that the author did not tell me?

4. Use examples to show how to draw a conclusion.
   Ask: How are the details and inference(s) related?
   What can I figure out because of the relationship?

5. Have students make inference(s) and draw a conclusion about a selection.

6. Have students explain their thinking.

STUDENT CHECKLIST

Inference

1. Look at stated details.

2. Think about your own experiences.

3. Ask: What do I "know" that the author did not tell me?

4. Tell *what* I know and explain *why* I know it.

Conclusion

5. Think about stated details, personal experiences, and inference(s).

6. Decide how they are related.

7. Ask: What can I figure out because of the relationships?

8. Tell *what* I figured out. Explain *why* I think that way.

STUDENT VISUAL—INFERENCE & CONCLUSION

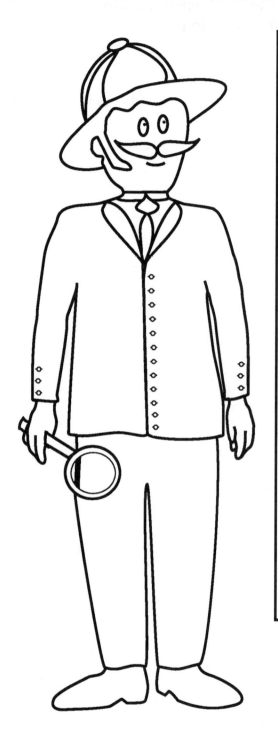

Inference

1. Look at stated details.

2. Think about your own experiences.

3. Ask: What do I "know" that the author did not tell me?

4. Tell <u>what</u> I know and explain <u>why</u> I know it.

Conclusion

5. Think about details, personal experiences, and inference(s).

6. Decide how they are related.

7. Ask: What can I figure out because of the relationships?

8. Tell <u>what</u> I figured out and explain <u>why</u> I think that way.

ANNOTATED BIBLIOGRAPHY

Ahlberg, Janet, and Allan Ahlberg. *The Jolly Postman*. Boston: Little, Brown & Co., 1986.
Twelve of the pages have been made into envelopes, and contain letters and other written material that help tell the story of the postman's delivery route one particular day.

Alexander, Martha. *Maggie's Moon*. New York: Dial Press, 1982.
A little girl and her dog set out to capture the moon and bring it home with them.

Brown, Margaret Wise. *When the Wind Blew*. Illustrated by Geoffrey Hayes. New York: Harper & Row, 1937.
An old lady living alone by the sea finds joy and comfort from her seventeen cats, and especially one small blue-eyed kitten.

Cleary, Beverly. *Dear Mr. Henshaw*. Illustrated by Paul O. Zelinsky. New York: William Morrow & Co., 1983.
In his letters to his favorite author, ten-year-old Leigh reveals his problems in coping with his parent's divorce, being the new boy in school, and generally finding his own place in the world.

Craven, Carolyn. *What the Mailman Brought*. Illustrated by Tomie de Paola. New York: G. P. Putnam's Sons, 1987.
While William is sick and unable to go to school, a mysterious mailman brings him unusual packages every day.

Gackenbach, Dick. *Ida Fanfanny*. New York: Harper & Row, 1978.
Ida lives in a land of no weather until a salesman sells her four magical paintings.

Holl, Adelaide. *The Runaway Giant*. Illustrated by Mamoru Funai. New York: Lothrop, Lee & Shepard Co., 1967.
The sleeping animals are awakened by the warnings of a squirrel that a giant is in the valley, so each animal goes to see. They all scare him away—the snowman melts.

Hutchins, Pat. *Tom and Sam*. New York: Macmillan, 1968.
Two friends try to outdo one another by building beautiful items for their gardens, but jealousy almost destroys their friendship.

_____. *You'll Soon Grow into Them, Titch*. New York: Greenwillow Books, 1983.
The tables turn at last for Titch, who has been inheriting his older siblings' outgrown clothes.

Lemieux, Michele. *What's That Noise?* New York: William Morrow & Co., 1984.
Brown Bear pursues a noise he hears and finally realizes its source, just as sleep overtakes him and his winter nap begins.

Lionni, Leo. *Swimmy*. New York: Pantheon Books, 1968.
A remarkable little fish instructs the rest of his school in the art of protection—swim in the formation of a gigantic fish!

Preston, Edna Mitchell. *Squawk to the Moon, Little Goose*. Illustrated by Barbara Cooney. New York: Viking Press, 1974.
Little Goose disobeys her mother one night and almost gets swallowed by the fox.

Steig, William. *Sylvester and the Magic Pebble*. Illustrated by Janet Stevens. New York: Prentice-Hall, 1969.

In a moment of fright, Sylvester the donkey asks his magic pebble to turn him into a rock, but then cannot hold the pebble to wish himself back to normal again.

Wood, Audrey. *The Napping House*. Illustrated by Don Wood. San Diego: Harcourt Brace Jovanovich, 1984.

In this cumulative tale, a wakeful flea atop a number of sleeping creatures causes a commotion with just one bite.

GAME 1

SELECTION TITLE:

> *Sylvester and the Magic Pebble*
> by William Steig

FOCUS:

Inference & Conclusion

HOW TO MAKE: Cut out selection title, focus, student directions, and answer card. Color and cut out all games pieces. Glue title onto folder tab and focus onto folder front. Glue Sylvester and the four bubbles onto the inside of the folder. Store student directions, answer card, and *grease pencil* in library pocket glued to back of folder.

STUDENT DIRECTIONS:

1. Read paragraph on Sylvester.
2. Read paragraph on bubble.
3. Read question.
4. Circle with grease pencil the phrase that best answers the question.
5. Do other paragraphs the same way.
6. Check your answers using answer card.

ANSWER CARD:

1. to keep tools in
2. to dry clothes when it rains
3. vacuum cleaner
4. roller skates

PIECES FOR GAME 1—INFERENCE & CONCLUSION

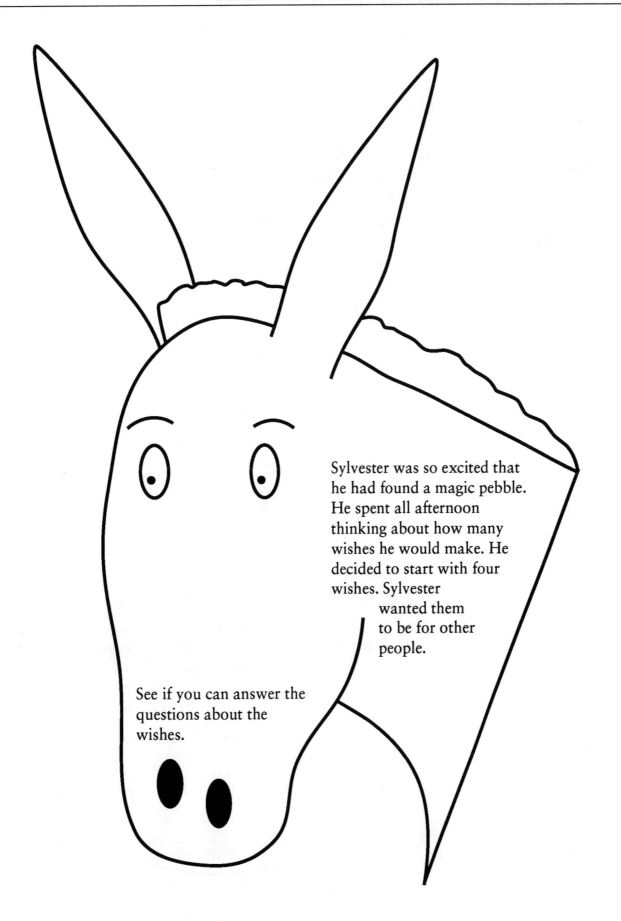

Sylvester was so excited that he had found a magic pebble. He spent all afternoon thinking about how many wishes he would make. He decided to start with four wishes. Sylvester wanted them to be for other people.

See if you can answer the questions about the wishes.

Wish 1

Sylvester's Uncle Fred is a carpenter. He has built many houses in the neighborhood. Uncle Fred has hammers, nails, screwdrivers, and a saw. He always has a difficult time remembering where he put them. Sylvester wishes for a tool box. Why?

it's a good Christmas present

to keep tools in

Wish 2

Aunt Emma always hung her clothes on a line outside. When it rained, the wash piled up. This made her quite upset. Sylvester wished for a clothes dryer. Why?

it was on sale

to dry clothes when it rains

Wish 3

Sylvester's mom always wanted the house to look nice. Every day she made the beds, washed the dishes, and swept the floor with a broom. Sylvester decided to wish for something that plugged into the wall and could be pushed by hand. What did Sylvester wish for?

vacuum cleaner

dishwasher

Wish 4

Amy, Sylvester's friend, always goes to the park and plays. She likes to watch the children ride their bikes and roller skate on the sidewalk. Sylvester has a great idea! He wishes for something that has wheels and is a size 5. What did he wish for?

roller skates

tricycle

GAME 2

SELECTION TITLE:

> *The Jolly Postman*
> by Janet and Allan Ahlberg

FOCUS:

Inference & Conclusion

HOW TO MAKE: You will need six envelopes, five of which are numbered. Cut the flaps off all envelopes. Type or print the following addresses, one on each numbered envelope:

1. The Seven Dwarfs, Little Cottage South, Whistle Garden
2. Mom and Dad, Gingerbread Farms, Meadowbrook Hills
3. Mr. Wolf, Red Brick Circle, Blowing Downs
4. Mr. Rumpelstiltskin, Spinning Gold Lane, South Woods
5. The Troll, Three Bridge Drive, Waterstation

Glue the unnumbered envelope to the front of the folder and address it to: Students, Direction Lane, The Classroom. Cut out selection title, focus, student directions, and answer card. Glue title onto folder tab and glue focus above the envelope addressed to students on the folder front. Glue the five numbered envelopes inside the folder; if protective covering is used for the folder, *remember* to make a slit at the top of each envelope! Cut letters apart. Store letters, answer card, and *grease pencil* in library pocket glued to back of folder. Store student directions in envelope on folder front.

STUDENT DIRECTIONS:

1. Read each letter.
2. Write who the letter is to and who the letter is from on the correct lines.
3. Put each letter into the envelope to whom the letter is addressed.
4. Check your answers using answer card.

ANSWER CARD:

1. Dear Seven Dwarfs, - Apples to you, Snow White
2. Dear Mom and Dad, - Happily running, Gingerbread Boy (Man)
3. Greetings, Wolf, - Living happily, Three Little Pigs
4. Hi, Rumpelstiltskin, - Yours sincerely, The Queen
5. Dear Troll, - Tramp, tramp, Three Billy Goats Gruff

PIECES FOR GAME 2—INFERENCE & CONCLUSION

○

Dear _____ ,

○

Bridges, bridges, bridges! We love to tramp over

them. No one tries to stop us anymore.

We hope you are letting animals cross your bridge.

It's not nice to scare anyone.

Tramp, tramp,

○

_____

○

Dear _____ ,

I think of you seven quite often. We had so much fun

○

working and whistling together.

I now own an apple store called, "An Apple A Day."

It's doing quite well. I keep a very close watch on all my

apples. I'm sure you know why!

Come and see me when you can. I miss you terribly!

Apples to you,

○

_____

Dear _____ ,

    How are you? I hope you don't miss me too much. I am still running and seeing the sights. The animals don't bother me as much anymore.

    One thing I'd like you to remember is if you want to keep your cookies, don't set them on the windowsill. I'm sure you know why!

                        Happily running,

                        _____

Greetings_____ ,

    We have built very nice homes out of brick. Each one has a very nice fireplace.

    Are you still huffing and puffing? We hope not, because trying to destroy someone's home is not nice.

                        Living happily,

                        _____

Hi, _____ ,

Have you shortened your name yet? Goodness, it sure was long!

My baby has grown into a young man. He was the only one in all his classes at school who could spell your name correctly.

Yours sincerely,

_____

ACTIVITIES

Pack Your Suitcase: Fill small suitcases or duffel bags with clothes and vacation supplies. If you can't collect the real items, pictures from catalogs will work just as well. Have your students study the items in the suitcase and then write an itinerary for the trip. The itinerary can be as simple as where they are going, or it can include how long they plan on staying and what they are going to do while they are there. The activity can also be reversed: Give your students an itinerary and have them use it to plan what to pack in their suitcases.

Missing Elements: Using "action-packed" pictures, cut out one or more things from the picture. Glue each picture onto another piece of paper. Students should study the pictures and draw in what is missing. This type of activity can also be done with short prose selections; students write their own elements for those missing from a selection.

Tools of the Trade: Gather items that people would use in various jobs or careers. Pictures can easily be substituted for actual items in this activity. Students can determine who would use the tools and how the tools are used.

Inference Boxes: Students select a picture or an object and put it inside a box. On the outside, they glue sentences or paragraphs that give information about the item in the box. Students trade boxes with each other and practice the inference procedure to determine what is in the box.

Candy Wrappers: Students should write descriptions of their favorite candy bars without naming them. Other students then match the descriptions to the correct candy wrapper, or even the candy itself. This activity can be done with lots of different food items.

Riddle Books: Riddles are a great way to practice making inferences. Students can create class books or their own books of favorite riddles. Better still, have the students write their own riddles about characters or events in a story.

Recipes: Students write recipes for their favorite foods, leaving out the name of the recipe. Share the recipes with other students and see if they can infer what is being made. The recipes do not even have to be food items. How about a recipe for a football player, a thunderstorm, a city, a teacher, or a character from a story?

Character Awards: After reading a selection, students create awards for the characters based on what happened in the story and the characters' traits. They can write and give speeches as they present the awards to the characters. They could also issue tickets or citations to characters who create problems in the story.

Setting Maps: After reading a selection, have students draw a map that shows the setting of the story. They can label places from the story, the location of action or characters, or show the route the characters followed in the story.

13—MAIN IDEA

Objective: The student will identify the main idea of a written selection.

TEACHER CHECKLIST FOR PLANNING

1. Define topic: words that indicate the substance of a selection.

2. Define main idea: most important idea of a selection that is supported by details.

3. Teach how to determine topic.
   a. Use name or title of selection to find topic.
   b. Use details to find topic when there is no title.
   Ask: What do the details tell about?

4. Teach how details are related to each other.
   Ask: What do the details tell about the topic?

5. Teach how to find stated main idea.
   Ask: Is the main idea the first sentence?
         Is the main idea the last sentence?
         Is the main idea in another sentence?

6. Teach how to use details to support chosen main idea.
   Ask: Do details support main idea?

7. Teach how to determine inferred main idea.
   Ask: What is the topic?
         What do the details tell about the topic?

STUDENT CHECKLIST

1. Determine topic.
   Ask: Is it the title?
   Ask: Do I need to use details to find topic?

2. Ask: What do details tell about topic?

3. Check first, last, and other sentences for main idea.

4. If not stated, use topic and details to figure out main idea.

5. Ask: Are there details to support the main idea?

STUDENT VISUAL—MAIN IDEA

Topic
(title)

Classify details to find topic

Main Idea

Check first, last, and other sentences.

Ask: Do details support main idea?

If not stated, use topic and details to figure out main idea.

Ask: Are there details to support the main idea?

Details

Look at picture and/or read selection.

Identify words and phrases that tell Who, What, When, Where, Why, and How.

ANNOTATED BIBLIOGRAPHY

Anno, Mitsumasa. *The King's Flower*. New York: Philomel, 1976.
The king discovers that bigger is not always better.

Carle, Eric. *The Very Busy Spider*. New York: Philomel, 1985.
The farm animals try to distract a busy little spider from spinning her web, but she persists and produces a thing of both beauty and usefulness.

Crowe, Robert. *Clyde Monster*. Illustrated by Kay Chorao. New York: E. P. Dutton, 1976.
A young monster is afraid of the dark because he believes that a person may be lurking under the bed or in a corner.

De Paola, Tomie. *The Cloud Book*. New York: Holiday House, 1975.
Introduces the ten most common types of clouds, the myths that have been inspired by their shapes, and what clouds can tell about coming weather changes.

Goble, Paul. *The Girl Who Loved Wild Horses*. New York: Bradbury Press, 1978.
Though she is fond of her people, a girl prefers to live among the wild horses where she is truly happy and free.

Hogrogian, Nonny. *One Fine Day*. New York: Macmillan, 1971.
An old woman cuts off a fox's tail when he steals her milk, and the fox must go through a long series of transactions before she will sew it back again.

Hutchins, Pat. *The Wind Blew*. New York: Macmillan, 1974.
A rhymed tale describing the antics of a capricious wind.

Kraus, Robert. *Leo, The Late Bloomer*. Illustrated by Jose Aruego. New York: Scholastic, 1979.
Leo, a young tiger, finally blooms under the anxious eyes of his parents.

Lobel, Arnold. *A Treeful of Pigs*. Illustrated by Anita Lobel. New York: Greenwillow Books, 1979.
A farmer's wife uses drastic measures to get her husband to abandon his lazy ways.

McDermott, Gerald. *Arrow to the Sun*. New York: Viking Press, 1974.
An adaptation of the Pueblo Indian myth explaining how the spirit of the Lord of the Sun was brought to the world of man.

Miles, Miska. *Annie and the Old One*. Illustrated by Peter Parnall. Boston: Little, Brown & Co., 1971.
A Navajo girl tries several ways to keep time from passing so that her grandmother will stay alive.

Mosel, Arlene. *Tikki Tikki Tembo*. Illustrated by Blair Lent. New York: Holt, Rinehart & Winston, 1968.
An old Chinese tale explaining why Chinese have short names.

Surat, Michele Maria. *Angel Child, Dragon Child*. Illustrated by Vo-Dinh Mai. Milwaukee, WI: Raintree Publishers, 1983.
　　Ut came to the United States from Vietnam, doesn't like school, and misses her mother, who eventually joins her family through the help of the schoolchildren.

Viorst, Judith. *Alexander and the Terrible, Horrible, No Good, Very Bad Day*. Illustrated by Ray Cruz. New York: Macmillan, 1972.
　　Alexander's day is filled with mishaps from the time he gets up until the time he goes to bed.

GAME 1

SELECTION TITLE:

> *A Treeful of Pigs*
> by Arnold Lobel

FOCUS:

> # MAIN IDEA

HOW TO MAKE: Cut out selection title, focus, student directions, and answer card. Color and cut out all game pieces. Glue title onto folder tab and focus onto folder front. Glue pigs and bucket onto the inside of the folder. Store student directions, answer card, and ears of corn in library pocket glued to back of folder.

STUDENT DIRECTIONS:

1. Read main idea sentences on pigs.
2. Read sentences on ears of corn.
3. Decide which main idea the sentences are describing and place on top of the main idea.
4. Sentences that do not belong can be placed on buckets.
5. Check your answers using answer card.

ANSWER CARD:

(order of answers not important)

1. a, d, e, h, i
2. b, c, f, g, j, k

PIECES FOR GAME 1—MAIN IDEA

The farmer was quite lazy.

The farmer decided never
to be lazy again.

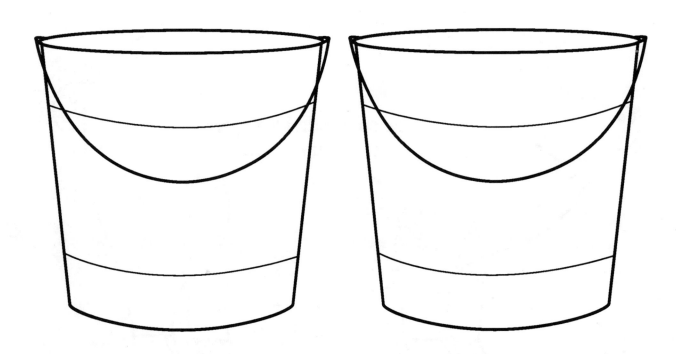

When the pigs bloom in the garden, the farmer will plant the corn. **a**

He put his head back down on the pillow. **d**

The farmer's wife had to do everything by herself. **e**

The farmer yawned and went back to sleep. **h**

He never got dressed. **i**

The farmer realized he made a big mistake. **b**

He wanted help to look for his lost pigs. **f**

The farmer jumped out of bed and put on his clothes. **c**

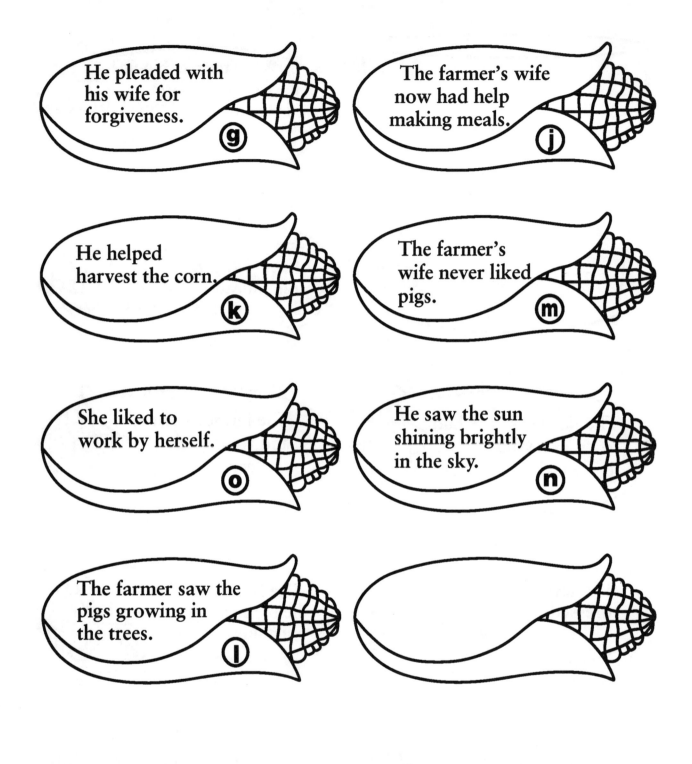

He pleaded with his wife for forgiveness. **g**

The farmer's wife now had help making meals. **j**

He helped harvest the corn. **k**

The farmer's wife never liked pigs. **m**

She liked to work by herself. **o**

He saw the sun shining brightly in the sky. **n**

The farmer saw the pigs growing in the trees. **l**

GAME 2

SELECTION TITLE:

> *The King's Flower*
> by Mitsumasa Anno

FOCUS:

> # Main Idea and Details

HOW TO MAKE: Cut out selection title, focus, student directions, and answer card. Color and cut out all game pieces. Glue title onto folder tab and focus onto folder front. Glue tulips onto the inside of the folder. Store student directions, answer card, and flower stems in library pocket glued to back of folder.

STUDENT DIRECTIONS:

1. Read details on flower petals.
2. Read main idea sentences on flower stems.
3. Decide which details support the main ideas.
4. Match details to main ideas to complete the flowers.
5. Check your answers using answer card.

ANSWER CARD:

1. The king's belongings were big.
2. The king had to have a tooth pulled because he ate too much chocolate.
3. The birds escaped from the cage.
4. The eagle could not get the birds in the cage.
5. The king caught a fish, but it was too heavy and he had to let it go.
6. The king realized that biggest is not always best.

PIECES FOR GAME 2—MAIN IDEA

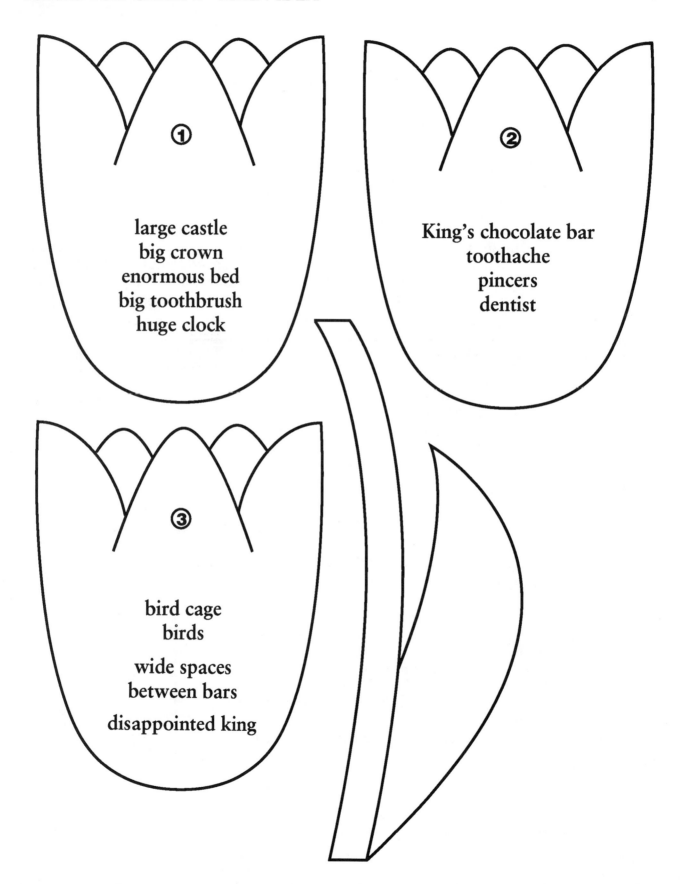

①
large castle
big crown
enormous bed
big toothbrush
huge clock

②
King's chocolate bar
toothache
pincers
dentist

③
bird cage
birds

wide spaces
between bars

disappointed king

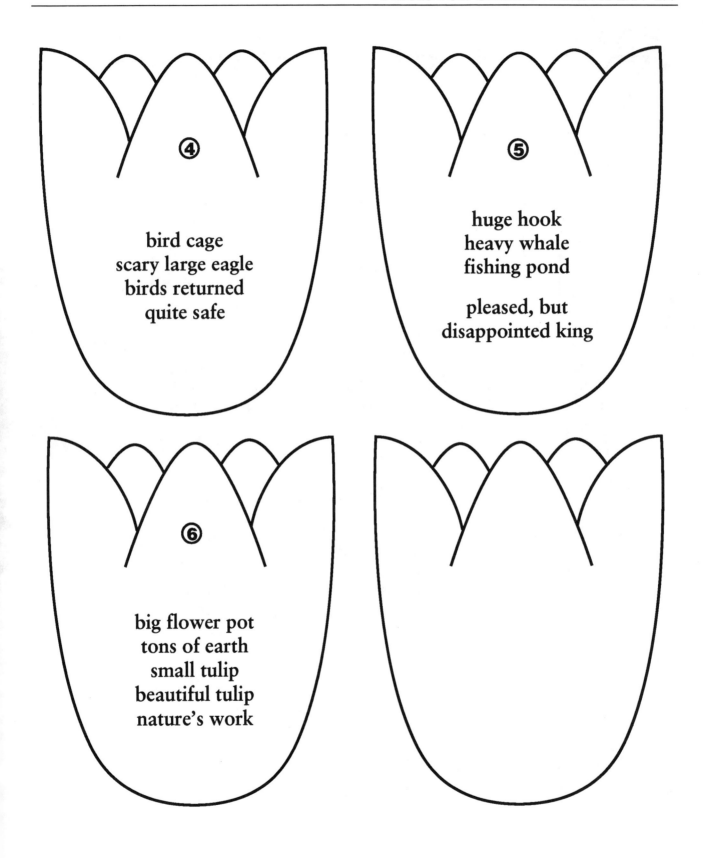

④
bird cage
scary large eagle
birds returned
quite safe

⑤
huge hook
heavy whale
fishing pond

pleased, but
disappointed king

⑥
big flower pot
tons of earth
small tulip
beautiful tulip
nature's work

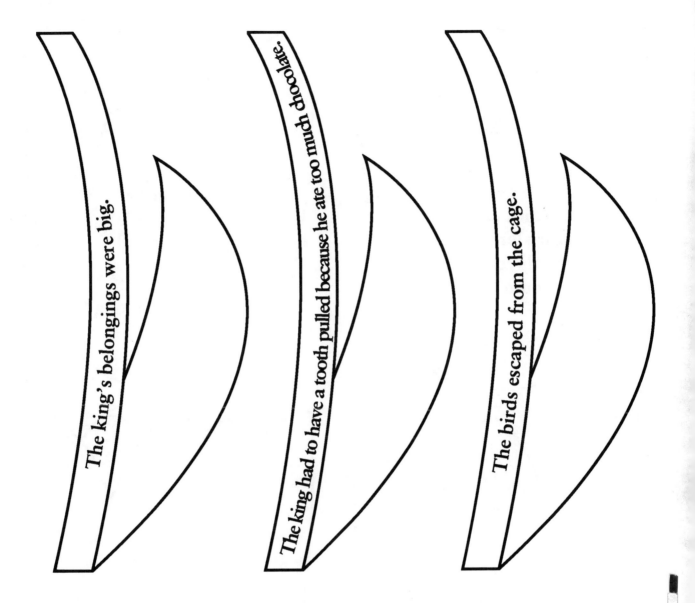

The king's belongings were big.

The king had to have a tooth pulled because he ate too much chocolate.

The birds escaped from the cage.

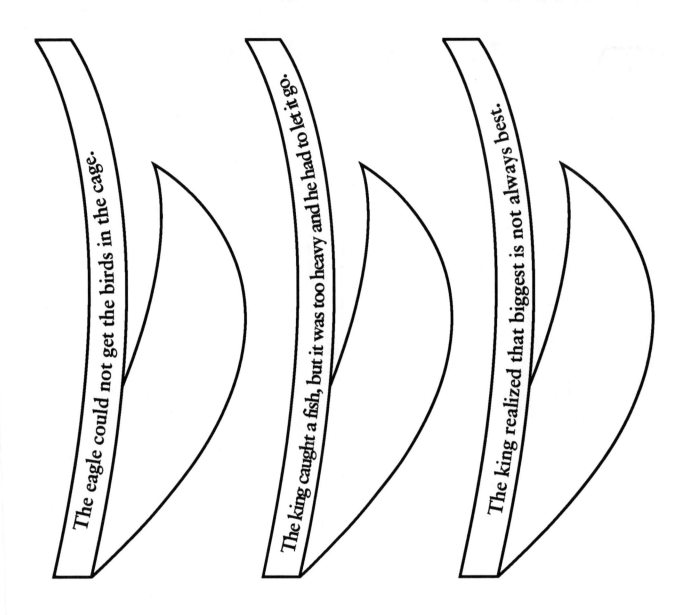

The eagle could not get the birds in the cage.

The king caught a fish, but it was too heavy and he had to let it go.

The king realized that biggest is not always best.

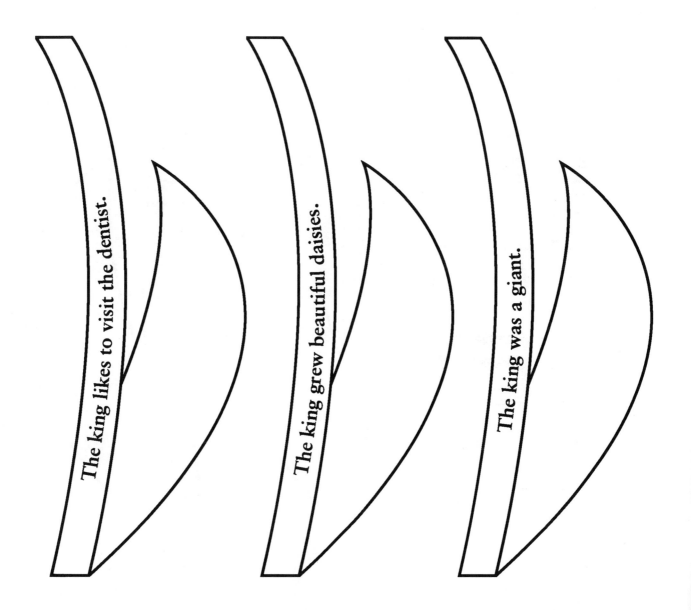

The king likes to visit the dentist.

The king grew beautiful daisies.

The king was a giant.

ACTIVITIES

Add a Heading: Find a non-fiction selection (social studies or science text) that uses headings and subheadings. Run off copies, but cover up the headings and subheadings. Students read a selection, determine its main idea, and create their own headings and subheadings.

Table of Contents: Give your students a narrative selection that is divided into numbered chapters. After students read the selection, they may create a new table of contents. Instead of numbers, they should title each chapter based on its main idea.

Picture Talk: Choose a wordless picture book to share with your students. After sharing and discussing, students determine the main ideas based on the illustrations. If possible, write the main idea, or have students write the main idea, and attach to the pages with paper clips.

Main Idea Match: Provide the students with several paragraphs and corresponding titles. Mix up the paragraphs and the titles. Students read the paragraphs and match them to titles. For advanced readers, all the paragraphs could be about the same topic.

Main Idea Mobile: Show students how to make and balance a mobile. Have students make mobiles, leaving sections blank. After reading a paragraph, students determine the main idea and supporting details. They then write the main idea on the top crossbar and the details on the hanging pieces.

Lost and Found: Prepare transparencies of well-constructed paragraphs, but omitting the main idea sentence. Leave a blank line where the main idea was located. Students read the paragraph and determine the main idea. Write the main idea sentence in the blank.

Name That Tune: Working with your school's music teacher, select an assortment of songs to teach your students. *Do not* let them know the titles of the songs. After students learn the songs, let them create the titles.

Stir It Up!: Gather an assortment of pictures. Pass out one picture to each student. Have students write about their pictures. Collect all the pictures and pieces of writing and stir them up. Pass out the pictures and pieces of writing and have students match them.

14—PARAPHRASE

Objective: The student will paraphrase the important ideas of a selection.

TEACHER CHECKLIST FOR PLANNING

1. Define paraphrase: a periodic check for understanding by putting important ideas in one's own words.

2. Teach paraphrasing by using sentences.

3. Have students paraphrase sentences.

4. Teach paraphrasing by using paragraphs.

5. Have students paraphrase paragraphs.

6. Teach paraphrasing a selection by stopping throughout the story.
    a. Stop at difficult words or passages.
    b. Stop at difficult ideas.
    c. Stop at end of paragraphs.
    d. Stop at end of chapters or sections.
    e. Stop at end of selection.

7. Have students read selection and paraphrase important ideas.

8. Have students explain their reasoning for paraphrasing.

STUDENT CHECKLIST

1. Begin reading selection.

2. Stop at the following:
    a. Difficult words or passages.
    b. Difficult ideas.
    c. End of paragraphs.
    d. End of chapters or sections.
    e. End of selection.

3. Ask: Do I understand the important ideas?

4. Ask: Can I tell the important ideas in my own words?

5. Ask: Do my words and the author's words mean about the same thing?

6. Reread and try again, if necessary.

No game provided in this unit.

STUDENT VISUAL—PARAPHRASE

Paraphrase

1. Begin reading selection.
2. Stop at the following:
   a. Difficult words or passages.
   b. Difficult ideas.
   c. End of paragraphs.
   d. End of chapters or sections.
   e. End of selection.
3. Ask: Do I understand the important ideas?
4. Ask: Can I tell the important ideas in my own words?
5. Ask: Do my words and the author's words mean about the same thing?
6. Reread and try again, if necessary.

ANNOTATED BIBLIOGRAPHY

Aliki. *Mummies Made in Egypt*. New York: Thomas Y. Crowell, 1979.
    Describes the techniques and the reasons for the use of mummification in ancient Egypt.

Branley, Franklyn M. *Sunshine Makes the Seasons*. Illustrated by Giulio Maestro. New York: Thomas Y. Crowell, 1985.
    Describes how sunshine and the tilt of the earth's axis are responsible for the changing seasons.

Charles, Oz. *How Is a Crayon Made?* New York: Simon & Schuster, 1988.
    Describes, in text and step-by-step photographs, the manufacture of a crayon, from wax to finished product.

Dorros, Arthur. *Me and My Shadow*. New York: Scholastic, 1990.
    Explains what shadows are, how and when they exist, and how they reveal the size and shape of things around us.

George, Jean Craighead. *Julie of the Wolves*. Illustrated by John Schoenherr. New York: Harper & Row, 1972.
    An Eskimo girl shows courage and the will to survive in potentially alien worlds.

Gibbons, Gail. *Sunken Treasure*. New York: Thomas Y. Crowell, 1988.
    Describes the many-years-long search for the treasure that went down with the Atocha, a Spanish galleon that sank off Florida in a hurricane in 1622.

_____. *Tunnels*. New York: Holiday House, 1984.
    A brief introduction to tunnels—their types, shapes, and parts—and how they are built.

Goble, Paul. *Death of the Iron Horse*. New York: Bradbury Press, 1987.
    In an act of bravery and defiance against the white men encroaching on their territory in 1867, a group of young Cheyenne braves derail and raid a freight train.

_____. *The Gift of the Sacred Dog*. New York: Macmillan, 1980.
    In response to an Indian boy's prayer for help for his hungry people, the Great Spirit sends the gift of the Sacred Dogs (horses), which enables the tribe to hunt for buffalo.

_____. *Iktomi and the Berries*. New York: Orchard Books, 1988.
    Relates Iktomi's fruitless efforts to pick some buffalo berries.

MacLachlan, Patricia. *Through Grandpa's Eyes*. Illustrated by Deborah Kogan Ray. New York: Harper & Row, 1980.
    A young boy learns a different way of seeing the world from his blind grandfather.

Mathis, Sharon Bell. *The Hundred Penny Box*. Illustrated by Leo Dillon and Diane Dillon. New York: Puffin Books, 1975.
    Michael's love for his great-great-aunt, who lives with them, leads him to intercede with his mother, who wants to toss out all her old aunt's things.

McGaw, Jessie Brewer. *Chief Red Horse Tells about Custer*. New York: Elsevier/Nelson Books, 1981.
Relates the account of the Battle of Little Bighorn, told five years later by Sioux Chief Red Horse, who fought in the conflict.

McMillan, Bruce. *Making Sneakers*. Boston: Houghton Mifflin, 1980.
Photographs and text explain the steps in manufacturing running shoes.

Showers, Paul. *What Happens to a Hamburger*. Illustrated by Anna Rockwell. New York: Thomas Y. Crowell, 1985.
Explains the processes by which a hamburger and other foods are used to make energy, strong bones, and solid muscles as they pass through all the parts of the digestive system.

Magazine

Cobblestone: The History Magazine for Young People. Cobblestone Publishing, Inc., 30 Grove Street, Peterborough, NH 03458.
Text and illustrations provide a walk through the history of the United States.

ACTIVITIES

What Does That Mean?: Students are always asking "What does that mean?" In everyday conversation, take the opportunity to use their questions. Keep a classroom chart on the wall. When students ask for clarification, write the sentence they don't understand on the chart. Help them use the context of the conversation and sentence to tell in their own words what was said. Write the new sentence under the original sentence.

Straight from the Horse's Mouth: Provide a small toy horse. When you are reading orally to your students, set the horse on a student's desk. Stopping throughout the selection, the student with the horse must paraphrase what you have read, "straight from the horse's mouth." Pass the horse around the group as you read.

Do the Shuffle: Select a story from a children's magazine, old basal, or old workbook (students could select the story). Cut the story into sections according to paragraphs and glue on heavy paper. Number the paragraphs in the correct order. Pass out a paragraph to each student. Have the students paraphrase the paragraphs (in order, one at a time). Write their paraphrasing on chart paper. When completed, read the paraphrased story and compare to the original to see if the author's story and the student's story mean the same thing.

Go Fly a Kite: Select a three- or four-paragraph story. Cut and paste onto a kite pattern. Add a tail string. Supply strips of paper for students' writing. The strips will complete the tail. They paraphrase the story, write their sentences on the strips, and glue them onto tail string.

Paraphrase Pudding: Using a simple pudding recipe, make it over-detailed (go to the refrigerator, open door, take milk out, put on counter, open top...). Students look for relevant parts of the recipe and paraphrase to write their own recipe. Students can test recipes by making the pudding.

Do You Read What I Read? Pass out the same short piece of literature to all students. Divide them into working groups and have each student paraphrase at the end of each paragraph. Share the paraphrasing within the group.

Definitely Difficult: Get an article from the newspaper that contains difficult passages, words, and/or ideas. It could be put on a transparency and presented to the whole class. Have students read article and stop as needed for paraphrasing. Write responses in the margin.

Grandma's Trunk: Create an old-fashioned trunk out of a box. Gather historical literature from sources such as *Cobblestone: The History Magazine for Young People*, Old West story books, etc. Make sure they contain words and ideas that are unfamiliar to students. Have students choose a selection to paraphrase and illustrate. Students' work could be used to decorate the trunk as a classroom exhibit.

Poetry to Prose: Select some examples of children's poetry. Let students determine which poem they would like to read. Students first read the poem and think about its meaning. They then paraphrase the poem, not necessarily in a poetry format, and share the paraphrases with the class.

15—PREDICTION

Objective: The student will predict a future action or probable ending.

TEACHER CHECKLIST FOR PLANNING

1. Define prediction: logical guess as to future action.

2. Demonstrate use of details in pictures, illustrations, and/or written selections to find out:
   a. What is happening.
   b. What has already happened.

3. Teach students to compare a situation to their personal experiences.

4. Have students make predictions using details and personal experiences.

5. Have students check to see if prediction is correct.

6. Potential obstacle: Students with a lack of background experiences. Solution: Provide extensive background information through the use of pictures, real-life situations, and related literature.

STUDENT CHECKLIST

1. Look at picture(s) and illustration(s).

2. Read selection.

3. Look for details.

4. Ask: What is happening?
   What has already happened?

5. Imagine the event happening to myself.

6. Make prediction.

7. Does the prediction make sense?

8. For stories, read on to see if prediction is correct.

STUDENT VISUAL—PREDICTION

Prediction

1. Look at pictures and illustrations.
2. Read selection.
3. Look for details.
4. Ask: What is happening?
   What has already happened?
5. Imagine the event happening to myself.
6. Make prediction.
7. Does the prediction make sense?
8. For stories, read on to see if prediction is correct.

ANNOTATED BIBLIOGRAPHY

Asch, Frank. *Sand Cake*. New York: Parent's Magazine Press, 1978.
Papa Bear uses his culinary skills and a little imagination to concoct a sand cake.

Briggs, Raymond. *The Snowman*. New York: Random House, 1978 (wordless).
When his snowman comes to life, a little boy invites him home and in return is taken on a flight above beautiful cities and strange lands.

Burningham, John. *Mr. Grumpy's Outing*. New York: Holt, Rinehart & Winston, 1970.
Mr. Grumpy accepts more and more riders on his boat until the inevitable occurs.

Burton, Virginia Lee. *Mike Mulligan and His Steam Shovel*. Boston: Houghton Mifflin, 1967.
Mary Anne, the steam shovel, is old-fashioned, but she and her owner prove they can still dig and be of use in the town of Popperville.

Carle, Eric. *Do You Want to Be My Friend?* New York: Thomas Y. Crowell, 1971.
A mouse searches everywhere for a friend.

Craven, Carolyn. *What the Mailman Brought*. Illustrated by Tomie de Paola. New York: G. P. Putnam's Sons, 1987.
While William is sick and unable to go to school, a mysterious mailman brings him unusual packages every day.

De Paola, Tomie. *Big Anthony and the Magic Ring*. San Diego: Harcourt Brace Jovanovich, 1979.
When Big Anthony borrows Strega Nona's magic ring to turn himself into a handsome man, he gets more trouble than fun.

_____. *Pancakes for Breakfast*. San Diego: Harcourt Brace Jovanovich, 1978 (wordless).
A little old lady's attempt to have pancakes for breakfast is hindered by a scarcity of supplies and the participation of her pets.

Ginsburg, Mirra. *How the Sun Was Brought Back into the Sky*. Illustrated by Jose Aruego and Ariane Dewey. New York: Macmillan, 1975.
This Slovenian folk tale describes how the chicks, magpie, rabbit, ducks, and hedgehog helped the sun to shine again.

Hoban, Tana. *Take Another Look*. New York: Greenwillow Books, 1981 (wordless).
By viewing nine subjects, both in full-page photos and through die-cut pages, the reader learns that things may be perceived in different ways.

Hughes, Shirley. *Alfie's Feet*. New York: Lothrop, Lee & Shepard Co., 1982.
Alfie is proud of being able to put his lovely new boots on by himself, but wonders why they feel funny.

Hutchins, Pat. *The Doorbell Rang*. New York: Greenwillow Books, 1986.
Each time the doorbell rings, there are more people who have come to share Ma's wonderful cookies.

Kimmell, Eric A. (retold). *Anansi and the Moss-Covered Rock*. New York: Holiday House, 1988.
Anansi the Spider uses a strange moss-covered rock in the forest to trick all the other animals, until little Bush Deer decides he needs to learn a lesson.

Lionni, Leo. *Fish Is Fish*. New York: Pantheon Books, 1970.
When his friend, the tadpole, becomes a frog and leaves the pond to explore the world, the little fish decides that maybe he doesn't have to remain in the pond either.

Numeroff, Laura Joffee. *If You Give a Mouse a Cookie*. Illustrated by Felicia Bond. New York: Harper & Row, 1985.
Describes how a little mouse was not satisfied with just one thing!

Prater, John. *The Gift*. New York: Viking Kestrel, 1985 (wordless).
Two children fly over their town, travel to the bottom of the ocean, and explore a jungle, in the cardboard box that had wrapped a gift.

GAME 1

SELECTION TITLE:

Anansi and the Moss-Covered Rock
retold by Eric A. Kimmell

FOCUS:

PREDICTION

HOW TO MAKE: Cut out selection title, focus, student directions, and answer card. Color and cut out all game pieces. Glue title onto folder tab and focus onto folder front. Glue animals onto the inside of the folder. Store student directions, answer card, and *grease pencil* in library pocket glued to back of folder.

STUDENT DIRECTIONS:

1.   Read paragraph on animals.
2.   Read question at end of paragraph.
3.   Circle your answer with grease pencil.
4.   Do other paragraphs the same way.
5.   Check your answers using answer card.

ANSWER CARD:

1.   Cook them
2.   Make a banana sandwich
3.   Learn a lesson
4.   Make pineapple punch

PIECES FOR GAME 1—PREDICTION

Anansi watched Lion take the yams to his porch. He started sorting them by size into large and small piles. All the time, Lion was thinking about a new recipe. The large yams were peeled and cut up. Anansi wondered, "What will Lion do with the large yams?"

freeze them   cook them   plant them

③

Anansi used a moss-covered rock to trick the animals. Little Bush Deer played along when Anansi took her to the rock. Pretending not to see the rock, she never said the magic words. What will Anansi do?

go home   learn a lesson
make her cry

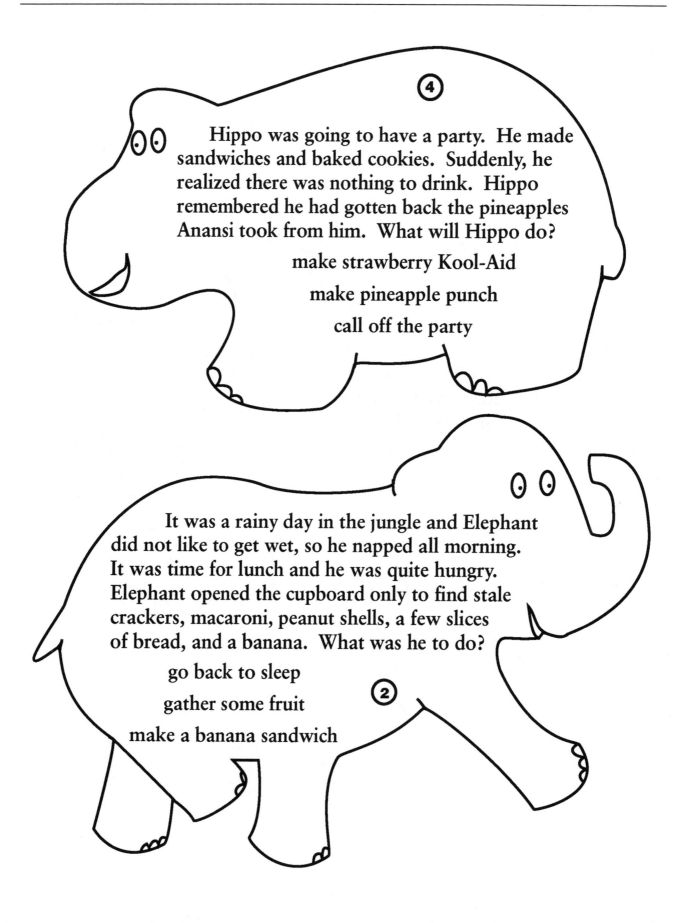

④

Hippo was going to have a party. He made sandwiches and baked cookies. Suddenly, he realized there was nothing to drink. Hippo remembered he had gotten back the pineapples Anansi took from him. What will Hippo do?

make strawberry Kool-Aid

make pineapple punch

call off the party

It was a rainy day in the jungle and Elephant did not like to get wet, so he napped all morning. It was time for lunch and he was quite hungry. Elephant opened the cupboard only to find stale crackers, macaroni, peanut shells, a few slices of bread, and a banana. What was he to do?

go back to sleep

gather some fruit

②

make a banana sandwich

GAME 2

SELECTION TITLE:

> *The Doorbell Rang*
> by Pat Hutchins

FOCUS:

> # PREDICTION

HOW TO MAKE: Cut out selection title, focus, student directions, and answer card. Color and cut out all game pieces. Glue title on folder tab and focus on folder front. Glue doors onto inside of folder. Store student directions, answer card, and cookies in the library pocket glued to the back of the folder.

STUDENT DIRECTIONS:

1. Read paragraph on each door.
2. Read sentences on each cookie.
3. Match correct prediction cookie with door.
4. Check your answers using answer card.

ANSWER CARD:

1. She sent out invitations.
2. The balloon popped.
3. He will call his friends and invite them to go.
4. She will punch the button marked 6.
5. They will go home.
6. Her dad will take her skiing.
7. They will wait for better weather.
8. He will enter his car sketch in the contest.

PIECES FOR GAME 2—PREDICTION

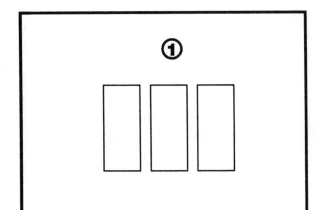

①

Susan's father said she could have a party. Susan made a list of her friends' addresses. What happened next?

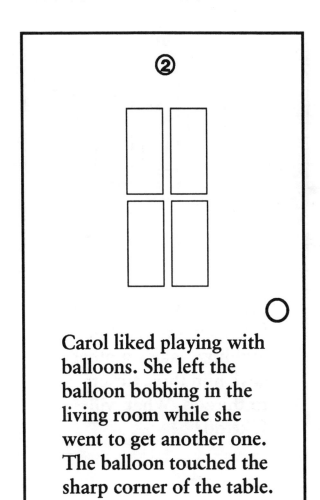

②

Carol liked playing with balloons. She left the balloon bobbing in the living room while she went to get another one. The balloon touched the sharp corner of the table. What happened next?

She sent out invitations.

The balloon popped.

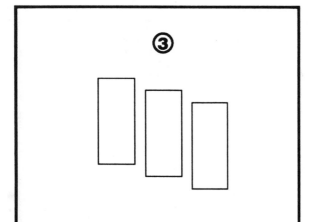

③

Jake had two very close friends in his apartment building. Jake's mother gave him three tickets to the zoo. What will Jake do?

He will call his friends and invite them to go.

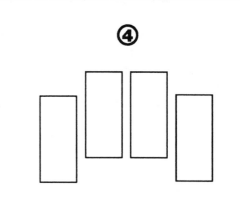

④

"The cafeteria is on the sixth floor," the man said to April. She got on the elevator. What will April do next?

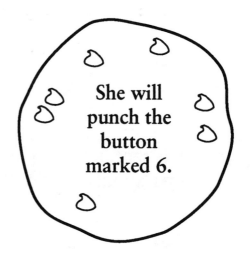

She will punch the button marked 6.

⑤

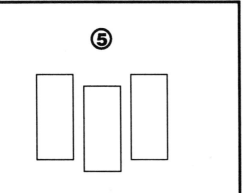

Mrs. Grey lined the students up at the door. It was 3:00 p.m. The students were getting their coats, lunch boxes, and books. What will the students do next?

⑥

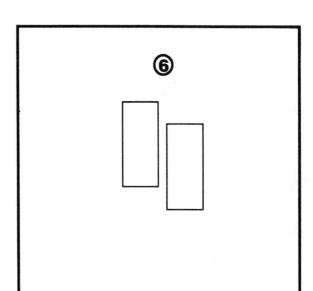

Niki loved to ski. Her father said he had a surprise for her. The next morning she found two lunches packed and two pairs of skis leaning against the door. What will they do next?

They will go home.

Her dad will take her skiing.

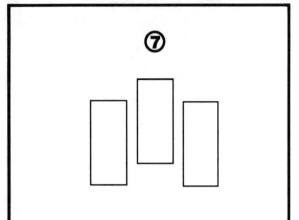

Beth and Connie were going to the beach. They packed their raft and towels in a bag and walked out the door. The sun was covered by a huge cloud and a few raindrops were falling. What will Beth and Connie do?

They will wait for better weather.

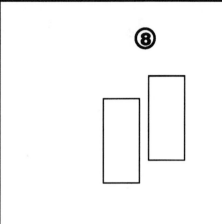

Matthew loved to draw. When he wasn't studying, he was making sketches of cars. At school he read an ad about a drawing contest. What will Matt do?

He will enter his car sketch in the contest.

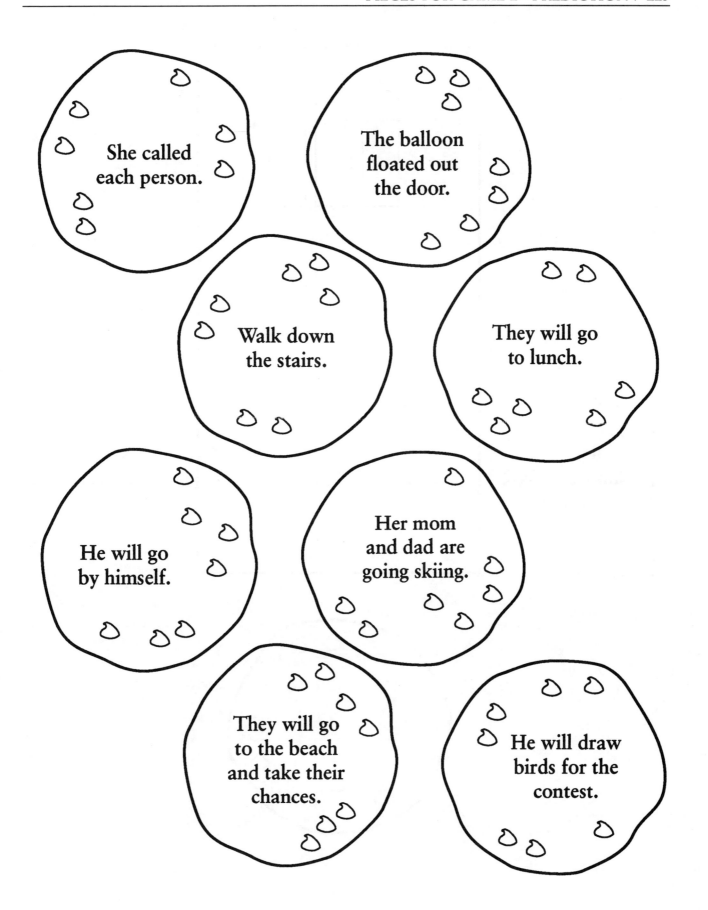

She called each person.

The balloon floated out the door.

Walk down the stairs.

They will go to lunch.

He will go by himself.

Her mom and dad are going skiing.

They will go to the beach and take their chances.

He will draw birds for the contest.

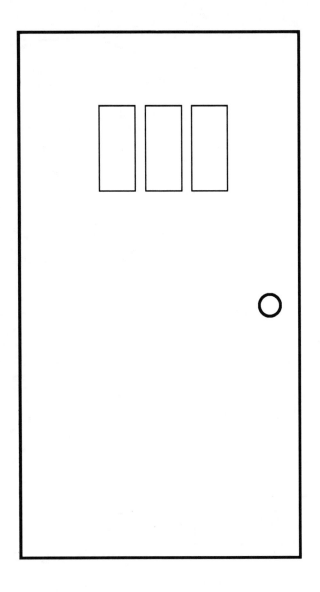

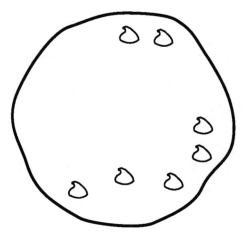

ACTIVITIES

Speech Balloons: Select pictures from old workbooks, magazines, cartoons, or other sources. Glue blank speech balloons next to the characters in the pictures. Have students tell orally or write what the characters might be saying. Have students explain why they think the characters said what they did.

Picture Puzzles: Instead of having students number a set of sequence pictures in the right order, cut the pictures apart. Give students an incomplete set. Have them add their own pictures to complete the set. This activity can also be done with sets of sentences or short paragraphs.

Test That Prediction: Select short selections for students to read. Provide them with several predictions, some logical and some illogical. Have students evaluate the predictions and choose the best. Then have them read the selection to check the predictions.

You Be the Author: When you read aloud to students, stop occasionally and let your students guess the word or event that is coming, before reading more of the selection.

Headline News: Have students read only part of a selected story. Then have them write headlines that tell how the story will end. The headlines might tell who the hero is, what the hero does, or what problem the characters are having. The activity can be extended by writing an article to go along with the headline. Be sure to finish reading the original selection to see how well the reporters did.

Picture Predictions: Using pictures from magazines, newspapers, or even old basals, have students write a description of what is happening. They can then write about what they think is going to happen next.

Captions: Photos from newspapers, especially the sports page, can be used. Cut off the captions. Have students write their own captions, including the final outcome. Then compare the students' versions to the original caption.

Real Life: Don't forget the opportunities in everyday situations for students to practice making predictions. Set up a float or sink activity center, a "weigh" station, a measurement center, a temperature center, a weather station, or a sweet-or-sour tasting center. Be sure to have students make a prediction and explain their thinking. Then provide the tools and the time for the students to test their predictions.

16—REALISM AND FANTASY

Objective: The student will identify a selection as realism or fantasy.

TEACHER CHECKLIST FOR PLANNING

1.   Define realism: something that could happen in real life.

2.   Share examples.
     Ask: Could this happen in real life?

3.   Define fantasy: something that could not happen in real life.

4.   Share examples.
     Ask: Are there talking animals?
            Is there magic?
            Is there exaggeration?
            Is it make-believe?

5.   Have students tell or write their own examples of realism and fantasy.

6.   Have students listen to or read selection.

7.   Have students find examples of realism and fantasy, using questions above.

8.   Have students identify selection as realism or fantasy.

STUDENT CHECKLIST

1.   Look for examples of realism.
     Ask: Could this happen in real life?

2.   Look for examples of fantasy.
     Ask: Are there talking animals?
            Is there magic?
            Is there exaggeration?
            Is it make-believe?

3.   Decide if selection is realism or fantasy.

4.   Explain my answer.

STUDENT VISUAL—REALISM AND FANTASY

Realism and Fantasy

1. Look for examples of realism.
   Ask: Could this happen in real life?

2. Look for examples of fantasy.
   Ask: Are there talking animals?
   Is there magic?
   Is there exaggeration?
   Is it make-believe?

3. Decide if selection is realism or fantasy.

4. Explain my answer.

ANNOTATED BIBLIOGRAPHY

Realism

Addy, Sharon Hart. *A Visit with Great-Grandma*. Illustrated by Lydia Halverson. Niles, IL: Albert Whitman & Co., 1981.
Even though Great-grandma speaks very little English and Baruska does not speak Czech, they enjoy a very special afternoon together while baking and looking at old photographs.

Baker, Jeannie. *Home in the Sky*. New York: Greenwillow Books, 1984.
A pigeon with a kindly owner and a home on the roof of a building meets a boy who wants to keep him.

Baker, Leslie. *The Third Story Cat*. Boston: Little, Brown & Co., 1987.
A house cat with a longing to visit the park across the street "escapes" her comfortable apartment, meets a streetwise cat, and is given a tour that results in a hair-raising encounter that sends her rushing home to stay, at least until tomorrow.

Edwards, Patricia Kiev. *Chester and Uncle Willoughby*. Illustrated by Diane Worfolk Allison. Boston: Little, Brown & Co., 1987.
Four vignettes in which Chester and his Uncle Willoughby sit together on their front porch and exchange thoughts and stories.

Hughes, Shirley. *The Big Alfie and Annie Rose Storybook*. New York: Lothrop, Lee & Shepard, 1988.
Presents experiences of nursery school student Alfie and his younger sister Annie Rose.

Shulevitz, Uri. *Dawn*. New York: Farrar, Straus & Giroux, 1974.
Describes the sights and sounds that an old man and his grandson experience around and on a lake.

Fantasy

Adoff, Arnold. *Flamboyan*. Illustrated by Karen Barbour. San Diego: Harcourt Brace Jovanovich, 1988.
One sunny afternoon while everyone is resting, Flamboyan, a young girl named after the tree whose red blossoms are the same color as her hair, dreamily flies over her Caribbean island home.

Alexander, Martha. *Maggie's Moon*. New York: Dial Press, 1982.
A little girl and her dog set out to capture the moon and bring it home with them.

Ernst, Lisa Campbell. *When Bluebell Sang*. New York: Bradbury Press, 1989.
Bluebell the cow's talent for singing brings her stardom, but she soon longs to be back at the farm, if she can get away from her greedy manager.

McCarthy, Bobette. *Buffalo Girls*. New York: Crown Publishers, 1987.
An illustrated version of the traditional folk song in which the buffalo girls sing by starlight and dance by the light of the moon.

Realism and Fantasy Contained in Each Selection

Aylesworth, Jim. *Two Terrible Frights*. Illustrated by Eileen Christelow. New York: Atheneum, 1987.
A little girl mouse and a little girl person meet while getting a snack in the kitchen at bedtime and scare each other, only to dream of each other later.

Burningham, John. *Where's Julius?* New York: Crown Publishers, 1986.
Julius uses his bold imagination while he plays to enjoy fabulous escapades, such as shooting South American rapids and riding camels up pyramids.

Euvremer, Teryl. *Sun's Up*. New York: Crown Publishers, 1987.
The sun rises from his bed in the morning, spends the day moving across the sky while engaged in different activities, and goes to sleep as night falls.

Schoberle, Cecile. *Beyond the Milky Way*. New York: Crown Publishers, 1986.
Looking out a city window and seeing the night sky between the buildings, a child describes the glowing wonder of outer space and imagines another child doing the same thing on a distant planet.

White, E. B. *Charlotte's Web*. Illustrated by Garth Williams. New York: Scholastic, 1952.
Wilbur the pig is desolate when he discovers that he is destined to be the farmer's Christmas dinner, until his spider friend, Charlotte, decides to help him.

Realism and Fantasy Compared between Selections

Locker, Thomas. *Sailing with the Wind*. New York: Dial Books, 1986.
A young girl discovers the ocean's majestic character when she joins her uncle on a sailing trip.

Sendak, Maurice. *Where the Wild Things Are*. New York: Harper & Row, 1963.
A mischievous boy takes a boat trip to the land of the wild things and becomes their king.

Baker, Leslie. *The Third Story Cat*. Boston: Little, Brown & Co., 1987.
A house cat with a longing to visit the park across the street "escapes" her comfortable apartment, meets a streetwise cat, and is given a tour that results in a hair-raising encounter that sends her rushing home to stay, at least until tomorrow.

Tafuri, Nancy. *Junglewalk*. New York: Greenwillow Books, 1988.
A little boy falls asleep after reading a book about animals in a jungle, and then meets them all in his dream.

Gerstein, Mordicai. *The Room*. New York: Harper & Row, 1984.
An artist recreates the many characters from years past who have lived in a room that is once again for rent.

Schlein, Miriam. *My House*. Illustrated by Joe Lasker. Chicago: Albert Whitman & Co., 1971.
    A boy tells why his house is a very special place.

Tejima, Keizaburo. *Owl Lake*. New York: Philomel Books, 1982.
    As the sun slips down behind the lake and the sky darkens, Father Owl comes out and hunts for fish to feed his hungry family.

Thaler, Mike. *Owly*. New York: Harper & Row, 1982.
    When Owly asks his mother question after question about the world, she finds just the right ways to help him find the answers.

GAME 1

SELECTION TITLE:

> *Owl Lake* by Keizaburo Tejima
> *Owly* by Mike Thaler

FOCUS:

Realism and Fantasy

HOW TO MAKE: Cut out selection title, focus, student directions, and answer card. Color and cut out all game pieces. Glue title onto folder tab and focus onto folder front. Glue owls onto the inside of the folder. Store student directions, answer card, and moons in library pocket glued to back of folder.

STUDENT DIRECTIONS:

1. Read sentences on moons.
2. Decide if the sentence is realism or fantasy.
3. Place realism sentences on realism owl and fantasy sentences on fantasy owl.
4. Check your answers using answer card.

ANSWER CARD:

(order of answers not important)

Realism - 1, 2, 4, 5, 8
Fantasy - 3, 6, 7, 9, 10

PIECES FOR GAME 1—REALISM AND FANTASY

① The owl came out at night.

② The owl searched for food after a day of sleep.

③ The owl started asking questions.

④

The owl liked to
eat fish.

⑤

The owl listened for
fish jumping.

⑥

The owl stayed up
all night and counted
the stars.

⑦

The owl flew to
the shore and
counted waves.

⑧

The owl's feathers
glistened in
the moonlight.

⑨

The owl was
hugged by
his mother.

⑩

The owl asked,
"How deep is the
ocean?"

GAME 2

SELECTION TITLE:

> *Two Terrible Frights*
> by Jim Aylesworth

FOCUS:

Realism and Fantasy

HOW TO MAKE: Cut out selection title, focus, student directions, and answer card. Color and cut out all game pieces. Glue title onto folder tab and focus onto folder front. Glue the girl and the mouse onto the inside of the folder. Store student directions, answer card, and teddy bears in library pocket glued to back of folder.

STUDENT DIRECTIONS:

1. Read sentences on teddy bears.
2. Decide if the sentence is realism or fantasy.
3. Place realism sentences on girl and fantasy sentences on mouse.
4. Check your answers using answer card.

ANSWER CARD:

(order of answers not important)

Realism - 1, 3, 6, 8, 10, 11
Fantasy - 2, 4, 5, 7, 9, 12

PIECES FOR GAME 2—REALISM AND FANTASY

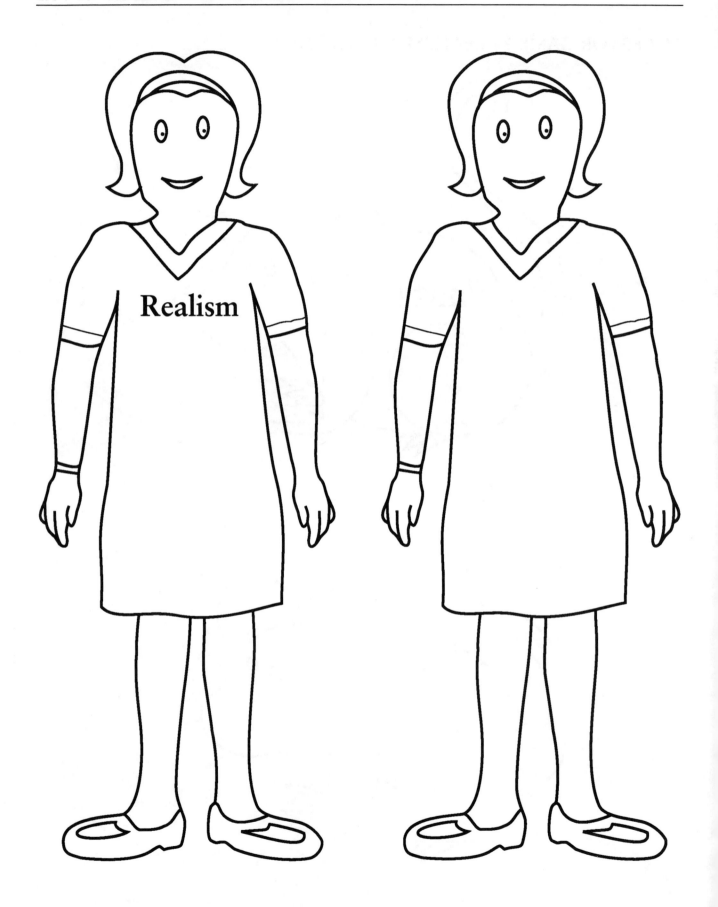

① There was a farmhouse in the country.

② A little mouse went to get a glass of milk.

③ The little girl asked for a glass of milk.

④ Mother mouse was tired from knitting.

5 Little mouse tiptoed to the kitchen.

6 The little girl went to the kitchen all by herself.

7 Little mouse slid down the radiator yelling, "Mommy!"

8 The little girl ran to her mother crying, "Mommy!"

9 The little mouse sobbed.

10 The little mouse crawled through a dark hole.

11 The little mouse crawled up the radiator pipe.

12 Mother mouse kissed the little mouse on the cheek and said, "Goodnight."

ACTIVITIES

Could Be—Couldn't Be: Prepare a sheet with two columns labeled "Could Be" and "Couldn't Be." While reading a selection, have students write examples of items from the selection under the correct heading.

Change That Character: After the students have read a realistic selection, have them pick one character and think of ways to change the character into a fantasy character. Students can do two illustrations or even two dioramas, one for the realistic character, the other for the fantasy character.

Ridiculous Reasons: Pattern this activity after *Just So Stories* by Rudyard Kipling ("How the Camel Got His Hump," "How the Leopard Got His Spots"). Have the students select an everyday item (book, paper, clock) and have them write their own stories (How the Book Got Its Pages, How the Paper Got Its Lines, How the Clock Got Its Hands).

Fantastic "Finds": Provide magazines, catalogs, and other sources of pictures that students can cut and paste. Have them cut out objects and put them together to create fantasy pictures. Students might make a picture showing a chair inside a big skillet, a horse sitting on a couch, or a car on skis. When students have finished their pictures, create a classroom or hall display. Talk about which parts of the picture are real and which parts are fantasy.

Have You Ever Seen a ...: To the tune of "The More We Get Together," sing this refrain: "Have you ever seen a butter-fly, a butter-fly, a butter-fly? Have you ever seen a butter-fly ... now you tell us one." The compound word has a realistic meaning. If you break the compound word apart, it is fantasy (stick of butter flying). Some other examples of appropriate compound words for this activity are *starfish, sunburn, firefly, sweetheart, toothbrush, weekday, headdress, headlight, bedrock, daydream, dragonfly, homesick.* Instead of singing, students could draw the realistic and fantasy versions of the compounds.

The Setting Shuffle: Provide students with a realistic piece of literature that includes an obvious or easy-to-describe setting. After students have read the selection, have them shuffle the setting by changing it into one with elements of fantasy. They may rewrite or retell the story using the fantasy setting.

Fashion Frenzy: Have students create a personal catalog of fashion items they like to wear. Then have students pretend they are aliens from a different planet, and create a second catalog of fashion items from their planet.

Dreamin': Discuss what happens when we are sleeping (we snore, we roll over, we kick the covers off, we stretch out). Have students create a four-panel cartoon that illustrates what they might do when they are sleeping. In four other panels above the completed panels, have them illustrate a fantasy dream.

17—SUMMARIZATION

Objective: The student will summarize a selection.

TEACHER CHECKLIST FOR PLANNING

1. Define summarizing: retelling the important ideas in a logical order.

2. Teach summarizing by using a selection.
   a. Determine important and unimportant information.
   b. Categorize important ideas.
   c. Determine logical order of ideas.
   d. Put ideas in own words.

3. Have students read selection and summarize.

4. Have students explain their reasoning of ideas, categories, and order.

STUDENT CHECKLIST

1. Read selection.

2. Ask: What is the important information?

3. Ask: What ideas can I put together?

4. Ask: In what order do I want to put the ideas?

5. Put this information in my own words.

6. Ask: Does my summary make sense?

No game provided in this unit.

STUDENT VISUAL—SUMMARIZATION

Summarization

1. Read selection.

2. Ask: What is the important information?

3. Ask: What ideas can I put together?

4. Ask: In what order do I want to put the ideas?

5. Put this information in my own words.

6. Ask: Does my summary make sense?

ANNOTATED BIBLIOGRAPHY

Aardema, Verna. *Who's in Rabbit's House?* Illustrated by Leo Dillon and Diane Dillon. New York: Dial Press, 1977.
Rabbit has a problem—someone is inside her house and won't let her in.

Arnold, Caroline. *The Terrible Hodag*. Illustrated by Lambert Davis. San Diego: Harcourt Brace Jovanovich, 1989.
A logger named Ole Swenson befriends the terrible Hodag, who helps him run the boss man out of the forest.

Barton, Byron. *Airport*. New York: Harper & Row, 1982.
Describes and pictures what happens from the time an airline passenger arrives at an airport and boards an airplane until the plane is in the air.

Blume, Judy. *Freckle Juice*. Illustrated by Sonia O. Lisker. New York: Four Winds Press, 1971.
Andrew wants freckles so badly that he buys Sharon's freckle juice recipe for fifty cents.

Cooney, Barbara. *Miss Rumphus*. New York: Viking Press, 1982.
Great Aunt Alice Rumphus was once a little girl who loved the sea, longed to visit faraway places, and wished to do something to make the world more beautiful.

De Paola, Tomie. *Nana Upstairs and Nana Downstairs*. New York: Puffin Books, 1972.
A small boy enjoys his relationship with his grandmother and his great-grandmother, but he learns to face their inevitable deaths.

_____. *Now One Foot, Now the Other*. New York: G. P. Putnam's Sons, 1980.
When his grandfather suffers a stroke, Bobby teaches him to walk, just as his grandfather once taught him.

Goor, Nancy, and Ron Goor. *All Kinds of Feet*. New York: Thomas Y. Crowell, 1984.
Text and photographs present the different types of feet found in the animal kingdom, and describe how each type is specifically suited to the needs of the particular animal to which it belongs.

Grifalconi, Ann. *Darkness and the Butterfly*. Boston: Little, Brown & Co., 1987.
Small Osa is fearless during the day, climbing the trees or exploring the African valley where she lives, but at night she becomes afraid of the strange and terrifying things that might lie in the dark.

Hirschi, Ron. *Who Lives in ... the Mountains?* Photographs by Galen Burrell. New York: G. P. Putnam's Sons, 1989.
A tiny bird in each photograph leads the reader through the mountain forests and streams to view the mountain goats, pikas, bluebirds, and other animals that live in the high country.

Kay, Helen. *The First Teddy Bear*. Illustrated by Susan Detwiler. Owings Mills, MD: Stemmer House Publishers, 1985.
Describes how the first teddy bear stuffed toy originated, inspired by President Theodore Roosevelt's refusal to shoot a little bear during a hunt.

MacLachlan, Patricia. *Sarah, Plain and Tall*. New York: Harper & Row, 1985.

When their father invites a mail-order bride to come live with them in their prairie home, Caleb and Anna are captivated by her and hope that she will stay.

Martin, Bill, and John A. Archambault. *The Ghost-Eye Tree*. Illustrated by Ted Rand. New York: Henry Holt & Co., 1985.

Walking down a dark, lonely road on an errand one night, a brother and a sister argue over who is afraid of the dreaded Ghost-Eye tree.

Moore, Elaine. *Grandma's Promise*. Illustrated by Elise Primavera. New York: Lothrop, Lee & Shepard, 1988.

Kim spends a week after Christmas with her grandmother and enjoys every minute—sleeping by the wood stove, ice skating on the pond, and feeding the birds.

Swanson, June. *The Spice of America*. Illustrated by Priscilla Kiedrowski. Minneapolis, MN: Carolrhoda Books, 1983.

Traces the little-known origins of such American phenomena as the doughnut, Mary's little lamb, the beaver hat, the Ferris wheel, the Raggedy Ann doll, and denim jeans.

Yolen, Jane. *Owl Moon*. Illustrated by John Schoenherr. New York: Philomel, 1987.

On a winter's night under a full moon, father and daughter trek into the woods to see the great horned owl.

ACTIVITIES

Time Capsule: Build a time capsule of book summaries that students have written. It might be opened by next year's students to give them ideas of good books to read.

Moral Madness: Share with students several fables, talking about the moral of each. Much of children's literature, although not fables, also have implied morals. Have students write morals for their reading selections as a form of summarization.

Book Jackets: Borrow book jackets from the media center. Have students observe and discuss the design and information found on the book jackets. Students may design and write a book jacket for one or more of their favorite selections.

Beat the Clock: When students are describing a favorite television show or movie, they often ramble on and on. Challenge the students to beat the clock. Set a timer for one or two minutes and have students try to complete their descriptions before the timer reaches zero. Give students some thinking time before starting the timer.

Urgent! Telegram: Have a telegram, real or fabricated, delivered to your class. Discuss with students how people sending telegrams need to be brief and to the point. Discuss how people sending telegrams are charged. Encourage students to send telegrams to each other, within the classroom, summarizing a favorite reading selection.

Hang It Up: Provide a non-working telephone for the classroom. Be sure to lead a discussion of phone etiquette, including the importance of not tying up the phone. After gathering information from more than one source, and summarizing what they learned, students might enjoy sharing the information over the telephone.

Be Brief: Supply students with 3" x 5" index cards. Have them summarize on the card knowledge gained about a topic they have researched. They will learn to be brief by including only important information and categorizing ideas when they use small cards instead of notebook paper.

Comparisons: Many workbook pages about summarizing are designed so that students simply read the selection and fill in the bubble next to the best summary. Collect short selections and the summaries from workbooks and worksheets. Instead of just marking which is the better selection, students may select the better summary and explain why it is the better choice. To extend the activity, have the students rewrite the poor summary, deleting and adding information as necessary.

Organize Those Thoughts: Using content-area text, have students observe how headings and sub-headings within a chapter can be clues and starting points when summarizing. Instead of having each student answer all the questions at the end of the chapter, divide the students into working groups and ask the groups to summarize specific sections of the text. Students can write their summaries on chart paper to share with the class, or make copies of the summaries to pass out to individuals. When all the summaries are put together, a summary of the entire chapter will be complete.

18—VISUALIZATION

Objective: The students will make visualizations to help them understand what they are reading.

TEACHER CHECKLIST FOR PLANNING

1. Define visualizing: creating a picture in one's mind about what has been read.

2. Explain to students when visualization will help with comprehension.
   a. Poetry.
   b. Figurative language.
   c. Following directions to create a model.
   d. Fables.
   e. Folktales.

3. Explain to students when visualization enhances enjoyment.
   a. Tall tales, fairy tales.
   b. Riddles.
   c. Adventure-packed reading.
   d. Humor.

STUDENT CHECKLIST

1. Read selection and think about who, what, when, where, why, and how.

2. Ask: How do my own experiences fit in?

3. Create a picture.

4. Ask: Does my picture fit with what I'm reading?

No game provided in this unit.

STUDENT VISUAL—VISUALIZATION

Visualization

1. Read selection and think about who, what, when, where, why, and how.

2. Ask: How do my own experiences fit in?

3. Create a picture.

4. Ask: Does my picture fit with what I'm reading?

ANNOTATED BIBLIOGRAPHY

Anderson, Hans Christian. *The Wild Swans*. Illustrated by Angela Barrett. New York: Peter Bedrick Books, 1984.
Eleven brothers who have been turned into swans by their evil stepmother are saved by their beautiful sister.

Anno, Mitsumasa. *In Shadowland*. New York: Orchard Books, 1988.
Chaos descends on Shadowland when the watchman leaves his post to join a little match girl on a snowy street in the real world.

Brown, Marcia. *Walk with Your Eyes*. New York: Franklin Watts, 1979.
Text and photographs encourage the reader to carefully observe the surroundings.

Clément, Claude. *The Voice of the Wood*. Illustrated by Frédéric Clément. New York: Dial Books, 1989.
An incomparable magical cello, made from a Venetian instrument maker's beloved tree, is played during the Grand Carnival only after a famous young musician lets down his public facade and faces the instrument with honesty and heartfelt desire.

Esbensen, Barbara Juster. *Words with Wrinkled Knees*. Illustrated by John Stadler. New York: Thomas Y. Crowell, 1986.
A collection of poems about words that express the essence of the animals they identify.

Jonas, Ann. *Reflections*. New York: Greenwillow Books, 1987.
Chronicles a child's busy day by the sea, in a forest, at a carnival, and then at dinner and a concert. The illustrations change when the book is turned upside down.

_____. *The Trek*. New York: Greenwillow Books, 1985.
A child describes her trip through a jungle and across a desert—all on the way to school.

Lobel, Arnold. *The Rose in My Garden*. Illustrated by Anita Lobel. New York: Greenwillow Books, 1984.
A variety of flowers grow near the hollyhocks that give shade to the bee who sleeps on the only rose in a garden.

Locker, Thomas. *Where the River Begins*. New York: Dial Books, 1984.
Two young boys and their grandfather go on a camping trip to find the source of the river that flows by their home.

Radin, Ruth Yaffe. *High in the Mountains*. Illustrated by Ed Young. New York: Macmillan, 1989.
A young child describes a day spent near grandpa's house in the mountains.

Rylant, Cynthia. *Night in the Country*. Illustrated by Mary Szilagyi. New York: Bradbury Press, 1986.
Text and illustrations describe the sights and sounds of nighttime in the country.

Van Allsburg, Chris. *Jumanji*. Boston: Houghton Mifflin, 1981.
    Left on their own for an afternoon, two bored and restless children find more excitement than they bargained for in a mysterious and mystical jungle adventure board game.

_____. *The Polar Express*. Boston: Houghton Mifflin, 1985.
    A magical train ride on Christmas Eve takes a boy to the North Pole to receive a special gift from Santa Claus.

_____. *The Wreck of the Zephyr*. Boston: Houghton Mifflin, 1983.
    A boy's ambition to be the greatest sailor in the world brings him to ruin when he misuses his new ability to sail his boat in the air.

Wood, Audrey. *Moonflute*. Illustrated by Don Wood. San Diego: Harcourt Brace Jovanovich, 1986.
    A moonbeam turns into a magic flute and takes Firen on a journey through the night sky to find out what the moon has done with her lost sleep.

Yolen, Jane. *The Seeing Stick*. Illustrated by Remy Charlip and Demetra Maraslis. New York: Thomas Y. Crowell, 1977.
    Relates how an old man teaches the emperor's blind daughter to see.

ACTIVITIES

Filmstrip Projector: Make a large homemade projector using a cardboard box. Cut off the top, and put slits on both sides. Using a roll-type paper, divide the paper into frames. Read a selection to students, without showing illustrations. Have students draw an illustration in each frame. Roll the paper around a dowel, through the slits, and onto a dowel on the other side. Reread the selection, letting the filmstrip be rolled as the story progresses, to share the illustrations.

What's the Picture: While you are reading a selection orally, stop frequently and ask students what "picture" they have in their minds. Ask questions about the action: What is Tommy doing? Ask questions about the setting: Is the sun shining? What noises do you hear?

What If ...: Give students "What if ..." statements, similar to "What if polar bears could ski?" Have students describe what it would look like and illustrate their visualizations. Students could write their own what-if statements.

Description of a Suspect: Share with students a description of a suspect, real or imaginary. Based on information, have them design and create a "Wanted" poster. The suspect could be a character from literature.

Sound Effects: Visualization is often only thought of as seeing things, but other senses can and should be utilized. Share a selection with students. Discuss what sounds could be added. Reread the selection, letting students supply the sound effects as you read.

Dynamic Dioramas: Students will enjoy building dioramas using a variety of materials (shoe boxes, clay, paper, wood, junk) based on visualizations they created while reading a selection. Display for all to see.

Where Am I?: Describe scenes from the neighborhood, the school, famous places, or literature. Students guess where they are by using clues in the descriptions. This activity could be done by matching written descriptions and photographs or pictures.

Model That Image: While describing an animal or common object, students create the image using modeling clay. Compare sculptures and determine if visualizations are accurate.

Pantomime Pictorials: Select students to pantomime characters' actions while you read aloud. An extension for this activity could have students working in small groups to create pantomimes of written descriptions. Share descriptions with the entire group. As the pantomimes are presented, students match the pantomimes with the correct descriptions. For older children, all descriptions could be related, with only subtle differences in the action.

Perspective: Share a selection that has an excellent description of something as seen from the eyes of a person. Have students rewrite the description as seen from the eyes of an ant or a giant and illustrate both descriptions. Compare and note the likenesses and differences.

Hey, That Doesn't Fit!: While reading a selection aloud to students, occasionally add a detail that doesn't belong. Students visualize while you are reading, and when they notice that a detail doesn't fit within the context, they raise their hand and respond with "Hey, That Doesn't Fit!"

Critical Evaluation

19—AUTHOR'S PURPOSE

Objective: The student will identify the author's purpose in writing a selection.

TEACHER CHECKLIST FOR PLANNING

1. Define purpose: reason for writing a selection.

2. Define types of purpose.
   a. To inform: give facts.
   b. To entertain or amuse: tell a story.
   c. To persuade: encourage to believe or do something.
   d. To teach: explain how to do something.
   e. To teach: give a moral or lesson.

3. Teach by using examples.

4. Have students give examples, oral or written, using types of purpose.

5. Potential obstacle: Students need to know that entertainment does not always make you laugh. Solution: Provide an assortment of articles from newspapers, magazines, books, etc., that entertain but do not necessarily make one laugh. Students could then look for examples on their own.

STUDENT CHECKLIST

1. Read selection.

2. Ask: Does this selection give *facts* about the topic?
   Does this selection *try* to get me to *agree* or *persuade* me about the topic?
   Does this selection make me *laugh* or *entertain* me?
   Does this selection give me *how-to* information?
   Does this selection *teach* me a lesson?

3. Use information in the selection to support the purpose I chose.

4. Potential obstacle: Some literature does not fall neatly into one category. Solution: It is acceptable to have more than one purpose for writing a selection.

_____

No game provided in this unit.

Author's Purpose

1. Read selection.

2. Does this selection give <u>facts</u> about the topic?

   Does this selection <u>try</u> to get me to <u>agree</u> or <u>persuade</u> me about the topic?

   Does this selection make me <u>laugh</u> or <u>entertain</u> me?

   Does this selection give me <u>how-to</u> information?

   Does this selection <u>teach</u> me a lesson.

3. Use the information in the selection to support the purpose I chose.

ANNOTATED BIBLIOGRAPHY

Anno, Mitsumasa (retold). *Anno's Aesop*. New York: Orchard Books, 1989.
Presents an illustrated collection of Aesop's fables, interwoven with Mr. Fox's own unique interpretations of the stories.

Booth, Jerry. *The Big Beast Book*. Illustrated by Martha Weston. Boston: Little, Brown & Co., 1988.
An introduction to dinosuars, with instructions for related projects.

Bowden, Joan Chase. *Why the Tides Ebb and Flow*. Boston: Houghton Mifflin, 1979.
In this folktale explaining why the sea has tides, an old woman threatens to pull the rock from the hole in the ocean floor if Sky Spirit does not honor his promise to give her shelter.

Demi. *A Chinese Zoo*. San Diego: Harcourt Brace Jovanovich, 1987.
A collection of thirteen adapted Chinese fables, in which an array of animal characters demonstrate principles such as "It is foolish to be greedy."

De Paola, Tomie. *The Popcorn Book*. New York: Holiday House, 1978.
Presents a variety of facts about popcorn and includes two recipes.

Donna, Natalie. *The Peanut Cookbook*. Illustrated by Robert Quackenbush. New York: Lothrop, Lee & Shepard Co., 1976.
Recipes using peanuts and peanut butter and featuring natural foods.

Heller, Ruth. *Chickens Aren't the Only Ones*. New York: Grosset & Dunlap, 1981.
A pictorial introduction to the animals that lay eggs, including chickens as well as other birds, reptiles, and amphibians, fishes, insects, and even a few mammals.

Holland, Penny. *Looking at Word Processing*. Illustrated by Patti Boyd. New York: Franklin Watts, 1986.
A beginners introduction to the many functions of a word processor, with brief projects to demonstrate them.

Mitgutsch, Ali. *From Fruit to Jam*. Minneapolis, MN: Carolrhoda Books, 1981.
Describes how jam is made from fresh fruit.

Ortiz, Simon. *The People Shall Continue*. Illustrated by Sharol Graves. San Francisco: Children's Book Press, 1988.
Traces the progress of the inhabitants of North America from the time of the creation to the present.

Paige, David. *A Day in the Life of a Marine Biologist*. Photographs by Roger Ruhlin. Mahwah, NJ: Troll Associates, 1981.
The text and photographs show all the duties of a marine biologist for the study of ocean life.

Raffi. *The Raffi Singable Songbook*. Illustrated by Joyce Yamamoto. New York: Crown Publishers, 1980.
A noted Canadian recording artist presents his own songs.

Ride, Sally, with Susan Okie. *To Space and Back*. New York: Lothrop, Lee & Shepard, 1986.
Describes in text and photographs what it is like to be an astronaut on the space shuttle.

Selsam, Millicent. *Popcorn*. Photographs by Jerome Wexler. New York: William Morrow & Co., 1976.
Describes the growth cycle of the type of corn used to make popcorn.

Surat, Michele Maria. *Angel Child, Dragon Child*. Illustrated by Vo-Dinh Mai. Milwaukee, WI: Raintree Publishers, 1983.
Ut, a Vietnamese girl attending school in the United States, who is lonely for her mother left behind in Vietnam, makes a new friend, who presents her with a wonderful gift.

Swenson, Judy Harris, and Roxane Brown Kunz. *Learning My Way, I'm a Winner*. Illustrated by Lynn J. Kratoska. Minneapolis, MN: Dillon Press, 1986.
Depicts a learning-disabled child, and shows many of the problems he faces in learning and the strategies that are used to compensate for these differences.

Thaler, Mike. *Cream of Creature from the School Cafeteria*. Illustrated by Jared Lee. New York: Avon Books, 1985.
When the food in the cafeteria takes on a life of its own and spreads out as a green blob eating everything in sight, the students find there is only one way to stop it.

_____. *The Teacher from the Black Lagoon*. Illustrated by Jared Lee. New York: Scholastic, 1989.
A small boy dreams what his teacher will be like on his first day of school.

Tokuda, Wendy, and Richard Hall. *Humphrey the Lost Whale*. Illustrated by Hanako Wakiyama. Union City, CA: Heian International, 1986.
Tells about the whale that entered San Francisco Bay and ended up in a shallow irrigation ditch, where hundreds of people were involved in the rescue.

Williams, Barbara. *Seven True Elephant Stories*. Illustrated by Carol Maisto. New York: Hastings House, 1978.
Dramatic-but-true stories about elephants of the past; also presents research findings about these amazing animals.

Wolf, Bernard. *In the Year of the Tiger*. New York: Macmillan, 1988.
Text and photographs present a brief history of China and introduce the daily life of members of the Chen family, who live in a rural village of Ai Shan.

Magazines

Colorado Fever. 2710 East Exposition Avenue, Denver, CO 80209.
Text and illustrations describe historical happenings in Colorado.

Highlights for Children. 2300 West Fifth Ave., P.O. Box 269, Columbus, OH 43272-0002.
Activities and articles help children grow in basic skills, knowledge, and creativity.

Kid City Magazine. P.O. Box 51277, Boulder, CO 80321-1277.
Makes reading, language skills, and learning fun for readers ages six to ten.

National Geographic World. P.O. Box 2330, Washington, DC 20077-9955.
Contains stories about people and places, science, sports, adventure, and animals, and also games, puzzles, and mazes.

Ranger Rick. National Wildlife Federation, 1400 Sixteenth Street, NW, Washington, DC 20036-2266.
Contains puzzles, games, articles, and illustrations that help children discover the world.

3-2-1 Contact Magazine. E=MC Square, P.O. Box 51177, Boulder, CO 80321-1177.
Award-winning articles about nature, science, and technology for readers ages eight to fourteen.

Your Big Backyard. National Wildlife Federation, 1400 Sixteenth Street, NW, Washington, DC 20036-2266.
Nature magazine helps build an appreciation for conservation and wildlife through animal pictures, stories, and facts, for readers ages six to twelve.

ACTIVITIES

Want Ads: Gather an assortment of want ads from the local newspaper. Divide a sheet of paper into three sections (Want to Buy, Want to Sell, Want to Trade). Students sort the want ads and glue them on the paper according to their purposes. Other categories could be developed based on the want ads. You may wish to extend this activity by having students write their own want ads for things they want to buy, sell, or trade.

Morning News Scavenger Hunt: Save a stack of newspapers for your students to use for this activity. Students can work independently or in small groups. Brainstorm a list of authors' purposes with the students. Send them on a scavenger hunt through the newspaper to find articles that demonstrate the different purposes. Students cut out the articles, glue them on paper, and write descriptions of the authors' purposes. The pages could be collected to make a class scrapbook.

Poster Sort: Gather an assortment of reading selections from magazines, old basals, textbooks, examples of children's literature, etc. The assortment could be about a single topic if students are working on a thematic or integrated unit. Have students read the selections, decide on the authors' purposes, and sort the selections by purpose. Posters could be designed and created by the students that would encourage others to read the sorted pieces if they want to find information, be entertained, etc.

Cereal Boxes: Just about everyone has spent time at breakfast reading cereal boxes. Most cereal boxes have writing that serves a variety of purposes. Collect and bring to your classroom empty cereal boxes. Have students read the boxes from flap-to-flap to see how many different purposes they can locate on one box.

What's the Big Picture?: Select several pieces of literature that have a common theme (*The Bookfinder* is an excellent source, see additional resources list.). Students read the selections and identify the authors' purposes. Then students can compare and contrast how the authors portrayed this purpose.

Select-a-Source: Create a list of titles, either from literature or invented titles, about a similar theme (A Technical Manual for Building Rockets, Willie's Wild Rocket Ride, Why Do We Need Rockets, The Rockets Built by NASA). Write the titles on the cover of blank books. Using the titles to aid in identifying the authors' purposes, have some of your students generate a list of questions that might be answered in the various selections. Cut the list apart and distribute to the other students. Have them read the questions and decide which book would most likely have the answer to the questions. They can then glue the questions on the pages of the blank book with the most appropriate title.

That's Entertainment: People have varying opinions about what is entertaining. Some people enjoy humor, while others find suspense or horror entertaining. One author's purpose is to entertain the reader. After students have finished reading a selection, have them identify the elements that they found entertaining. They might share their choices with others and also defend those choices.

T.V. Guide: Bring an assortment of television schedules and guides that include brief descriptions of the programs. Have students select several programs. Using the name of the program and the description, students decide the writer's purpose. If possible, have students view the show to verify the purpose.

20—AUTHOR'S POINT OF VIEW

Objective: The student will identify the author's point of
view in a selection.

TEACHER CHECKLIST FOR PLANNING

1.   Define point of view: author's feelings, beliefs, emotions, and/or opinions about a topic.

2.   Review clue words.
Examples: *Believe, think, feel, worried, suspect*

3.   Teach students to look for adjectives, colorful language, and other "power" words.
Examples: *Nutro* yogurt, *unfortunate* news

4.   Teach using comparing and contrasting examples.
Examples: School newsletters, magazines, newspapers, television commercials, pictorial ads

5.   Teach by having students give examples, oral or written, by using the author's strategies in isolation.

6.   Teach students to identify "who" wrote the article.
Examples: Parent, child, school principal, reporter, salesman, politician

7.   Have students decide point of view.

8.   Have students support their answers.

STUDENT CHECKLIST

1.   Read selection and/or look at illustration.

2.   Find clue and/or "power" words.

3.   Identify author.

4.   Decide author's point of view.

5.   Support my answer.

No game provided in this unit.

STUDENT VISUAL—AUTHOR'S POINT OF VIEW

Author's Point of View

1. Read selection and/or look at illustration.

2. Find clue and/or "power" words.

3. Identify author.

4. Decide author's point of view.

5. Support my answer.

ANNOTATED BIBLIOGRAPHY

Blume, Judy. *Freckle Juice*. Illustrated by Sonia O. Lisker. New York: Four Winds Press, 1971.
Andrew wants freckles so badly that he buys Sharon's freckle juice recipe for fifty cents.

Coerr, Eleanor. *Sadako and the Thousand Paper Cranes*. Illustrated by Ronald Himler. New York: G. P. Putnam's Sons, 1977.
Hospitalized with the dreaded atom-bomb disease, leukemia, a child in Hiroshima races against time to fold one thousand paper cranes to verify the legend that by doing so a sick person will become healthy.

Cole, Joanne. *The New Baby at Your House*. Photographs by Helen Hammid. New York: William Morrow & Co., 1985.
Describes the activities and changes involved in having a new baby in the house, and the feelings experienced by the older brothers and sisters.

Ferris, Jeri. *Walking the Road to Freedom*. Illustrated by Peter E. Hanson. Minneapolis, MN: Carolrhoda Books, 1988.
Traces the life of a black woman orator who spoke out against slavery throughout New England and the Midwest.

Friedman, Ina R. *How My Parents Learned to Eat*. Illustrated by Alan Say. Boston: Houghton Mifflin, 1984.
An American sailor courts a Japanese girl and each tries, in secret, to learn the other's way of eating.

Gay, Kathlyn. *Be a Smart Shopper*. Photographs by David C. Sassman. New York: Julian Messner, 1974.
Explains advertising psychology, comparative shopping, and consumer protection, and advises the reader on being a more responsible shopper.

Greenberg, Polly. *Oh Lord, I Wish I Was a Buzzard*. Illustrated by Aliki. New York: Macmillan, 1968.
As she works in a cotton field, a little girl dreams of changing places with the many creatures in the field.

Greene, Laura. *Help: Getting to Know about Needing and Giving*. Illustrated by Gretchen Mayo. New York: Human Sciences Press, 1981.
Illustrates that giving and accepting help makes most tasks easier.

Halliburton, Warren J. *The Picture Life of Jesse Jackson*. New York: Franklin Watts, 1984.
Traces the life of the Afro-American minister and civil rights worker from his childhood in South Carolina through his 1984 campaign for the Democratic presidential nomination.

Kunjufu, Jawanza. *Lessons from History: A Celebration in Blackness*. Illustrated by Yaounde Olu and Cornell Barnes. Chicago: African-American Images, 1987.
A comprehensive black history textbook.

Lee, Jeanne M. *Ba-Nam*. New York: Henry Holt & Co., 1987.
   A young Vietnamese girl visiting the graves of her ancestors finds the old gravekeeper frightening, until a severe storm reveals the old woman's kindness.

Levin, Jack E. *Abraham Lincoln's Gettysburg Address Illustrated*. Philadelphia: Chilton Co., 1965.
   Selected photographs taken by Civil War photographers are used as graphic complements to the words of the Gettysburg Address.

Mayle, Peter. *Why Are We Getting a Divorce?* Illustrated by Arthur Robins. New York: Harmony Books, 1988.
   A handbook offering "reassurance, sympathy, and sound advice on how to cope with a family that is splitting up."

McGraw, Eric. *Population Growth*. Vero Beach, FL: Rourke Enterprises, 1987.
   Presents information on the issue of population in various countries and the problems caused by population growth.

Mohr, Nicholasa. *Felita*. Illustrated by Ray Cruz. New York: Dial Press, 1979.
   The everyday experiences of an eight-year-old Puerto Rican girl growing up in a close-knit, urban community.

Parnall, Peter. *The Mountain*. New York: Doubleday & Co., 1971.
   Drawings and a brief text reveal how an effort to preserve a wilderness area brought about its destruction.

Seixas, Judith S. *Junk Food—What It Is, What It Does*. Illustrated by Tom Huffman. New York: Greenwillow Books, 1984.
   An introduction to facts about junk food—what it is, where it is found, and how it affects the body—with suggestions for snacking more nutritionally.

Simon, Norma. *All Kinds of Families*. Illustrated by Joe Lasker. Chicago: Albert Whitman & Co., 1976.
   Explores in words and pictures what a family is and how families vary in makeup and lifestyles.

Turner, Ann. *Dakota Dugout*. Illustrated by Ronald Himler. New York: Macmillan, 1985.
   A woman describes her experiences living with her husband in a sod house on the Dakota prairie.

Magazines

Cobblestone: The History Magazine for Young People. Cobblestone Publishing, Inc., 30 Grove Street, Peterborough, NH 03458.
   Text and illustrations provide a walk through the history of the United States.

National Geographic World. P.O. Box 2330, Washington, DC 20077-9955.
   Contains stories about people and places, science, sports, adventure, and animals, and also games, puzzles, and mazes.

Ranger Rick. National Wildlife Federation, 1400 Sixteenth Street, NW, Washington, DC 20036-2266.
Contains puzzles, games, articles, and illustrations that help children discover the world.

Sports Illustrated for Kids. P.O. Box 830606, Birmingham, AL 35282-9487.
Text and colorful photography entertain and challenge children in the area of sports; for readers ages eight and up.

Zoobooks. Wildlife Federation, Ltd., 930 West Washington Street, San Diego, CA 92103.
Dedicated to the student who wants to learn about nature and animals through articles and illustrations.

ACTIVITIES

Editorial Cartoons: Using newspapers, gather an assortment of editorial cartoons. Students select a cartoon, read it, and determine the author's point of view. They could also draw a cartoon illustrating the opposing point of view.

Get the Scoop: Have students develop a survey about a topic of their interest, such as, "Do children need more recess," or "Should chocolate milk be served every day in the cafeteria?" Divide students into working groups. Some students should survey teachers, some should survey other students, some should survey parents, etc. When students have compiled their results, the class should study the results to determine if the surveyed groups have differing points of view.

Vegetable Debate: Survey the class to determine students' favorite and least favorite vegetables. From this survey, select three or four vegetables that are both liked and disliked. Divide students into teams to verbally give reasons why they like or dislike the vegetables.

Letters to the Editor: Have students write letters to the editor after a discussion about how a character in a selection would feel about a topic (How did Andrew Marcus feel about freckles in Judy Blume's *Freckle Juice*?). Students can assume the role of the character and write the letter from the character's point of view.

Bare Facts: Using articles from the magazines listed in the annotated bibliography, select important facts from the articles. Write the facts on index cards, one article per card. Pass out the cards to students. By using the facts, students determine the author's point of view. Have students read article to check their thinking.

Through Someone Else's Eyes: People view the same event differently. Select a current event such as a space shuttle launch. Make a list of people who would watch the event. Have students write about the event by assuming the role of one of the people watching. Compare the writings and the points of view.

Soap Box: Let students brainstorm various occupations while you make a list for them. Cut this list apart and put all occupation strips into a soap box. Have each student draw a strip from the box but keep the occupation a secret. They then write about a topic dealing with their occupation. For example, a fireman might write about how to prevent fires. After sharing the articles orally, students determine who (which occupation) wrote the article.

Community Spirit: As students think about the places where they live, have them draw an illustration that shows their point of view about their town, their city, or their community. Display the pictures throughout the classroom. Have the other students determine the illustrator's point of view. If the students are negative, brainstorm ways to change that point of view.

21—FACT VERSUS OPINION

Objective: The student will identify a statement as fact or opinion.

TEACHER CHECKLIST FOR PLANNING

1. Define fact: information that can be observed, checked by using reference material, and/or stated factually.

2. Teach clue words for some fact statements.
   Examples: Numbers, dates, ages

3. Work through examples.

4. Define opinion: information that cannot be checked or observed, and/or relates to someone's feeling.

5. Teach clue words used for some opinion statements.
   a. *Believe, think, felt, probably, it seems, perhaps, as well as*, etc.
   b. Adjectives: *beautiful* house, *noisy* room, *good* work
   c. Adverbs: ran *swiftly*, yelled *loudly*, whispered *quietly*

6. Work through examples.

7. Have students give oral and written fact and opinion statements.

8. Have students read statements and determine if they are fact or opinion.

9. Have students check by using definitions.

10. Potential obstacle: Students read selection and then decide if statements are fact or opinion. Students might label opinion statements as fact because they were written as fact in a selection. Solution: Students need to understand that authors use both fact and opinion statements in their writing. Just because an author wrote the statement and the student can find it in the selection does *not* mean that the statement is a fact. Direct students to definitions and clue words.

STUDENT CHECKLIST

1. Read statement.

2. Look for clue words.

3. Determine if statement is fact or opinion.

4. Check by using definitions.

STUDENT VISUAL—FACT VERSUS OPINION

FACT VS. OPINION

Define fact.
a. Can be observed
b. Can be checked using reference material
c. Stated factually

Define opinion.
a. Can't be checked or observed
b. Relates to someone's feelings about something

1. Read statement.
2. Look for clue words.
3. Determine if statement is fact or opinion.
4. Check by using definitions.

ANNOTATED BIBLIOGRAPHY

Cobb, Vicki. *The Scoop on Ice Cream*. Illustrated by G. Brian Karas. Boston: Little, Brown & Co., 1985.
Outlines the ingredients and making of ice cream and the role played by the manufacturers, retailers, and suppliers of this popular dessert, plus a taste test and recipe for the homemade variety.

Estrem, Paul. *ATV'S*. Mankato, MN: Crestwood House, 1987.
Describes a variety of ATV's (all-terrain vehicles) and their uses; includes a glossary of terms.

Fritz, Jean. *Who's That Stepping on Plymouth Rock?* Illustrated by J. B. Handelsman. New York: Coward, McCann & Geoghegan, 1975.
Relates the history of Plymouth Rock since the Pilgrims first landed on it to the present day.

Gibbons, Gail. *Sun Up, Sun Down*. San Diego: Harcourt Brace Jovanovich, 1983.
Describes the characteristics of the sun and the ways in which it regulates life on earth.

Haddock, Patricia. *San Francisco*. Minneapolis, MN: Dillon Press, 1989.
Describes the past and present, neighborhoods, attractions, and festivals of San Francisco.

Kaufman, Meryl. *Jesse Owens*. Illustrated by Larry Johnson. New York: Thomas Y. Crowell, 1973.
An easy-to-read biography of the black athlete who won four gold medals in the 1936 Olympics.

Lerner, Mark. *Racquetball Is for Me*. Photographs by Bob Wolfe and Diane Wolfe. Minneapolis, MN: Lerner Publications, 1983.
Jonathan discusses his experiences while learning to play racquetball.

Lyon, Nancy. *The Mystery of Stonehenge*. Milwaukee, WI: Raintree Publishers, 1977.
Discusses the theories and the superstitions that have arisen throughout the years to explain the existence of the circle of stones at Stonehenge.

Maberry, D. L. *Julian Lennon*. Minneapolis, MN: Lerner Publications, 1986.
A biography of the first son of John Lennon, a member of the Beatles. Julian is now a recording star himself.

Martin, Patricia Stone. *Jesse Jackson*. Illustrated by Bernard Doctor. Vero Beach, FL: Rourke Enterprises, 1987.
Examines the life of the black leader and civil rights worker from his childhood to the present, describing how he achieved his goal of obtaining more rights for blacks.

Newlands, Anne. *Meet Edgar Degas*. New York: J. B. Lippincott, 1989.
Presents the life and paintings of Edgar Degas in a first-person narrative drawn from people's stories about the artist and his own letters and notebooks.

Osinski, Alice. *The Nez Perce*. Chicago: Children's Press, 1988.
Describes the history, beliefs, customs, homes, and day-to-day life of the Nez Perce Indians and how they live today.

Preston-Mauks, Susan. *Field Hockey Is for Me*. Minneapolis, MN: Lerner Publications, 1983.
Allison discusses her experiences while learning the basic rules and techniques of field hockey.

Sandak, Cass R. *Skyscrapers*. New York: Franklin Watts, 1984.
Discusses the development of skyscrapers, how they are constructed, and new techniques for building them.

Thypin, Marilyn, and Lynne Glasner. *Wheels and Deals*. Photographs by Ira Berger. St. Paul, MN: EMC Corp., 1979.
With the help of a mechanic friend, Dick shops around for a reasonably priced car that still meets his needs.

Magazine

Sports Illustrated for Kids. P.O. Box 830606, Birmingham, AL 35282-9487.
Text and colorful photography entertain and challenge children in the area of sports; for readers ages eight and up.

GAME 1

SELECTION TITLE:

> *San Francisco*
> by Patricia Haddock

FOCUS:

Fact versus Opinion

HOW TO MAKE: Cut out selection title, focus, student directions, and answer card. Color and cut out all game pieces. Glue title onto folder tab and focus onto folder front. Glue city skyline and sentences onto inside of the folder. Store student directions, answer card, and footballs in library pocket glued to back of folder.

STUDENT DIRECTIONS:

1. Read sentences on skylines.
2. If the sentence is a fact, place a fact football on the skyline.
3. If the sentence is an opinion, place an opinion football on the skyline.
4. Check answer using answer card.

ANSWER CARD:

1. fact	4. fact	7. opinion	10. fact
2. opinion	5. opinion	8. fact	
3. opinion	6. opinion	9. fact	

PIECES FOR GAME 1—FACT VERSUS OPINION

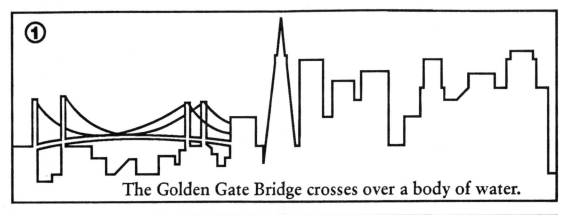

The Golden Gate Bridge crosses over a body of water.

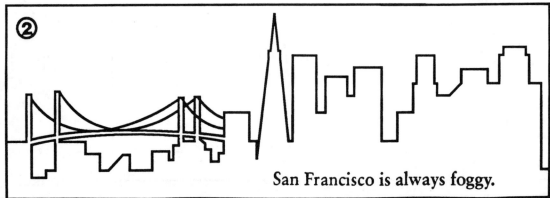

Super Bowl champions, the Forty-Niners, are based in San Francisco.

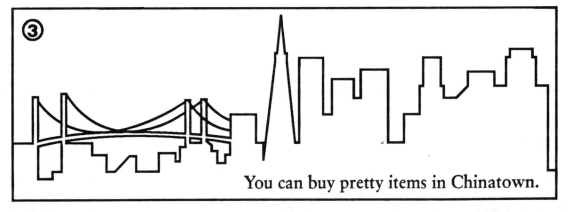

You can buy pretty items in Chinatown.

San Francisco is always foggy.

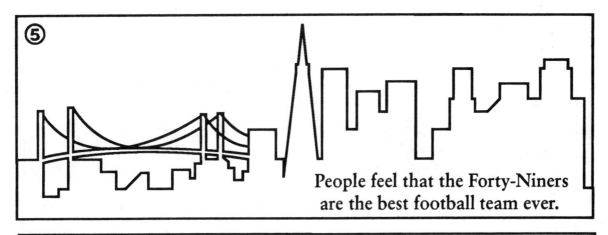

People feel that the Forty-Niners are the best football team ever.

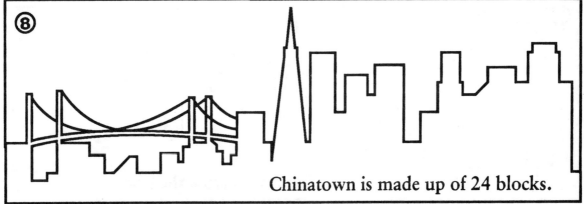

Chinatown is made up of 24 blocks.

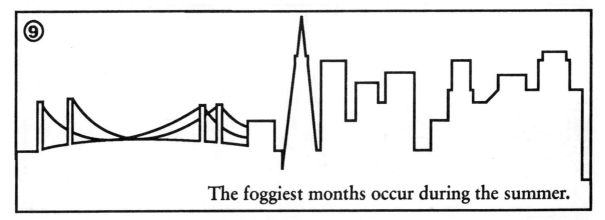

The foggiest months occur during the summer.

Someday San Francisco will be totally destroyed by an earthquake.

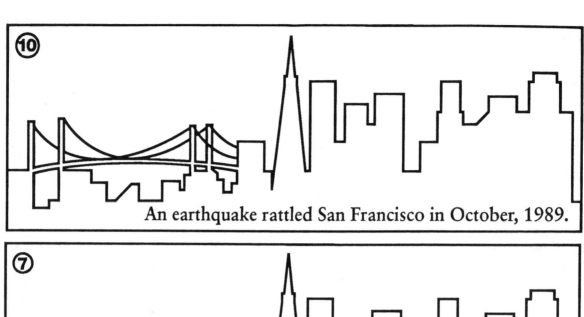

An earthquake rattled San Francisco in October, 1989.

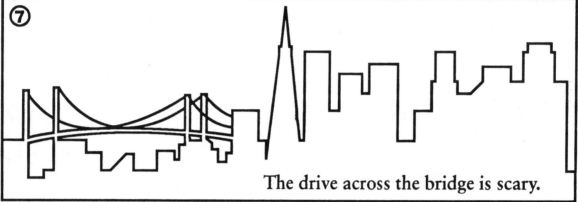

The drive across the bridge is scary.

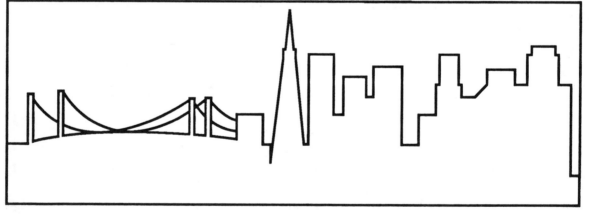

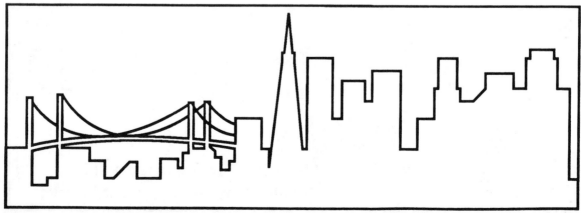

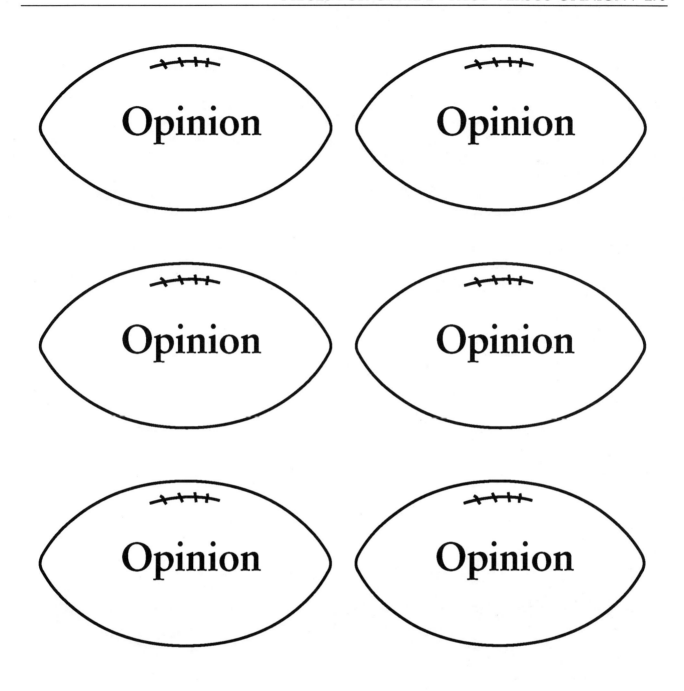

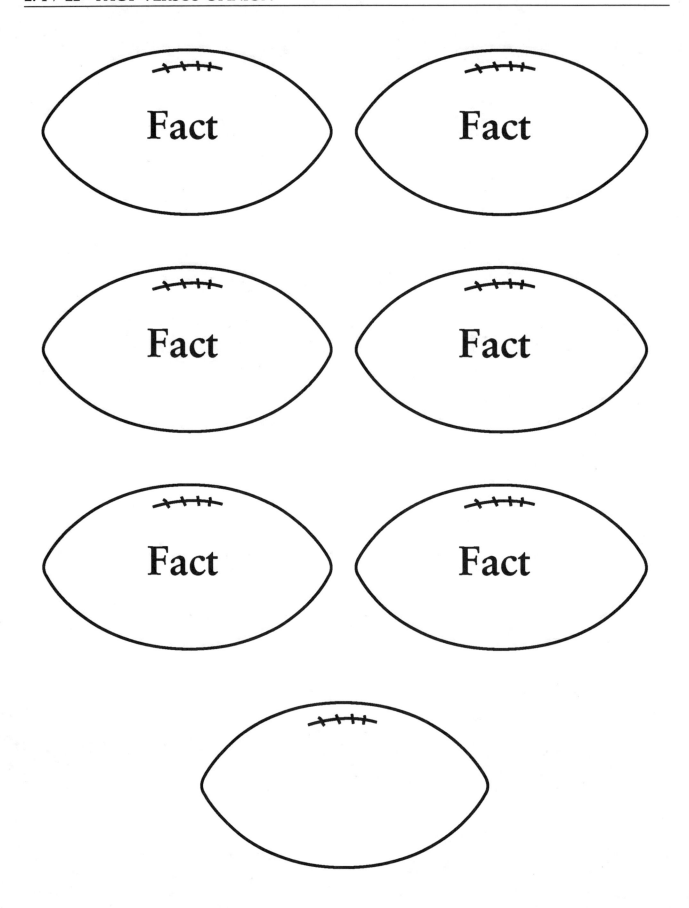

GAME 2

SELECTION TITLE:

> *The Scoop on Ice Cream*
> by Vicki Cobb

FOCUS:

Fact versus Opinion

HOW TO MAKE: Cut out selection title, focus, student directions, and answer card. Color and cut out all game pieces. Glue title onto folder tab and focus onto folder front. Glue book, child, and think bubble onto inside of folder. Store student directions, answer card, and ice cream cones in library pocket glued to back of folder.

STUDENT DIRECTIONS:

1. Read sentences on ice cream cones.
2. Place factual sentences on the book and opinion sentences on the bubble.
3. Check your answers using answer card.

ANSWER CARD:

(order of answers not important)

Fact - 1, 4, 6, 8, 9, 10

Opinion - 2, 3, 5, 7

PIECES FOR GAME 2—FACT VERSUS OPINION

FACT

Butterfat gives ice cream its creamy taste.
①

Ice-cream-making equipment is washed every day.
④

ACTIVITIES

I Don't Know about That: Many times, when writers have strong opinions about something that they want the reader to believe, they do not use clue words to express their opinions. Have students look through a *loaded* selection (an editorial, an advertisement). Chart the facts and opinions after careful study. Rewrite the selection using clue words when an opinion is expressed.

Think or Know: Students are always willing to share what they think they *know* about a topic. The problem is that sometimes what they know isn't a fact, but an opinion. Make a list of *facts* known by students about a topic. Assemble resource books about the topics. Give students the opportunity to research their facts to prove to others what they really do know.

Put Those Opinions to Work: "Boy, if I were a teacher I would...." Challenge students to finish this statement with thoughtful opinions about how to improve the class or the school. Compile the best of the opinions. Select one or several opinions that can be tried out in class for an afternoon or a day. Give the suggestion an honest try. After the trial, have students give honest opinions about the suggestion. Did it work? Did you enjoy it? Did you learn from the suggestion?

Getting the Facts: Take a nature walk. Students use their senses of sight, hearing, smell, and touch to get the facts about their surroundings. After returning to the classroom, compile a list of information gathered. Determine if each item of information is a fact or an opinion. Explain why.

Believe It ... or Not?: Hand out a page or parts of a page of a newspaper. Students read through the paper. When they locate a fact, they circle it in red. When they locate an opinion, they circle it in blue. Students can share their findings with the class and explain why the items are fact or opinion.

Vacation Travel Guide: Have students select a location they have visited and create a travel guide to be shared with other students. When students are designing and creating the guide, have them use a code (red for facts, blue for opinions) that differentiates facts from opinions about the location.

Take Me Out to the Ball Game: Have students observe a ball game (on television, on the playground) or read about a ball game (in the newspaper or *Sports Illustrated for Kids*). Explain to students that a play-by-play announcer tells the action and events of the game. The color commentator expresses opinions about the players and the game. Have students work in pairs to create a dialogue about a ball game. One will tell the facts (play-by-play announcer). The other will share opinions about the game (the color commentator). Present the dialogues to the class.

How Does Your Garden Grow?: Have students plan the perfect garden using their *opinions* about vegetables. Then students should research the topic (What vitamins does my body need and what vegetables supply those vitamins?). Have students plan a second perfect garden based on this factual information. Compare the two gardens.

22—NARRATIVE AND EXPOSITORY WRITING

Objective: The student will identify a selection as either narrative or expository writing.

TEACHER CHECKLIST FOR PLANNING

1.   Define narrative writing: selection written in story form.

2.   Teach elements of narrative writing.
Examples: Plot, characters, setting, problem, events, solution

3.   Define expository writing: selection that explains or helps to explain.

4.   Teach elements of expository writing.
Examples: Table of contents, headings, headnotes, footnotes, bold print, italics, maps, glossary

5.   Have students identify elements found in a selection.

6.   Have students identify type of writing by elements found.

STUDENT CHECKLIST

1.   Can I find narrative writing clues?
Examples: Plot, characters, setting, problem, events, solution

2.   Can I find expository writing clues?
Examples: Table of contents, headings, maps, glossary, headnotes, footnotes, bold print, italics

3.   Identify selection as narrative or expository.

4.   Explain my answer.

_____

No game provided in this unit.

STUDENT VISUAL—NARRATIVE AND EXPOSITORY WRITING

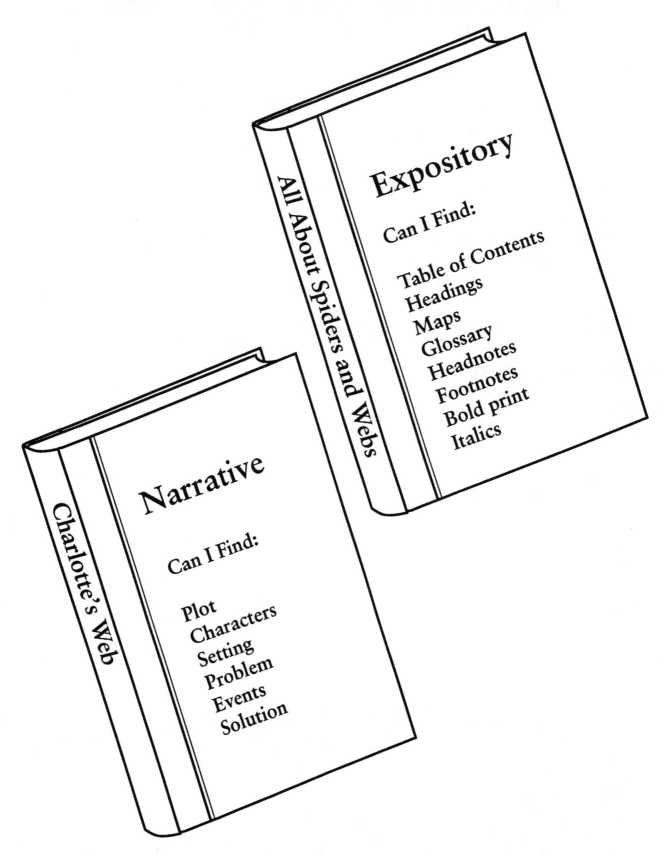

ANNOTATED BIBLIOGRAPHY

Narrative

Cleary, Beverly. *The Real Hole*. Illustrated by DyAnne DiSalvo-Ryan. New York: William Morrow & Co., 1960.
With interference and suggestions from his twin sister Janet, four-year-old Jimmy sets out to dig the biggest hole in the world.

Dahl, Roald. *George's Marvelous Medicine*. Illustrated by Quentin Blake. New York: Bantam Books, 1981.
George creates a fierce and fantastic bubbling brew to cure his horrible grandmother, but he is the one surprised.

Grahame, Kenneth. *The Reluctant Dragon*. Illustrated by Michael Hague. New York: Holt, Rinehart & Winston, 1983.
The boy who finds the dragon in the cave knows it is a kindly, harmless one, but how can he convince the frightened villagers and, especially, St. George the dragon-killer that there is no cause for concern.

Jukes, Mavis. *Blackberries in the Dark*. Illustrated by Thomas B. Allen. New York: Alfred A. Knopf, 1985.
Nine-year-old Austin visits his grandmother the summer after his grandfather dies, and together they try to come to terms with their loss.

Kipling, Rudyard. *The Elephant's Child*. Illustrated by Lorinda Bryan Cauley. San Diego: Harcourt Brace Jovanovich, 1983.
Because of his "satiable curiosity" about what the crocodile has for dinner, the elephant's child and all elephants thereafter have long trunks.

Levy, Elizabeth. *Something Queer at the Lemonade Stand*. Illustrated by Mordicai Gerstein. New York: Delacorte Press, 1982.
When Gwen and Jill open a lemonade stand, something strange happens to their lemonade every time their dog Fletcher disappears.

Locker, Thomas. *The Young Artist*. New York: Dial Books, 1989.
A talented young artist, commanded to paint the king's courtiers, all of whom wish to be portrayed with improved appearances, struggles with his sense of integrity that demands honest portraiture.

Mendez, Phil. *The Black Snowman*. Illustrated by Carole Byard. New York: Scholastic, 1989.
Through the powers of a magical "kente," a black snowman comes to life and helps young Jacob discover the beauty of his black heritage as well as his own self-worth.

Purdy, Carol. *Least of All*. Illustrated by Tim Arnold. New York: Macmillan, 1987.
A little girl in a big farm family teaches herself to read using the Bible, and shares this knowledge with her brothers, parents, and grandmother during a long, cold, Vermont winter.

Robart, Rose. *The Cake That Mack Ate*. Illustrated by Maryann Kovalski. Boston: Little, Brown & Co., 1986.
A cumulative verse that relates everything that went into Mack's cake.

Sharat, Marjorie, and Mitchell Sharat. *The Pizza Monster*. Illustrated by Denise Brunkus. New York: Delacorte Press, 1989.
   Wealthy secret agent Olivia Sharp helps depressed Duncan find a friend.

Steffy, Jan. *The School Picnic*. Illustrated by Denny Bond. Intercourse, PA: Good Books, 1987.
   Twenty-eight Amish children, their teacher, and their parents celebrate the last day of school with a picnic.

Stevens, Janet. *The Town Mouse and the Country Mouse*. New York: Holiday House, 1987.
   A town mouse and a country mouse exchange visits and discover each is suited to his own home.

Willard, Nancy. *The Mountains of Quilt*. Illustrated by Tomie de Paola. San Diego: Harcourt Brace Jovanovich, 1987.
   Four magicians lose their magic carpet, which eventually finds its way into the center of a grandmother's quilt.

Winthrop, Elizabeth. *The Best Friends Club*. Illustrated by Martha Weston. New York: Lothrop, Lee & Shepard, 1989.
   Lizzie learns to share her best friend and enjoy it, too.

Expository Writing

Dunrea, Olivier. *Skara Brae: The Story of a Prehistoric Village*. New York: Holiday House, 1985.
   Describes the stone-age settlement preserved almost intact in the sand dunes of one of the Orkney Islands, how it came to be discovered in the mid-nineteenth century, and what it reveals about the life and culture of this prehistoric community.

Graham, Ada. *Six Little Chickadees*. New York: Four Winds Press, 1982.
   Presents some of the career work done by Cordelia Stanwood, who began her study of birds when ornithology was a very young science.

Jaspersohn, William. *Ice Cream*. New York: Macmillan, 1988.
   Takes the reader on a tour of Ben and Jerry's ice cream plant to explain where ice cream comes from and how it is made.

Johnston, Tom. *Air, Air Everywhere*. Illustrated by Sarah Pooley. Milwaukee, WI: Gareth Stevens Publishing, 1985.
   Illustrates the properties of air, how air works for us, and how we use and abuse it.

LaBonte, Gail. *The Arctic Fox*. Minneapolis, MN: Dillon Press, 1989.
   Examines the appearance, habitat, and behavior of the arctic fox, discusses its relationship with humans, and describes a year in the life of an arctic fox.

Langley, Andrew. *Under the Ground*. New York: Bookwright Press, 1968.
   Takes a journey through underground workings from earthworms to caves to cables.

Muirden, James. *Going to the Moon*. Illustrated by Nigel Code. New York: Random House, 1987.
   Simple text describes the preparations, lift off, voyage, and exploration activities of the first Apollo team to land on the moon.

Oleksy, Walter. *The Video Revolution*. Chicago: Childrens Press, 1986.
    Examines the history, formats, features, and uses of videotape records, and discusses aspects such as music video, piracy, and possible future developments.

Robinson, Marlene M. *Who Knows This Nose?* New York: Dodd, Mead & Co., 1983.
    Text and photos discuss the appearance and function of the noses of humans and a variety of animals, including a pig, sugar gliders, kiwis, and cheetahs.

Sandak, Cass R. *Dams*. New York: Franklin Watts, 1983.
    Describes various kinds of dams, how they function, how they are planned and built, and some problems and failures.

Sattler, Helen Roney. *Tyrannosaurus Rex and Its Kin: The Mesozoic Monsters*. Illustrated by Joyce Powzyk. New York: Lothrop, Lee & Shepard, 1989.
    Discusses the fossil remains, probable appearance, and possible behavior of the gigantic flesh-eating dinosaurs of the Mesozoic, including Tyrannosaurus rex, Allosaurus, and such lesser-known relatives as Acrocanthosaurus and Baryonyx walkeri.

Spies, Karen. *Denver*. Minneapolis, MN: Dillon Press, 1988.
    Describes the past and present, neighborhoods, historic sites, attractions, and festivals of Denver.

White, Sandra Verrill, and Michael Filisky. *Sterling: The Rescue of u Baby Harbor Seal*. New York: Crown Publishers, 1989.
    Text and photographs follow the story of an abandoned harbor seal pup who is rescued and cared for at the New England Aquarium until she is strong enough to return to her natural environment.

Narrative and Expository Writing Compared between Selections

Jennings, Terry. *Earthworms*. Illustrated by David Anstey. New York: Gloucester Press, 1988.
    Describes where earthworms live, what they like to eat, how they move, and how they help the soil.

Rockwell, Thomas. *How to Eat Fried Worms*. Illustrated by Emily McCully. New York: Franklin Watts, 1973.
    Two boys set out to prove that worms can make a delicious meal.

Dixon, Dougal. *The Last Dinosaurs*. Photography by Jane Burton. Milwaukee, WI: Gareth Stevens Publishing, 1987.
    Text and photographic illustrations describe the characteristics and habits of several dinosaurs and other prehistoric reptiles that roamed the earth during the Cretaceous period.

Murphy, Jim. *The Last Dinosaurs*. Illustrated by Mark Alan Weatherby. New York: Scholastic, 1988.
    Depicts what life might have been like for the last dinosaurs on earth.

Nixon, Joan Lowery. *Beats Me, Claude*. Illustrated by Tracey Campbell Pearson. New York: Viking Kestrel, 1986.
Exciting escapades follow Shirley's attempts to make an apple pie for Claude, until one day an orphan boy makes a pie that wins him Claude's favor.

Thompson, Kathleen. *Texas*. Milwaukee, WI: Raintree Publishers, 1986.
Discusses the history, economy, culture, and future of Texas.

Bender, Lionel. *Spiders*. New York: Gloucester Press, 1988.
Text and pictures describe all the different types of spiders in the world, what they look like, what they eat, and where and how they live.

Jukes, Mavis. *Like Jake and Me*. Illustrated by Lloyd Bloom. New York: Alfred A. Knopf, 1984.
Alex feels that he does not have much in common with his stepfather Jake, until a fuzzy spider brings them together.

Berger, Melvin. *Switch On, Switch Off*. Illustrated by Carolyn Croll. New York: Thomas Y. Crowell, 1989.
Explains how electricity is produced and transmitted, how to create electricity using wire and a magnet, how generators supply electricity for cities, and how electricity works in homes.

Hoban, Russell. *Arthur's New Power*. Illustrated by Byron Barton. New York: Thomas Y. Crowell, 1978.
A crocodile family tries to conserve energy at home.

Rawlins, Donna. *Digging to China*. New York: Orchard Books, 1988.
Hearing her friend Marj, the elderly lady next door, speak wistfully of China, Alexis digs a hole all the way through the earth to that exotic country and brings back a postcard for Marj's birthday.

Tolan, Sally, and Rhonda Sherwood, eds. *Children of the World: China*. Photographs by Yasuhiko Miyozima. Milwaukee, WI: Gareth Stevens Publishing, 1988.
Presents the life of a fifth-grader and her family living in Beijing, China; describes her home and school, daily activities, and the ethnic groups, religion, government, education, industry, geography, and history of her country.

Broekel, Ray. *Storms*. Chicago: Childrens Press, 1982.
Describes the weather conditions that produce storms and the damage that can be done by rain, snow, wind, dust, ice, thunder, lightning, and hail.

Szilagyi, Mary. *Thunderstorms*. New York: Bradbury Press, 1985.
A little girl is comforted by her mother during a thunderstorm and she in turn comforts the family dog.

Isenbart, Hans-Heinrich. *A Duckling Is Born*. Photographs by Othmar Baumli. New York: G. P. Putnam's Sons, 1979.
Follows the development of a mallard duckling from the mating of his parents to his first swim, less than an hour after his birth.

McClosky, Robert. *Make Way for Ducklings*. New York: Viking Press, 1969.
Traffic is stopped by a policeman so Mrs. Mallard can cross the street with her ducklings to meet Mr. Mallard at the pond in Public Garden.

Santrey, Laurence. *What Makes the Wind?* Illustrated by Bert Dodson. Mahwah, NJ: Troll Associates, 1982.
Describes different kinds of winds and the effects they can have on Earth.

Yolen, Jane. *The Girl Who Loved the Wind*. Illustrated by Ed Young. New York: Thomas Y. Crowell, 1972.
Though her father seeks to protect her from all unpleasant things, a young princess is intrigued by the voice of the wind that tells her of worlds beyond the palace walls.

ACTIVITIES

Graph It: After students have read an example of expository material with information that is quantitative, have students construct graphs to share the information (bar graphs, line graphs, pie charts). This activity could be reversed: Have student write about the information presented on a graph.

Flow Chart: Flow charts are an excellent device to use for plot development. Have students think about the relevant events leading up to the climax, or the solution to the problem in a selection. Students write the events on rectangular strips and connect the rectangles with arrows to illustrate the events.

Headnotes, Footnotes, Sidenotes: Student textbooks often include these notes to give additional information, to define a word, or help students understand a concept. Cut apart old textbooks. Have students select a page or a section. Reading through the material, students can locate "hard spots" and add their own notes to the text. They could use colored pencils or write their notes on strips of paper to be glued to the texts.

Survey Sense: On a 3" x 5" index card, print a checklist. On one side, the checklist should include the elements of narrative writing. On the back side, the checklist should include the elements of expository writing. Provide cards for each student, or tuck a card inside each book. Provide an assortment of materials for students to survey and skim. Using the checklist, have the students determine the type of writing, narrative or expository. They share the information with others and explain their decisions.

Graphic Organizers: When working with expository texts, graphic organizers are very helpful. There are a variety of kinds and an organizer can be easily adjusted for the materials and student levels (Richgels 1989). Students, after much guided practice, can even design their own organizers, after surveying a selection.

Great Glossary: Glossaries are added to the back of texts for students to use in understanding word meaning specific to the text. Students might construct glossaries for texts when they are not provided. The glossaries could be completed using blank books. Store the glossaries in a central location or with the companion books so other students can use them.

Literature Logs: Many different formats are used by teachers for keeping track of children's reading. Think about adding an entry asking whether the selection is narrative or expository. Be sure to ask students to explain their answers.

Story Maps: Story maps are an excellent tool to help students think about narrative text. Several examples are available (Davis and McPherson 1989). Begin by modeling story maps, and designing with students the kind of story map appropriate to the text. When students have lots of guided experience, they can try to design and complete their own story maps.

23—PROPAGANDA

Objective: The student will identify and explain the use of propaganda.

TEACHER CHECKLIST FOR PLANNING

1. Define propaganda: ideas or information used to try to influence the thinking of people.

2. Explain the use of propaganda in real-life situations.
   Examples: Advertisement and commercials, school elections

3. Explain devices used in propaganda.
   Examples: Famous people, exaggeration, name-calling, generalities

4. Explain how propaganda is used to influence a person's thinking.
   Examples: Buy certain products, vote for certain candidates, change opinion

5. Have students identify and explain the use of propaganda, both oral and written.

6. Have students look for examples of propaganda and explain the use(s).

7. Explain how to determine the purpose, truthfulness, and validity of propaganda.

8. Have students determine and explain the purpose, truthfulness, and validity of examples of propaganda.

STUDENT CHECKLIST

1. Read or listen to example.

2. Ask: Is propaganda used?

3. Ask: What devices are used?

4. Ask: What am I to believe?

5. Ask: Is it valid and truthful?

6. Ask: Does this change my thinking?

7. Explain why or why not.

No game provided in this unit.

STUDENT VISUAL—PROPAGANDA

Propaganda

1. Read or listen to example.

2. Ask: Is propaganda used?

3. Ask: What devices are used?

4. Ask: What am I to believe?

5. Ask: Is it valid and truthful?

6. Ask: Does this change my thinking?

7. Explain why or why not.

ANNOTATED BIBLIOGRAPHY

Armstrong, Louise. *How to Turn Up into Down into Up*. Illustrated by Bill Basso. New York: Harcourt Brace Jovanovich, 1978.
A child's guide to inflation, depression, and economic recovery through a child's own private enterprise.

Cleary, Beverly. *Ramona Quimby, Age 8*. Illustrated by Alan Tiegreen. New York: Dell Publishing, 1981.
The further adventures of the Quimby family as Ramona enters the third grade.

Dahl, Roald. *Charlie and the Chocolate Factory*. Illustrated by Joseph Schindelman. New York: Puffin Books, 1964.
Each of the five children lucky enough to discover an entry ticket into Mr. Willy Wonka's mysterious chocolate factory takes advantage of the situation in his own way.

Facklam, Margery. *The Trouble with Mothers*. New York: Clarion Books, 1989.
What is a boy to do when his teacher-mother's historical novel is given as an example of the kind of "pornography" that should be banned from schools and libraries?

Geisel, Theodor Seuss. *The Butter Battle Book*. New York: Random House, 1984.
Engaged in a long-running battle, the Yooks and the Zooks develop more and more weaponry as they attempt to outdo each other.

Lubin, Leonard B. *Christmas Gift-Bringers*. New York: Lothrop, Lee & Shepard, 1989.
Stories of the traditional bringers of Christmas gifts around the world persuade a skeptical youngster to believe in Santa Claus.

Marek, Margot. *Matt's Crusade*. New York: Four Winds Press, 1988.
Seventh grader Matt Tyson is tempted to join his new friend Allie in a public protest against the Army's decision to stockpile nuclear missiles outside their town, even though the demonstration conflicts with a big football game in which he is needed to play.

McGough, Elizabeth. *Dollars and Sense*. Illustrated by Tom Huffman. New York: William Morrow & Co., 1975.
A factual guide to many consumer problems encountered by teenagers when making large purchases, looking for work, and applying for credit.

Pomerantz, Charlotte. *The Piggy in the Puddle*. Illustrated by James Marshall. New York: Macmillan, 1974.
One little pig was enjoying a puddle, while the others would not join in until they jumped on the bandwagon and enjoyed the puddle too.

Storms, Laura. *Careers with an Advertising Agency*. Photographs by Milton J. Blumenfeld. Minneapolis, MN: Lerner Publications, 1984.
Describes fifteen career possibilities in an advertising agency, including such jobs as account executive, art director, office manager, media buyer, and copy writer.

Weiss, Ann E. *Polls and Surveys*. New York: Franklin Watts, 1979.
Examines scientific polling; its history, techniques, and uses; and possible polling methods of the future.

Magazines

Consumer Reports. Box 53009, Boulder, CO 80321-3009.
    Text provides articles and information for consumers.

Zillions Consumer Reports for Kids. P.O. Box 54841, Boulder, CO 80321-4841.
    Text provides information about the products kids purchase. Articles about commercials and advertisements are also included for readers ages eight to fourteen.

Note: Other sources of propaganda are newspapers, other magazines, television, and radio.

ACTIVITIES

Anti-Ads: Have students select advertisements from written media. Good ads to use are ads for merchandise that appeals to children; soda pop, candy, junk food, and cereal ads are especially good. After determining how propaganda is used in the ads, have students create, design, and write an advertisement that convinces others not to buy the product.

Book Commercials: Have students read, or read to them, the commercial written by Ramona in *Ramona Quimby, Age 8*, by Beverly Cleary. Students will enjoy writing their own commercials for their favorite books.

Propaganda Scrapbook: Students can collect examples of propaganda from magazines, newspapers, and campaign literature. Put the examples into a class scrapbook. On the opposite page, have students write their reaction to the information, including both positive and negative comments.

Ingenious Invention: Have students design and make models of inventions. Of course, to sell their inventions, students need to plan an advertising campaign.

Pick the Propaganda: After students complete a study of the devices used in propaganda (bandwagon, plain folks, etc.), have them sort through a set of advertisements collected from newspapers and magazines. Students should identify the devices used to influence readers. Then students may select an ad, choose a different device, and write a new ad for the product using the new device.

Who's the Audience?: Most toy and sweet cereal advertisements are intended for a young audience. The hope is that the youngsters will convince their parents to buy the product for them. Collect several of these ads and, after discussing the intent, have students write an ad for the product that is aimed directly at their parents. Encourage the students to use similar propaganda devices in their ads.

Pick the Picture: How good would a dog food advertisement be if the dog looked sick? Have students discuss the impact of pictures and illustrations on the effectiveness of the overall advertisements.

Get Their Attention: Make a class book of words and phrases cut from advertisements that are trying to grab the emotions of the reader. Students could use the class book to help them write persuasive advertisements.

Small Print: Few advertisements or persuasively written articles give the negative aspects of the product. Using advertisements, students identify the important negative information they think the writer left out. They can then add the "small print" on strips of paper. Glue them onto the advertisement to give more information.

Consumer Experts: Select several items from a mail-order house to order that interest your students. Order the items and wait with excitement for them to arrive. When they arrive, compare the items to the advertisements. Do the items live up to the claims in the advertisements? What misleading claims are in the advertisements?

REFERENCES AND ADDITIONAL TEACHER RESOURCES

REFERENCES

Davis, Zephaniah T., and Michael D. McPherson. 1989. "Story Map Instruction: A Road Map for Reading Comprehension." *The Reading Teacher* 43(3): 232-40.

Richgels, Donald J., Lea M. McGee, and Edith A. Slaton. 1989. "Teaching Expository Text Structure in Reading and Writing." In *Children's Comprehension of Text*, edited by K. Denise Muth. Newark, DE: International Reading Association.

ADDITIONAL TEACHER RESOURCES

Barchers, Suzanne I. 1990. *Creating and Managing the Literate Classroom*. Englewood, CO: Teacher Ideas Press.

Butler, Andrea, and Jan Turnbill. 1984. *Towards a Reading-Writing Classroom*. Portsmouth, NH: Distributed by Heinemann Educational Books, Inc.

Cullinan, Bernice. 1983. *Children's Literature in the Reading Program*. Newark, DE: International Reading Association.

Dreyer, Sharon Spredemann. 1985. *The Bookfinder*. Vol. 3. Circle Pines, MN: American Guidance Service, Inc.

Graves, Donald H. 1983. *Writing: Teachers and Children at Work*. Portsmouth, NH: Heinemann Educational Books, Inc.

Hoffman, James V. 1986. *Effective Teaching of Reading: Research and Practice*. Newark, DE: International Reading Association.

Johnson, Terry D., and Daphne R. Louis. 1987. *Literacy through Literature*. Portsmouth, NH: Heinemann Educational Books, Inc.

Kruise, Carol Sue. 1987. *Those Bloomin' Books*. Littleton, CO: Libraries Unlimited, Inc.

Muth, K. Denise. 1989. *Children's Comprehension of Text*. Newark, DE: International Reading Association.

Orasanu, Judith. 1986. *Reading Comprehension from Research to Practice*. Hillsdale, NJ: Lawrence Erlbaum Associates.

Roser, N., and M. Firth, eds. 1983. *Children's Choices: Teaching with Books Children Like*. New York: G. P. Putnam's Sons.

Watson, Dorothy J., ed. 1987. *Language Arts in the Elementary School*. Urbana, IL: National Council of Teachers of English.

Wilson, Robert M., and Linda B. Gambrell. 1988. *Reading Comprehension in the Elementary School*. Boston: Allyn & Bacon.

ABOUT THE AUTHORS

PATRICIA R. CONLEY

PATRICIA R. CONLEY is a graduate of the University of Southern Mississippi. She has a Master's degree in Curriculum and Instruction with a specialization in elementary and is working on an endorsement in reading. She has taught for sixteen years in Florida and Colorado schools where she has taught kindergarten, first and second grades. Presently, she is an Instructional Support Teacher in the area of reading, problem-solving, and thinking skills, working with grades K-5 at Crawford Elementary School in Aurora, Colorado.

BERDELL J. AKIN is a graduate of The Colorado College in Colorado Springs, Colorado. She has fourteen years of teaching experience in public schools where she has taught kindergarten, first, third, fourth, fifth, sixth and Chapter 1 Reading. She is currently an Instructional Support Teacher at Crawford Elementary in Aurora, Colorado.

BERDELL J. AKIN

ps

Grades 1-5

BA-15

Comprehension Check-up
Grades 1-5

AUTHOR

TITLE

DATE DUE	BORROWER'S NAME	ROOM NUMBER
	a. amaral	103

DATE DUE

MAR 04 2019	